Management of Development Projects
(PPS-11)

Pergamon Titles of Related Interest

PERGAMON
POLICY
STUDIES

Management of Development Projects

An International Case Study Approach

Edited by
Louis J. Goodman
Ralph Ngatata Love

Published in cooperation with the
East-West Center, Hawaii

Pergamon Press

NEW YORK • OXFORD • TORONTO • SYDNEY • FRANKFURT • PARIS

Pergamon Press Offices:

U.S.A.　　　　　Pergamon Press Inc., Maxwell House, Fairview Park, Elmsford, New York 10523, U.S.A.

U.K.　　　　　Pergamon Press Ltd., Headington Hill Hall, Oxford OX3 0BW, England

CANADA　　　　　Pergamon of Canada, Ltd., 150 Consumers Road, Willowdale, Ontario M2J, 1P9, Canada

AUSTRALIA　　　　　Pergamon Press (Aust) Pty. Ltd., P O Box 544, Potts Point, NSW 2011, Australia

FRANCE　　　　　Pergamon Press SARL, 24 rue des Ecoles, 75240 Paris, Cedex 05, France

FEDERAL REPUBLIC
OF GERMANY　　　　　Pergamon Press GmbH, 6242 Kronberg/Taunus, Pferdstrasse 1, Federal Republic of Germany

Copyright © 1979 Pergamon Press Inc.

Library of Congress Cataloging in Publication Data
Main entry under title:

Management of development projects.

(Pergamon policy studies)
Bibliography: p.
Includes index.
1. Economic development projects—Management—Case studies. I. Goodman, Louis J. II. Love, Ralph Ngatata.
HC60.M298　1979　658.4'04　78-26673
ISBN 0-08-022493-8

The East-West Center gratefully extends special acknowledgement to the Exxon Education Foundation for its grant to support the case studies on development projects

Printed in the United States of America

Contents

PREFACE   vii

CHAPTER

1   THE INTEGRATED PROJECT PLANNING AND
MANAGEMENT CYCLE (IPPMC)
Louis J. Goodman and Ralph Ngatata Love   1

2   PACIFIC ISLAND LIVESTOCK DEVELOPMENT:
SOUTH PACIFIC
Ralph Ngatata Love   14

3   THE WAY ABUNG TRANSMIGRATION PROJECT:
INDONESIA
Bintoro Tjokroamidjojo   52

4   LAGUNA RURAL SOCIAL DEVELOPMENT
PROJECT: PHILIPPINES
Ernesto Garilao   97

5   BANGKOK METROPOLITAN IMMEDIATE WATER
IMPROVEMENT PROGRAM: THAILAND
Chakrit Noranitipadungkarn   145

6   THE MALIA COAST COMPREHENSIVE HEALTH
CENTER: UNITED STATES
Nancy Crocco and Tetsuo Miyabara   176

7   CONCLUSION: MAJOR FACTORS AND ISSUES
IN THE IPPMC
Louis J. Goodman and Ralph Ngatata Love   235

SELECTED BIBLIOGRAPHY   249

INDEX   253

ABOUT THE AUTHORS   257

v

Preface

The ultimate objective of development in all societies, it is generally agreed, must be sustained improvement in the well-being of the individual. To meet this objective, the problems of employment, income distribution, and the allocation, distribution and utilization of resources must be dealt with directly. Increasing attention by national governments, international funding agencies, and private organizations is being given to these problem areas and to related social, economic, technological, and political issues in developing and developed countries.

The rapid and pervasive social, economic, technological, and political changes of the 1960s and early 1970s have created a multiplicity of problems that mutually affect all countries, from highly industrialized to predominantly rural societies. But even though vast resources are channeled into development projects, evidence clearly demonstrates that intensive project investment has not had the anticipated impact on the achievement of developmental goals. One of the primary reasons is that lack of viable policies, coupled with poor management, has wasted valuable resources and even led to counterproductive disharmony and tension. Another reason is that planning and project development take place within a social and economic environment which molds and limits the actions of the implementing agency.

A major obstacle to the achievement of developmental goals, as well as to an increase in the flow of capital to developing areas, continues to be the inability to identify, to formulate plans, and to implement projects properly. The majority of studies of the problem have found that most nations simply do not have adequate institutional capacity or trained manpower to plan and execute projects effectively. One of the most persistent and difficult problems facing local, national, and international cooperative development efforts, particularly in developing countries, is the scarcity of managerial capability to put into effect and to sustain, innovative policies, social and technological plans, and resource development programs. Problem solving, policy making, and planning are ineffective unless manpower resources and administrative procedures can be created to realize national and local decisions.

Traditional management education and training programs are not meeting the needs that both developing and developed countries have for project-oriented managers who can provide unified control to achieve a given objective over a specific time period in projects comprehending all sectors: agricultural, industrial, public works, and social. Experience demonstrates that ineffective administration results in costly mistakes in all nations.

It follows, then, that early attention must be given to education and training programs for developing the indigenous skilled manpower needed to formulate and implement national and regional development goals. There is a need for greater cooperation among university, government, industry, and civic groups to maximize the contribution of each in the development process. Viable local and national policies must be generated to provide the necessary support for manpower planning and education. At the same time, international cooperation is vitally needed in a continuing study of relationships and policy implications among international assistance agencies, national policy makers and planners, and managers of development projects.

The East-West Center* has recognized problems in the area of public policy implementation and project management for some years. From 1972 to 1978, the Center has worked cooperatively with a total of over 50 organizations in 15 countries on a manpower development program directed at educating and training project managers. This new program for project managers is aimed at increasing their understanding of the integrated project cycle: the entire spectrum of a given project, ranging from planning through evaluation. The program is also designed to broaden the perspectives of international assistance policy makers, local planners, and project implementers in understanding the relationship between national goals and local projects.

Part of the East-West Center manpower development program involves the cooperative development of teaching materials within a prototype curriculum for training project managers for countries with different cultural and social values. An essential feature of the prototype curriculum is the collection of case histories such as those that appear in this volume. Designed to cover the whole project cycle, these five studies are drawn from the records of developing and developed countries and provide valuable data in a relatively neglected area. They illustrate common management factors while clearly indicating the importance of the environment on management decisions and methods. These cases can be used for training personnel responsible for managing projects, and for reference in academic programs at universities, community colleges, and technical institutes in all nations.

The accelerated pace of development in most countries means that there is now an acute need for more effective project managers. With increasingly limited resources, the world can no longer afford either inefficient

---

* The East-West Center is a nonprofit educational institution established in Hawaii, U.S.A., by the United States Congress in 1960. Its purpose is to promote better relations and understanding between the United States and the nations of Asia and the Pacific through cooperative study, training, and research.

implementation of projects or failures due to mismanagement. No exact quantification exists of the number of project managers who will be required; senior officials from both public and private sectors of many countries agree, however, that action-oriented programs must be developed and implemented immediately for an integrated approach to more effective project management. The severe strain on existing resources will worsen, not improve, with time; indeed project management will play a vital role in the constructive use or further waste of these resources.

This book would not have been made possible without the collaboration and cooperation of many senior scholars and practitioners and their institutions in Asia, the Pacific, and the United States. The editors wish to convey warmest thanks and deepest appreciation for the many contributions. Space does not permit adequate acknowledgment of each person and institution involved in this international cooperative project effort at the East-West Center. Special thanks are conveyed to the authors of the case histories and to their institutions for the splendid cooperation received. Particular acknowledgment is due to former East-West Center Senior Fellows Dr. Dennis Rondinelli, Dr. Leonard Mason, Dr. Clark Bloom, and Dr. Victor Ordoñez.

It is hoped that the impact of this cooperative project will have profound implications in the context of international efforts to improve the planning and management of development projects for all sectors of the economy and society. This should result in more efficient and effective use of critical resources for the mutual benefit of many countries and the well-being of their people.

Louis J. Goodman
Ralph Ngatata Love

1 The Integrated Project Planning and Management Cycle (IPPMC)

Louis J. Goodman
Ralph Ngatata Love

The challenge of managing resources to meet the demands of society is one of the most complex tasks facing decision makers in all nations. Although the problem is found in all countries, it is more acute for decision makers in developing countries, faced as they are with satisfying the rapidly rising expectations of an increasing population.

Since the Second World War, attempts to satisfy these expectations have centered around development programs. A development program in this context may be defined as a form of organized social activity with a specific objective, limited in time and space. (1) A development program normally consists of an interrelated group of "projects"; a project being an activity of minimum size, specific in location, and an essential element of the development process. (2) Project activities are brought under a unified form of management to achieve a given objective over a specified time period. Although each development project is unique, projects have several characteristics in common. They are a vital part of the overall development process, have a limited lifespan and narrow objectives. Development projects may be implemented to fulfill an immediate need within society, or they may result from a structured planning process and, in effect, be the starting point for converting the plans and policies of a nation into reality. Thus, the total development process may be viewed as a pyramid, with basic infrastructure projects making up the base. As projects which satisfy basic needs within society reach a satisfactory level, other projects and development programs of a more specialized and sophisticated nature can be built upon the foundation.

Today, international assistance policies, while vitally concerned with economic growth, place increasing emphasis on social equity, spatial and social redistribution of income, and increased employment of the poorest groups in developing nations. The trend is to couple economic growth through industrial and capital infrastructure projects with multipurpose, multisectoral integrated projects in social sectors such as rural development, population planning, agriculture, and education - to promote overall growth

1

linked with equity. Yet most studies show that the new strategies and policies are extremely complex and that both assistance agencies and developing countries have serious problems in implementing them.

Part of the problem with implementation lies in the fact that traditional management methods and techniques, as used in most organizations, are not appropriate for dealing with projects which have a relatively short life and cut across established organizational boundaries to obtain resources. Traditional management methods often consist of a fragmented departmental approach that cannot effectively integrate the various elements within the complete project cycle. Resource groups contributing to and participating in projects must have as their main concern the achievement of the projects' objectives.

A fundamental problem facing project managers is the need to create a temporary organization which can bring together in a meaningful way the numerous policies and decisions emanating from different organizations which have an influence on the implementation of the project. In established organizations, this problem is not so acute because policies, procedures, rules, and regulations are based on long experience, out of which accepted methods of operation have developed. The nonrepetitive, short-term nature of projects, however, presents special difficulties in decision making. In this setting, the role of the manager of development projects is a difficult one requiring special skills and abilities.

WHAT IS THE IPPMC?

To clarify the mass of procedures, methods, and possibilities relating to the management of projects, it is useful to have a framework within which development projects may be viewed. Projects, in fact, reflect an underlying unity of process that remains the same even though they differ in individual detail. Projects from all sectors - whether social services, agriculture, industry, or public works - follow a similar path in moving from conception to reality.

The Integrated Project Planning and Management Cycle (IPPMC) is a conceptual tool for observing and analyzing the single process that constitutes the life of a development project (see Fig. 1.1). The self-renewing IPPMC may be divided into four major phases: 1) Planning, Appraisal, and Design; 2) Selection, Approval, and Activation; 3) Operation, Control, and Handover; and 4) Evaluation and Refinement. Specific tasks may be further identified within these four phases.

Figure 1.1 illustrates the relationships among the phases of the project cycle, the tasks within each of the phases, and the overall dependency on central policy relationships. The tasks of the cycle are not necessarily sequential, for some activities may not be required, or they can take place at the same time or in a different order. Each activity, however, is dependent on and influenced by the others. Thus, a continual feedback and dependency relationship exists among the tasks.

A two-way flow of information and decision making exists between those

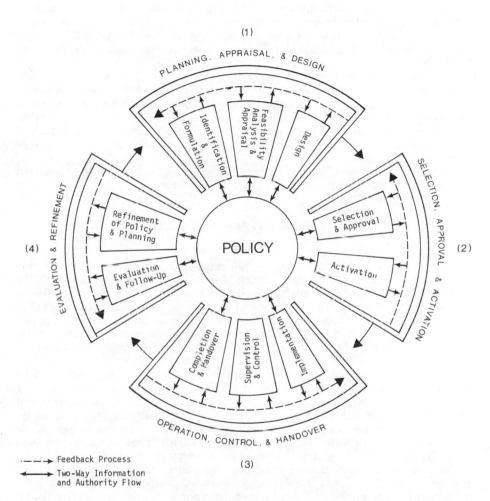

FIGURE 1.1   Integrated Project Planning and
            Management Cycle: The Four Phases.

responsible for policy and those concerned with managing each of the project tasks. This feedback to policy makers, and management's response to their decisions, is an important part of the integrated project cycle. Decisions on project implementation, although vested on a day-to-day basis in the hands of the manager, are closely linked to the policy framework in which the project operates. Thus, all tasks within the four phases of the IPPMC are tied together by policies emanating from the various authorities concerned with the projects.

As a result of the feedback and policy-making process, it should be noted, some projects may not proceed beyond the first phase. After the tasks within the planning, appraisal, and design phase have been completed, the information supplied to policy makers may lead to a decision to cancel any further allocation of resources to the project. However, for economic, technical, and other reasons, it may not be desirable to stop a project once it has moved past the first phase.

Given this overview of the integrated project planning and management cycle, each of the four phases can be examined in turn.

Phase 1: Planning, Appraisal, and Design

The first phase of the project is planning, appraisal, and design. Within this phase are three basic tasks: 1) the identification and formulation of the project, 2) the feasibility analysis and appraisal of the project, and 3) the design of the project. The first task is <u>identification</u> and <u>formulation</u>. The actual conception or identification of a project may occur in several ways. Basic needs within a country will prompt the implementation of projects to satisfy the needs. The planning process often identifies project possibilities for each sector in society.

The major source of projects in developing countries, however, will be through existing departments or ministries, including central planning agencies. Projects may be identified by political parties or government officials. In this case, the motivation may be a political one, such as an attempt to gain the support of electors in particular sectors or regions. In some countries, private entrepreneurs or multinational corporations will identify projects that meet the criteria set down by government.

International agencies have their own procedures for identifying projects; for example, the World Health Organization, in its manual on project preparation, identifies a step-by-step approach to problem analysis. (3) Starting with the initial concept of the problem, it suggests that the problem be viewed in terms of the consequences, critical elements, objectives and targets, followed by the identification of potential obstacles. The World Bank identifies projects through a "repeater" system whereby new opportunities develop out of ongoing development programs and projects. Thus existing projects lead to the identification of other projects, and a "piggyback" system operates where, as part of one project, funding may be obtained for feasibility studies for subsequent projects. The identification of projects, then, is a process that must take into account various needs, preconditions, and policies if the project idea is to proceed to operational reality.

Within the first phase, the second set of tasks, feasibility analysis and appraisal, is a critical one, involving in effect two distinct operations. A prior requirement to this set of tasks, however, is the development of preliminary designs for the project. The early designs must be detailed enough to enable cost estimates to be prepared and decisions on various dimensions of the project to be made.

Feasibility analysis is the process of determining if the ability of the individual areas of operation and the combined inputs are capable of implementing the project. Appraisal is the evaluation of the overall ability of the project to succeed. Projects will only proceed to the feasibility stage if they are considered to be desirable by decision makers.

While the feasibility analysis and appraisal are being conducted, several critical decisions need to be made. These decisions will determine if the project is capable of achieving its objective in the limits set by decision makers and whether it will proceed as an ongoing proposition. Preliminary estimates must be made of the resources required, as well as basic decisions about size, location, technology, and administrative needs.

Feasibility and appraisal need to be approached in a systematic manner. Time spent in researching the feasibility of a project is normally time well spent. The findings at this point of the project's life will be useful during other phases of the project, particularly in Phase 3.

The degree to which it is possible to determine project feasibility will depend on the precision of project information. Even though the final detailed design of the project can only be undertaken after approval has been given, the preliminary designs determine the foundation on which future decisions will be made. In most developing countries, a shortage of design capabilities, as well as research and development capabilities, exists. This situation may result in lack of attention to critical aspects of the project.

Some projects may require a pilot study as part of the feasibility process. Pilot studies provide data to enable more meaningful decisions to be made about larger projects. Or the appraisal process may require a comparative study to determine the merits of one project over another. Although the project identified may be feasible to implement, a comparative study determines whether resources are best used in the project or in some other form.

Many governments and international agencies have set down rigid procedures to be followed when their funds are required. While actual details vary from project to project and from organization to organization, a trend over recent years is for more sophisticated and more systematic studies.

Many alternatives are also possible in preparing a feasibility report. Studies may relate to the feasibility of the technical, economic, commercial, financial, managerial, administrative, organizational, and other aspects of the project. Political, social, environmental, and cultural factors relating to the project may also be included.

Technical studies, concerned with ensuring that the optimum technical solution is forthcoming, must also be made, and various technical alternatives must be considered to ensure that the suggested approach fulfills the project needs.

Economic studies examine the overall sector in which the project falls, and take into consideration how the project fits into the broader sector and national planning framework. Related to economic feasibility studies, commercial studies may be necessary to determine the overall competitive nature of the proposed project. They will examine the market demands for the output of the project, consider the costs of production, and look at all aspects of the project to determine if it is a viable proposition.

Financial studies determine what funds are required to complete the project. These studies determine whether the project could sustain its financial obligations, have adequate working capital, and generate enough funds to ensure adequate cash flow to keep the project operational.

Managerial and administrative studies determine the adequacy of procedures to control and direct the project. Their objective is to determine whether a project that is economically, financially, and commercially sound can, in fact, be properly implemented by available managerial and administrative procedures.

Once the feasibility studies have been completed, a meaningful appraisal of the project as an overall concept is possible. Appraisal may be carried out by policy and decision makers and by potential lending institutions. The policy and decision makers satisfy themselves that the project meets the conditions that enable it to proceed. Their concern is to determine whether or not the project is the best means of reaching the objectives they have set. They may review the project itself and alternative means of reaching the objective.

Potential lending institutions may approach their appraisal with a healthy skepticism toward all phases of the project. They endeavor to determine whether or not the project is intrinsically sound and whether or not all the circumstances that surround it are also viable.

The last task within this phase of the integrated project cycle is design. As mentioned earlier, preliminary design criteria must be established before the project feasibility and appraisal task. Once it has been determined that the project will continue, the design task proceeds. Design is a critical function. It establishes the basic programs, allocates responsibilities, determines activities and resources, and sets down in operational form the areas of priority and functions to be carried out. All input relating to projects, including personnel, skills, technical data, and so on, must be determined at this point. Environmental factors, social criteria, technological requirements, and procedures must be assessed and included.

The design task also includes the preparation of blueprints and specifications for construction, facilities, and equipment. Operating plans and work schedules are prepared and brought together in a formal implementation plan; contingency plans may also be prepared. Designers must bring together the views of policy and decision makers and technical experts in such a way that the design reflects the inputs of all those contributing to the project.

Phase 2: Selection, Approval, and Activation

This phase of the project has two major tasks: 1) selection and approval, and 2) activation. Project selection takes place after the project has been accepted by policy makers and funding organizations as meeting the feasibility criteria. At this point, the design function, including the formal implementation plan, has been completed. The project will be well defined, with key elements identified and the inputs required from organizational personnel, technicians, and outside consultants clearly identified. The selection of one project for implementation over another is made on the basis of several criteria. Policy makers consider the overall feasibility of the project and the priority of the project area. If a project fulfills a major need or contributes to national or sector goals and is politically desirable, it may be selected for implementation over a competing project that is not politically important. Funding agencies, however, have a variety of techniques for determining whether resources will be allocated to a particular project. These techniques may range from cost-benefit to other complex forms of analysis. (4) The overall requirement, however, is that the policy makers and the funding agency conclude that the project itself has a priority claim for resources required for the project. The selection process is, therefore, normally a competitive one.

The selection of a project for implementation requires negotiations to be undertaken to obtain formal approval from national authorities, funding agencies, and others contributing to the project. This requires the finalization of funding proposals, agreements, contract documents, including tenders and other contracts and the introduction by government or some other organization of appropriate regulations.

Activation of the program involves the coordination and allocation of resources to make the project operational. Activation is a complex process in which the project manager has to bring together an appropriate project team which may include professionals, technicians, and resource personnel. Other contributions to the project may come from other groups, such as outside consultants, contractors, suppliers, and policy makers in other agencies. The outside input must be coordinated with the work of the project team. Responsibility and authority for executing the project must be assigned at this point. This will include the granting of authority to make decisions in areas relating to personnel, and to legal, financial, organization, procurement and administration matters.

The activation task must ensure that planning for all phases is undertaken so that delays in vital input do not occur. Organizational and administrative procedures, together with feedback and response to policy makers' decisions, will have an important bearing on implementation. Concern for detail and proper planning during activation can save a great deal of time and resources during later phases of the project.

Phase 3: Operation, Control, and Handover

This phase of the project has three sets of tasks: 1) implementation, 2) supervision and control, and 3) completion and handover. Implementation involves the allocation of tasks to groups within the project organization. Implementation of the project will be based on procedures set down during the two earlier phases. At this point, a final review of the project design and timetable will be undertaken, and any necessary changes or adjustments included. Decisions about the procurement of equipment, resources, and manpower also need to be made. Schedules and time frames need to be established, efficient feedback and communication systems, and other management information systems must be set up. The appointment of a project manager means that responsibility for implementation will fall within his jurisdiction. He will need to work with policy makers, authorities, and organizations related to the project as well as with policy makers controlling the project. His task is a complex one, requiring him to steer the project through many obstacles.

The second set of tasks is supervision and control. Supervision and control procedures must be activated to provide feedback to policy makers and the project manager. Control procedures must identify and isolate problem areas; the limited time span of a project means that fast action is necessary if costly delays are to be avoided. At this point, specific management tools, such as the critical path method (CPM), the program and evaluation review techniques (PERT), and other forms of network analysis, are particularly useful. (5) These control and supervision techniques break down a project into detailed activities and establish the interrelationships between and among the various activities. This allows the project manager to organize the project into manageable components, to coordinate all activities, and to set a time-sequence schedule for project implementation. (6) Although using such techniques means spending more time prior to implementation, it is time well spent. Not only will these techniques give the project internal coherence, but they will also save implementation time by isolating any problems to the appropriate project component.

In addition to internal control, those providing funding for projects will maintain an independent monitoring and control system for the project. The project manager will thus have to meet control criteria set down by the government, or some other controlling agency, and perhaps the funding institution. This may involve using specified procedures, such as international competitive bidding, for supply contracts. Formal procedures are set down by many international organizations for the procurement and control of resources.

Whatever supervision and control techniques are used, they must take into account the changing patterns that occur during the project's life. These may include changes within the policy and political structures, difficulties with procurement, and poor performance by project team members and contractors. Often, a review of the overall project design may be necessary. Many technicians are involved in the supervision and control processes, and adequate information flow in all directions - from the project manager, and from those within his organization charged with special responsibilities - is essential if these procedures are to be effective. As part of supervision and control, any problems relating to environmental factors must also be identified and appropriate action taken.

Control procedures, however, are only useful if action is taken to rectify any deviation. It should also be noted that changing personnel and changing patterns of inputs occur naturally as the project goes through its phases. As work on some tasks is completed, other personnel, experts, and contractors move in. Personnel must adjust to their new environment, and procedures need to be reviewed and updated to meet the changing situation.

Project completion prepares the project for phasing out and handover to another form of administration. These are the third tasks of this phase. Project completion consists of scaling down and dismantling the project organization. It also involves the transfer of project personnel to other areas of operation. Assets and other facilities, including equipment and technology, may not be required by the operational project. Provision for transferring these must be made, since it is not always possible to have an automatic transition from the developmental to the operational stage. Completion may occur over a considerable period. As various parts of a project are completed, however, they may be taken over by a new organization, and handover may therefore be accomplished in a piecemeal manner. It is essential that development resource linkages between scaled-down projects and those projects in the elementary stages of implementation be planned systematically to ensure optimal use of limited project resources, particularly in the context of broader development programs. (7) The new project, when operational, will have an effect on other aspects within the sector. As the project becomes operational, the new controlling organization must have the skills, personnel, and technical backup required. Often, key personnel working in the development stage will transfer over to the new controlling organization.

In cases where technical, financial, political, or other factors prevent projects from being completed in the terms originally set down, handover and termination procedures may have to be implemented at an earlier stage. This may involve considerable loss as far as the project is concerned. In this situation, the objective is to liquidate the project in a way that will obtain the most benefit.

As a project nears completion, special reporting systems should be set up so that full information relating to the project is available. Completion reports will be prepared for various authorities, including funding organizations and policy makers.

The actual handover of the operation of the project involves finalization of contracts, termination of loan facilities, and so on. Handover also includes the transfer of the project activity and resources to the new administration. This is a critical task. While the development of the project can be viewed initially as a creative phase, once the project is completed, it must be viewed as a long-term operational program.

Phase 4: Evaluation and Refinement

The final phase of the project is the evaluation and refinement of policy and planning factors. The first task is evaluation and followup. While an immediate evaluation of results is possible, actual benefits, both anticipated and unanticipated, together with side effects, may not become apparent until the project has been operating for some time. Evaluation thus needs to cover several time periods. Evaluation normally includes an ex-post examination of the project in attaining its intended goals within the framework of both the timetable and the budget. However, experience clearly demonstrates the need to consider evaluation as an ongoing process integrated with each phase of the IPPMC. For example, evaluation procedures must be designed to analyze and propose solutions to problems that may arise during the tasks of activation, implementation, supervision, and control. Ongoing evaluation, which includes ex-post evaluation, should result in a careful documentation of experiences which can provide both insights and lessons for improving project planning and project management in the future.

Evaluation of a project can take several forms. These include evaluation by the body responsible for implementing the project and by others with an interest in the project, including funding organizations, contractors, and other groups. Those funding the project will undertake a thorough investigation of financial aspects of the project, including an effectiveness study of goal attainment. The agency responsible for the project will be concerned with determining whether goals have been attained and whether the expected impact on a sector or on national development will be achieved. The studies should also consider, in addition to the impact on the target group, the impact of the project on the political, social, cultural, and environmental factors relating to the project. An exhaustive evaluation of each phase to determine its contribution to the project in regard to budget, timetable, etc. is most desirable. In most cases, however, the project as a whole is evaluated with little effort made to analyze each phase or each task separately.

International agencies, such as the World Bank and the United Nations, have their own procedures for evaluating projects. These may be useful to policy makers, since they provide the opportunity for comparative analysis with similar projects.

Related to, and often arising from, the evaluation of a project is the need for project followup. Such activity may vary from determining how unmet needs can be satisfied to action on project tasks not properly fulfilled. The "piggyback" or followup projects mentioned earlier may come into play at this point. For a project to achieve its full objective, smaller or related projects may need to be implemented almost immediately. There is then a clear need to relate followup action closely to evaluation of projects. This action is one aspect of the project manager's role which could involve considerably more commitment than he at first envisaged. If followup means the difference between the project's being fully operational or not, then it is a wise investment to undertake these activities as quickly as possible. Aspects arising from the followup procedures may be useful in the future. If the project is successful, guidelines can be set down for the project to be repeated in another setting.

The second and last task is <u>refinement of policy and planning</u>. Policy makers and managers will need to refine their procedures in the light of each completed project. Experiences and lessons learned should be the foundation on which planning and policy tasks are reviewed. As the essential controlling force, policy procedures must be continually updated to meet challenges in the future. Planning must also be able to meet any new demands or new situations. Refinement of these procedures is an important contribution that the project can make to future development programs.

As a flexible model, then, the IPPMC provides an insight into all phases of a project from conception through completion. Linking the phases and tasks together is the power and authority relationship vested in various policy makers, ranging from top government and political decision makers to those with authority for one aspect of the project. The project manager, the staff, and those contributing to the project as consultants or contractors are bound by, and exist within, the framework of policy decisions. Analysis of these changing power relationships through the IPPMC model can provide a comprehensive overview of a development project. (8)

THE IPPMC AND THE CASE HISTORY APPROACH

The need for trained manpower for managing projects is a common problem in all nations. Although this need has been recognized by both local and national administrators and by international funding agencies, relatively little attention has been given to training in the complex task of managing development projects. Furthermore, the training that is available is often narrow in focus and usually concentrates on only a few aspects of the project manager's role.

One of the best tools for examining the complex role of the development project manager is case histories, which provide an intimate view of the workings of projects, as well as a realistic context for analysis of management. Cases also help pinpoint the many techniques, relationships, and other factors that contribute to either the success or the failure of projects. They are especially valuable in training project managers in all aspects of the IPPMC.

The case histories in this volume are a record of events and issues that have actually been faced by managers: events interwoven with actual facts, opinions, prejudices, and data upon which the manager's decision depended. They record the experience of government officials, consultants, international assistance officials, and project managers so that others can learn from their successes and mistakes. The projects presented here vary in country, sector, form of management, and funding. Each, however, represents an investment of resources aimed at achieving a well-defined set of goals, and each focuses on the inextricably related set of phases that make up the Integrated Project Planning and Management Cycle: 1) Planning, Appraisal, and Design; 2) Selection, Approval, and Activation; 3) Operation, Control, and Handover; and 4) Evaluation and Refinement.

These case histories were written within the framework of the IPPMC, which provides an orderly model for examining critical issues that may contribute to the success or failure of a project. Within each of the four phases of the project cycle, managers are faced with a different set of problems and responsibilities, some of which are described in Chapter 7. Each case history examines these different sets of problems in turn. Additionally, the cases attempt to determine four basic points: 1) the management functions performed in the project's planning and implementation, 2) how well and how effectively they were performed, 3) factors that seemed to contribute to or inhibit the project's success, and 4) how project management could be improved. A key that quality managers must have is the ability to understand the potential meanings and relationships of facts and events relating to environment and people.

Management is not an exact science. These cases present no single correct answer to a management problem. Alternatives always exist - as well as the expectation that the best answer has not yet been found. Each project is a new situation; each requires imaginative understanding; each provides a new axis for personal relations. Although they have been placed within the flexible model of the IPPMC for analysis, the cases are not designed to provide examples of the "rules" or "principles" of managing projects. What they do provide is an opportunity for practitioners and scholars alike to analyze and evaluate projects from the same basic original data.

NOTES - Chapter 1

(1) Administration of Development Programmes and Projects: Some Major Issues, United Nations pub. no. E 71 IIh 4 (New York, 1971).

(2) A.O. Hirschman, Development Projects Observed (Washington, D.C., The Brookings Institution, 1967).

(3) Hugh F. Ripman, "Project Appraisal," Finance and Development 1:3 (December, 1964): 178-183.

(4) See United Nations Economic Commission for Asia and the Far East, "Criteria for Allocating Investment Resources among Various Fields of Development and Underdeveloped Countries," Economic Bulletin for Asia and the Far East (June 1961): 30-45.

(5) CPM and PERT are methods for developiong detailed flow charts for the management of a project. CPM is a technique that reduces the implementation time of a project by breaking down the project into its critical activites, and then determining which set of activities constitute a critical path of implementations to be completed on schedule. PERT views the project as a total system and establishes a schedule of dates for using various systems of management control. These dates are then monitored through project progress reports. For detailed discussions of CPM, PERT, and other forms of network analysis, see: Edward Falkner, Project Management with CPM (Means, Robert Snow, Co., Inc. Duxbury, Massachusetts, 1973); Joseph Modern and Cecil Phillips, Project Management with CPM and PERT, (Van Nostrand and Reinhold: New York, 1970). See also the selected references on pp. 23-24.

(6) Administration of Development Programmes and Projects: Some Major Issues, (United Nations pub. no. E71 IIh 4 (New York, 1971, 83-85).

(7) Raymond Radosevich et al., "Divesting Project Resources" (Graduate School of Management, Vanderbilt, 1974); "Developing Project Organizational Systems" (Graduate School of Management, Vanderbilt, 1974).

(8) This section is essentially an overview of the IPPMC. The authors, in conjunction with collaborators from Asia, the Pacific, and the United States, are currently developing a companion volume that elaborates on IPPMC and analyzes the theory and practice in managing development projects. This second volume (see Chapter 7) presents an integrated and a balanced and comprehensive approach that provides a valuable contribution to the available literature on the subject.

2 Pacific Island Livestock Development: South Pacific
Ralph Ngatata Love

PROJECT BACKGROUND

Rabona, A South Pacific Community*

Rabona is an independent island nation in the southern tropics. It is made up of many small islands with a total land area of several hundred square miles. Many of the islands are uninhabited. The largest is Rabona Island, which supports the greatest concentration of the country's population of a little over 100,000. Rabona has been independent since the 1960s. It has a parliamentary system of government with a prime minister as the head of state.

Subsistence cultivation is the basis of economic life. There are such planted crops as coconuts, yams, taro, bananas, corn, and melons, as well as several other crops planted on a three-year rotation cycle. Returns from this agricultural activity are satisfactory because of the fertile soils. Little attempt has been made to develop export crops, even though countries and territories close by are unable to produce sufficient food crops for their own needs.

Land tenure practices are complex and are based on a traditional structure whereby the land is collectively owned by village groups. Private ownership of land is not possible. Members of each village group are able to cultivate sections of the land only with the agreement of elders whose authority is sanctioned by tradition. The Rabonan government, however, does

---

* For reasons relating to political and personal sensitivity, the names of specific places and individuals are disguised in this case study. All other factual description is accurately represented.

have some state-owned land.

The people of Rabona have retained a very strong affection for their ancestral soil, an association which extends far beyond its immediate productive value as a source of food. The land where the ancestors once lived and now lie buried is an object of the deepest feeling. This affection for the land is expressed in a number of ways and can be likened to a religious or spiritual attachment.

In 1965-1970 and again in 1970-1975, development plans were formulated by the Rabonan government with particular attention to the replanting of coconut trees for rehabilitating the islands' copra industry, and to the production of certain food crops with the objective of achieving a modest export trade. When Rabona's balance of payments reached a critical point in 1970, the government decided that everything possible should be done to encourage production of local substitutes to reduce the flow of imports.

Need for Livestock Development

One problem facing the country was the high cost of imported meat. Imports accounted for approximately 30 percent of Rabona's total meat consumption. It was highly desirable to reduce such large-scale reliance on meat imports as rapidly as possible. The continuing rise of prices for meat products related to the increase in freight charges prompted a special committee, established by the prime minister to investigate ways of decreasing import expenditures, strongly to recommend an increase in local livestock production as a substitute for meat importation.

The Rabonan Department of Agriculture estimated that between 7,000 and 8,000 cattle were already in the country, but few of these were managed in large herds. Most of the animals belonged to small landholders who kept only a few cows and had little or no experience in farm management. Outside observers had noted, however, that cattle did particularly well in Rabona. Existing deficiencies in this area were largely due to inbreeding and mismanagement rather than to any problem associated with the local climate or land ecology.

Since achieving independence, the Rabonan government has pursued a policy of localization (indigenization) of employment. Recently, with vigorous enforcement of this policy, expatriates from New Zealand and other noncitizens of Rabona were employed only where a qualified local person could not be found to undertake a particular job. This provision applied to hiring in government departments and also in private organizations. A noncitizen could be employed for only two years, and during that time was required to train a local counterpart who could take over his job at the end of his contract.

The primary stimulus for the idea to establish a livestock project came from deliberations in 1971 by the special committee mentioned earlier. The structure of agricultural development in Rabona was such that it was entirely possible to increase local meat production. Existing problems of land tenure and operating capital meant only that the project would have to be undertaken by a government agency rather than by a private corporation or private citizens.

The decisions of the special committee about where projects for import substitution could be introduced were based upon analysis of the country's historic dependence on imports. The committee itself was made up of officials from the Planning Department, none of whom had any direct responsibility or experience in the agricultural sector. The Department of Agriculture, for its part, was mainly concerned with the development of copra and pineapple plantations and with crops cultivated by growers who were producing on a small scale.

The special committee's recommendation for a project directed toward increasing local meat production was accepted by the cabinet. The Minister of Agriculture was asked to determine the means by which such a project could be implemented. The Honorable T. H. Rangi, who held that responsibility, sent a memorandum to the Director of Agriculture, Harvey Enoka, requesting him to "prepare a proposal to increase meat production through a livestock development scheme."

The major factor influencing the establishment of the project was the anticipation of economic benefits it would bring by reducing the amount of meat imported by Rabonans. Initially, social benefits, such as might accrue from land development, increased employment, and better health standards, were not considered. However, these became important elements in the overall planning as the project was formulated.

The need for and identification of a livestock development scheme, therefore, was a decision made primarily on economic grounds. The project was seen as a means of assisting in the solution of a vital economic problem. The Department of Agriculture became involved in the matter only after that decision had been made. Although officers of the department possessed technical knowledge in the general field of agriculture, they were not invited to judge the feasibility or rationality of the projected idea. Once the decision had been made by the special committee, the single role of the Agriculture Department as expert in its area of responsibility was to advise and assist in implementation.

Officers of the department, however, lacked experience in livestock production on the scale envisaged, and had no firsthand knowledge of either operations of this type or of the technical skills and backup services required. The overall objective of the scheme, while readily accepted by government leadership, was quietly opposed by some Ministry officials on the grounds that the livestock industry was one in which the department had virtually no experience. Moreover, the problems associated with acquiring rights to land and obtaining cooperation from landowners, in order to make the scheme viable in the long term, were issues that greatly concerned the department.

The primary task for Agriculture officials now became that of developing a proposal to implement the operation mandated by the government. Director of Agriculture Harvey Enoka, although not convinced that livestock development in Rabona was either feasible or desirable, was of the opinion that if the cabinet maintained its position, some outside assistance must be sought to investigate the prospects of such a scheme and to prepare an implementation plan. Reluctantly, he recommended to his minister that a request be made to the New Zealand government to provide experts who could assist the department with the proposed development. The Minister of Agriculture, recognizing the department's lack of experience in this field, readily agreed to his director's suggestion and said he would recommend this action to the Rabonan cabinet.

PHASE 1: PLANNING, APPRAISAL, AND DESIGN

Formulation of The Project

Rabonan Initiative for Action

On August 22, 1971, the Rabonan cabinet resolved that the livestock development program it had already mandated should be handled as a priority matter, considering the urgent necessity to make the country more self-sufficient in meat production. The cabinet also agreed to the Minister of Agriculture's suggestion that outside experts be asked to assist with the project. The Honorable T. H. Rangi, as minister, was given authority to take whatever measures were necessary to implement the cabinet's decisions.

On August 25, the minister met with his Director of Agriculture, Harvey Enoka, and told him of the two decisions reached by the cabinet. The minister said that the cabinet regarded the scheme as most important because it would not only provide a reduction in the expenditure of funds overseas but because it would also increase employment opportunities for the people in Rabona.

Director Enoka, still full of doubts, anticipated that the decision to undertake a new livestock program without adequately trained local personnel would create some problems. He also thought that the resources allocated to develop such a scheme would far better be utilized to stimulate production of copra, bananas, and other crops for which overseas markets could provide needed income for Rabonans. Because the people of Rabona were traditionally familiar with and experienced in crop production, he believed that expansion in that area was more advisable than initiating a new livestock program without understanding the problems and pitfalls involved.

The minister was not unsympathetic with the points raised by Enoka but told him that the cabinet decision to proceed with the livestock scheme had been unanimous. After hours of discussion, the two officials finally agreed that the New Zealand government should be approached about the possibility of utilizing that country's overseas aid funds to assist with the scheme in providing the expertise required for planning.

Following their meeting, Enoka checked with the Rabonan Ministry of Foreign Affairs and found that the overseas aid grant from New Zealand was not yet fully committed. There was approximately NZ$300,000 (1) that could still be allocated to new projects. He therefore submitted a report to his minister advising that funds were available and suggested that permission be obtained from the cabinet to ask the New Zealand government to allocate, from the unexpended funds, on a priority basis, whatever amount might be required for the livestock development scheme. The cabinet's executive committee, which was empowered to make such decisions, agreed to this proposal, and the Agriculture Minister advised Enoka that he should proceed with whatever action was necessary for approaching the New Zealand government on the matter (see Fig. 2.1).

On September 15, 1971, Enoka wrote to the New Zealand High Commissioner in Rabona, informing him of the cabinet's decision and asking that part of the overseas aid allocation be used to support the project to increase livestock production within the country with the ultimate objective of making Rabona self-sufficient in its meat supply. He further requested that an expert from New Zealand be sent to Rabona to look into the possibilities for implementing such a scheme. On the same date, the Rabonan Central Planning Office formally submitted an identical request to the New Zealand government, specifically to the External Aid Division in the Ministry of Foreign Affairs.

Overseas Aid From New Zealand

The Rabonan application to the New Zealand government under the latter's development assistance program had to pass through several stages of review in New Zealand. Responsibility for overall coordination and execution of this program rested with the Ministry of Foreign Affairs and its External Aid Division (EAD), which reviewed overseas applications for aid (see Fig. 2.2).

Foreign assistance policy was formulated by the New Zealand government caucus and was watched over by a cabinet subcommittee on Foreign Aid. Formal requests for bilateral assistance were forwarded to EAD in the Ministry of Foreign Affairs and checked for consistency with the aid policy. Planning was normally done for a three-year period and included major elements of the bilateral programs and all multilateral contributions. Ministry officials each year prepared a more detailed outline of foreign aid. In this context, the Rabona foreign aid program for 1971 was budgeted overall for NZ$1,500,000. Each specific project that drew upon funds from this program had to be approved by both the Ministry of Foreign Affairs and the cabinet.

The normal procedure for supervision of overseas aid programs called for them to be looked after by officers of the New Zealand diplomatic mission to the country concerned. Where it was necessary, experts would be recruited from New Zealand government departments and universities, or as private consultants. In the South Pacific, small aid programs were administered directly by specialist departments in the New Zealand government. In the present case, this would be the Department of Agriculture. EAD was responsible for recruiting and briefing the experts or consultants.

The Rabona livestock project would fall within the jurisdiction of the EAD officer in charge of the Rabona foreign aid program, Michael Bennett. He had been with the division for four years, having joined it after obtaining an honors degree in economics from a New Zealand university. He possessed little overseas experience, having served only in Australia for six months. His

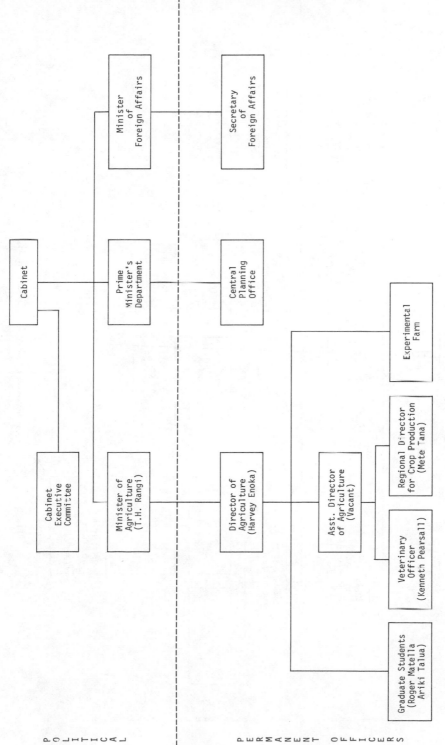

FIGURE 2.1 Rabona Government Structure as Related to the Rabonan Livestock Development Project

POLITICAL

PERMANENT OFFICERS

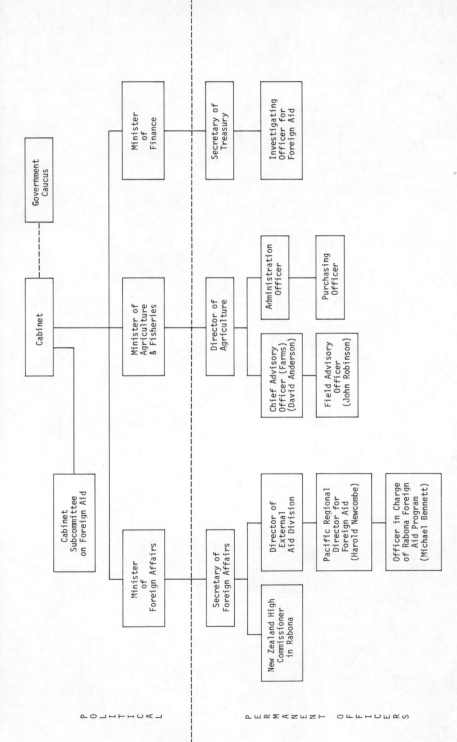

FIGURE 2.2   New Zealand Government Structure as Related to the
Rabonan Livestock Development Project

responsibility was to the Pacific Regional Director for Foreign Aid, a post then held by Harold Newcombe. All regional directors answered to the head of EAD.

The Rabonan application for assistance in livestock development was reviewed by EAD officer Bennett to determine: 1) if the proposal could be supported within the budget allocation for Rabona, and 2) if it fell within one of the general sectors that New Zealand had agreed to assist.   After checking, Bennett reported to Pacific Regional Director Newcombe that the project met both criteria.   He also noted that the Robonan cabinet had clearly identified this as a priority project. Accepting Bennett's evaluation, Newcombe reported these findings to the director of EAD, adding that since the Rabonan cabinet considered this a priority matter, the New Zealand government should proceed immediately with recruitment of an expert to be sent to Rabona.

On October 21, the director of EAD wrote to the New Zealand High Commissioner in Rabona advising him that the government was prepared to appraise the feasibility of a livestock development project in Rabona. He suggested that the High Commissioner inform the Rabonan government that an expert would probably be available early in 1972 to make the necessary study.   On the same date, the director of EAD sent a letter to the New Zealand Ministry of AGriculture and Fisheries requesting that a suitable person be recruited to "understand an appraisal of livestock development in Rabona with a view to assisting the country in its aim, to become self-sufficient in meat products within the foreseeable future."

Copies of this correspondence were sent to Pacific Regional Director Newcombe and to Michael Bennett. The EAD director noted on Bennett's copy that he should follow up with the New Zealand Ministry of Agriculture and Fisheries if nothing was heard within three weeks. On November 2, the director of EAD was informed that none of the Agriculture Department's officers could be released in early 1972. However, a recommendation was included that a suitable person for the job would be John Robinson, who was retiring as a field advisory officer after forty years with the department. Furthermore, the department could be prepared to give Robinson any support in the form of technical advice which might be required in carrying out the assignment. Robinson had had wide experience in all categories of farming. During his early years with the department, he had also farmed on his own property. Although familiar with New Zealand conditions, he never had been concerned with projects outside New Zealand and had no experience whatever in tropical agriculture.

The director of EAD passed this information on to Newcombe and Bennett with a note to the latter suggesting that "he contact John Robinson and bring him in for a chat." Bennett wrote to Robinson, asking him to come in for discussion of the proposed project. Robinson, already briefed on the matter by the Agriculture people, agreed to meet with Bennett and the other Foreign Affairs officials on December 15. Unfortunately, both Harold Newcombe and the director of EAD had to be away on that date, but Newcombe told Bennett to brief Robinson and to have him fill out the necessary papers should he be willing to take on the assignment.

The December meeting between Bennett and Robinson was fairly brief.

Bennett outlined the nature of the Rabonan request. He gave Robinson some general background information about Rabona, and also wrote down the details of the agricultural officer's experience with livestock development. The latter was eager to undertake the assignment, for he had never before had the opportunity of visiting the South Pacific islands. He felt that in his retirement he would be in a good position to devote some of his time to the proposed task. Bennett was impressed with Robinson's experience and knowledge of the livestock industry, and was convinced that the expert could easily handle the exploratory study, with support from the Agriculture Department if necessary. The two men agreed that the investigation should take place as soon as possible in 1972. Meanwhile, Robinson was to prepare a proposal with estimates of the time he would require to research the possibilities for livestock development and the cost estimates for completing that job.

Early in 1972, John Robinson wrote to Bennett advising him that it would take about two weeks to complete the study of Rabona's livestock potential and that he was prepared to do the work in February. The cost of the survey, apart from a consultant fee, would include travel fares and living expenses at 50 dollars a day. Bennett advised his superior, Pacific Regional Director Newcombe, that a time schedule and costs had been set and were in order. He requested approval for the study to be carried out. Newcombe agreed and sent a memorandum to the director of EAD relating the progress achieved to date. This information was forwarded to the New Zealand Minister of Foreign Affairs in a routine weekly report from the External Aid Division (EAD).

John Robinson, since retirement, had kept fairly busy reorganizing his personal affairs and actually did not have a great deal of time to undertake extensive research on Rabona before going there. He had read the brief background documents supplied by the Ministry of Foreign Affairs and was confident that his prior experience with livestock management in New Zealand would be sufficient preparation. From his former colleagues in the Agriculture Department who had been to Rabona, he learned more about the general nature of the country and local attitudes about livestock development. However, he really gained very little from these talks except to hear about the difficulties his colleagues had experienced in communicating with Rabonans and understanding their land tenure system.

Full details on the proposed study dates and John Robinson's background were sent to the New Zealand High Commissioner in Rabona, who in turn notified Harvey Enoka. The latter informed the Rabonan Minister of Agriculture about the progress that was being made.

Bennett was anxious to have Robinson conduct a very comprehensive review of Rabonan "livestock improvement in general." In his final briefing, he emphasized the need for Robinson to build "a sound general base" for conclusions drawn in his report. Bennett's enthusiasm for the prospect of livestock development in Rabona had prompted his superior, Harold Newcombe, to give him a free hand in overseeing the project.

It was formally agreed by Robinson and the Foreign Affairs officials that he would conduct the feasibility study during the last two weeks of February 1972. He was advised of his contact at the New Zealand High Commissioner's

Office in Rabona, and was given more background papers on Rabonan social, cultural, and land tenure matters.

An Informal Rabonan Proposal

It was noted earlier that Harvey Enoka, Director of Agriculture in Rabona, was skeptical about the cabinet proposal to diversify into livestock production. He considered it far more prudent to develop local resources with which Rabonans already had training and expertise. However, in late November 1971, he decided independently to make use of the services of two graduate students to prepare a proposal on livestock development. Roger Matella and Ariki Talua, both native Rabonans, had just completed a field study with the department two months ahead of schedule and had some weeks before leaving for their university studies in Australia. Both had worked for the department for three years before being granted a year's study leave to obtain postgraduate degrees in agricultural science in Australia. They had earned their bachelor's degrees in agriculture in New Zealand, where they had received a sound theoretical and practical training in cattle and dairy farming.

The project undertaken by the two men was personally supervised by Director Enoka, and they reported directly, and only, to him on an informal basis as temporary departmental officers. He gave them wide latitude in preparing a proposal for a livestock production scheme intended to reduce the high rate of meat imports into the country.

The student researchers decided at the start that the problem must be approached from a local point of view. Both were well aware that heretofore the major restriction on land development schemes of any kind in Rabona had been the complex nature of the traditional land tenure system, in which land was collectively owned by the members of village groups. Existing coconut plantations were, in effect, owned by the whole group as a corporate collectivity, even though the individual trees might belong to or be used by certain member families. Such customs were strictly adhered to by all Rabonans. Under this system, it was essential that development of land on a scale larger than that of a family garden plot should be approved by the entire group owning the land. This normally involved a long and detailed discussion with a large number of landholders as to the terms they would agree to for use of the land in question.

Matella and Talua realized that their first consideration was to determine the willingness of the people to participate in a major scheme that would require the cooperation of many landholders. The initial approach, they believed, should be to those Rabonans who held land in areas judged to be most suitable for grazing cattle. Most of the accessible land in this category was already devoted to coconut plantation use. This meant that a need existed to develop a program of cattle grazing under the coconut palms. The trees were normally spaced several yards apart amidst the understory vegetation and grew to a considerable height above the browse level. The student investigators would have to determine whether cattle could be grazed successfully under these conditions and achieve acceptable weight gains in the process. With their intimate knowledge of local conditions, they felt that one advantage of grazing "cattle under coconuts" was that the shade under the trees provided a more tolerable environment for cattle than did open pasture. An equally important consideration, at least during the initial phase of the scheme, was that if the cattle were restricted to utilizing the existing vegetation under the trees, there would be no urgency in planning pasture improvement.

Matella and Talua guessed that it might not be possible to assess the feasibility of this form of grazing in purely economic terms. It would take some time before one could determine whether the weight gains of cattle would be acceptable in relation to the capital invested. The costs of management in a tropical country would be strongly influenced by the different grazing conditions and stocking rates as compared with New Zealand. Whether the net result was positive or negative, however, it would have to be judged against the value of reducing the amount of imported beef and the consequent savings of local funds that would otherwise be expended overseas. There were also social gains to the nation implicit in an increased beef herd, both in employment opportunities and cash returns for landholders cooperating in the scheme. Overall, it was believed that the livestock development plan would create little social disruption and would not diminish copra revenues from the coconut plantations.

Discussions held by the two students with various Rabonan landholders proved to be successful. They obtained full cooperation as well as a firm offer by one village to make available two 400-hectare areas of land relatively close to each other and providing a good range of coconut tree age classes. One of these areas, which could be utilized for an experimental grazing project, possessed a topography varying from steep to gently rolling hills, with some bare earth and rocky outcrops. The land was adequately provided with a number of wells and permanent streams of good-quality water. Soils were reasonably fertile. The existing vegetation growing in symbiotic association with the trees of the coconut plantations could be grouped into several classes, that is, either mission grass or bracken and other low weeds in the drier areas, reeds in the moister locations, and residual broadleaf forest in the valley bottoms along stream edges. It was likely to be uneconomical to try improving the pasturage with fertilizers, because the results would be only marginal. The other of the two land areas was much the same, except for minor differences in vegetative cover and soil qualities.

General Recommendations

In submitting their final report to Director Enoka, Matella and Talua, concluded that, at least initially, the government should undertake an experimental program to explore the possibility of grazing "cattle under coconuts" in support of the national mandate to reduce meat imports by increasing local beef production. First, they argued, it would take some time to build up an organization and sufficient cattle stock to operate on a larger scale in Rabona. Thus, the urgent need was for a pilot project which, if successful, could serve as the nucleus for later expansion. The trial project could be conducted on the two 400-hectare land areas offered by Rabonans, which were generally representative of the principal soil types and coconut tree age classes in the country.

They acknowledged that a calculated risk existed in setting up such a trial project, because it would involve large expenditures for the initial investment in cattle herds and living accommodations for new staff.   However, if the trial should prove impracticable, the cattle might be disposed of locally at little or no loss to the government, and the accommodations could be turned over to Rabonans who needed housing.   Overall, it was considered that the degree of risk was minimal and acceptable, considering the government's sense of urgency about this undertaking.

The major problem facing large-scale livestock development in Rabona, as they saw it, was the lack of sufficient expert knowledge for conducting the required experimentation.   While unskilled labor was readily obtainable, individuals with some experience in cattle and farm management were scarce.   There was virtually no one in the local community with a thorough understanding of this type of farming.

The principal recommendations submitted by Matella and Talua to Director Enoka were to:

1. establish a pilot cattle-grazing project in the area as soon as possible,

2. recruit a cattle manager to set up and operate a special cattle unit within the Department of Agriculture for a four-year trial period,

3. superimpose on the grazing experiment a number of tests designed to provide more precise information on which to base future plans for expansion,

4. order and acquire housing and other domestic requirements, as well as stores for the first year of the project, before the cattle manager was appointed.

The last recommendation was included as a necessary precondition to recruiting a manager of sufficiently high caliber to supervise the development scheme and to ensure that training of local people was carried out in the best possible manner.   Thus, proper advance attention to the domestic accommo-dations for the manager and his family should guarantee that the new man would be able to spend his available time to the best advantage of the project.

The kind of livestock specialist best suited to the present situation, in the opinion of Matella and Talua, was a person who possessed the practical skills and capabilities of hill-country cattle farming, as well as experience with livestock in the tropics.   He should have an innovative approach to the task, and a sensitive appreciation for the cultural and social needs and values of the people of Rabona.   Preferably, he would be an active, younger man with a cooperative attitude, particularly in the management aspects of such a project, and in the training of local farmers.   It was essential that he be willing and able to work with Rabonan stockmen and to pass his knowledge on to them.   He would also be required to select local Rabonans having the basic qualifications to enable them, with training and experience, eventually to play significant managerial roles in the program.

To bring in an expatriate cattle manager, probably from New Zealand, would require that domestic arrangements include provision for schooling as well as housing. The initial appointment should be for a two-year term with an extension of two years if desirable. It was felt by the two investigators that whoever was appointed as cattle manager should maintain residence in Rabona throughout the initial period of the development scheme.

The experimental livestock development project, as proposed by Matella and Talua, would be oriented toward achieving the following benefits:

1. Provide experience in the large-scale management of "cattle under coconuts" in a manner that would not interfere with copra production of the plantations;

2. Allow the buildup of breeding herds;

3. Enable the development of technologies relating to:

    a. optimum grazing intensity, with reference to soil types, terrain, existing vegetation, and possible erosion,

    b. optimum paddock size and design,

    c. animal management practices, such as rotational grazing pattern,

    d. management organization,

    e. overall economics of the project,

    f. pasture improvements;

4. Advance as quickly as possible to a suitable situation permitting general expansion rapidly if the scheme proved practicable;

5. Provide information useful for further development of pasture farming.

Expanding on these recommendations, Matella and Talua provided further details and points for Director Enoka's consideration. They pointed out that present staff members of the Department of Agriculture were already fully occupied with their normal duties, and none of the field staff had adequate training in livestock management. Therefore, the recommended cattle unit, intended to operate separately and with direct responsibility to the Agriculture Director, would need a cattle manager, two stockmen, and casual labor on demand. The number of stockmen would be increased as the trial progressed. Clerical and logistical servicing would be carried out by existing departmental personnel.

In the plantation areas where no pasture improvement was planned, cattle would be raised until the age of two or two-and-a-half years, when they would be ready for final fattening on high-quality pasture. Cattle of this quality were already in demand and no difficulty was anticipated in finding a market for them. Because there was a national shortage of good-quality breeding cows, it was recommended that 100 of these and two bulls be acquired from overseas to provide the nucleus of a breeding herd. Additional yearlings could be obtained from local farmers wherever available to make up the balance of the projected herd when fencing had been completed. Local Santa Gertrudis and Brahmin crossbred cattle were well suited to the Rabonan conditions of rough grazing; temperate zone beef breeds, such as Herefords, would be useful primarily to expand the herd by breeding back to the locally adapted animal.

The development scheme would have to give careful attention to problems of cattle disease and animal health in general. Only a limited veterinary service was available, but every effort should be made to insure against an outbreak of disease during the trial period.

In pasture management, the aim would be to build the paddocks as large as possible, consistent with complete coverage by the cattle and without risk of erosion or deterioration of pasture grasses. As already indicated, the existing vegetation under the coconut trees would be utilized initially. Paddock size under these conditions might be set at 20 hectares to start with. Optimum size could be ascertained only after experimentation. Topography, water supply, herd control, and plantation management would also be governing factors.

The trial area would have to be large enough to fully cover the range of coconut tree age classes, understory vegetation types, and soil types, and to allow a comprehensive appreciation of management and administrative requirements. The size of the area should be economically consistent with the size and time available of the minimum staff provided. Costing and staffing for the trial project was estimated on the basis of the two 400-hectare areas of land available, and could be scaled up or down as experience and funding dictated. A schedule of costs was prepared for the project that would begin with only 200 hectares under grazing management and would build up each year over a four-year period to the 800 hectares projected for the trial. Costs for each year were estimated for personnel, housing, transport, cattle stock, paddock and stockyard construction, and veterinary services. The first year's projected outlay would amount to approximately NZ$50,000, which together with increments of about NZ$30,000 for each of the following three years would round off to NZ$145,000 as the total project cost.

Director Enoka was impressed with the thought which had gone into the report, and he spent several hours discussing the proposal with Matella and Talua. Their inquiries and understanding of the local situation had resulted in a report which in his opinion was eminently feasible in its attention to the land tenure problem. He considered the total cost estimate of NZ$145,000 to be quite realistic. Enoka was encouraged by the quality of the work produced by the two graduate students, and he believed they would make a very significant contribution to their country when they returned to Rabona in twelve months' time.

Enoka foresaw a major political problem in the fact that the recommendations made it clear that the cabinet's mandate to effect a high level of meat production was not going to be achieved for some years. Enoka was certain that the Minister of Agriculture would not like to be told of such a conclusion. The scheme put forward by Matella and Talua was frankly an experiment intended to test the feasibility of the cabinet's objective. It did not propose a major effort toward immediate development of a national beef production program. For that reason, Director Enoka did not forward the report to his minister, but waited instead for a reply to the cabinet's request to bring in a livestock specialist from New Zealand to undertake a feasibility study with overseas grant aid available to the Rabonan government.

An Expatriate Feasibility Study

Early in 1972, Harvey Enoka took six months' leave to attend an international conference in Asia and to visit various agricultural projects in Europe and North America. He turned over all of the immediate problems of his office to his veterinary officer, expatriate Kenneth Pearsall, who had been loaned to the department by the British government for a term of two years. At this time the post of Assistant Director of Agriculture was unoccupied, because Enoka had decided to leave it vacant until a suitably qualified Rabonan could be identified. In fact, he felt that Roger Matella, one of the two authors of the livestock report, would be quite capable of assuming that responsibility when he completed his graduate studies in Australia.

Kenneth Pearsall had arrived in Rabona only six months earlier. He had, however, acquired considerable experience in 14 years of service with the British government in Africa, and was well acquainted with the problems of livestock management in developing countries. He tended to be a bit aloof, it was said, and he still did not understand the cultural and social values of the people of Rabona. But so far he had proved to be efficient and competent in his work in the department.   Director Enoka had every confidence in Pearsall's ability to carry on the day-to-day tasks as acting director and to handle any problem that might arise in his absence. It should be noted here that Pearsall had not been told about the proposal for a livestock development scheme prepared by Matella and Talua a short time before. Enoka viewed the report as an unofficial study and saw no reason to share it with Pearsall before going on leave.

Shortly after Enoka departed on his journey overseas, the New Zealand High Commissioner in Rabona contacted the department with notice of the impending arrival of John Robinson, the livestock expert who had been appointed by the New Zealand government to study the feasibility of a development scheme in Rabona.   Pearsall, as acting director of the department, was only partially acquainted with details of this plan. Upon checking the department's files, he learned more about the Rabonan cabinet's decision, the earlier correspondence with the High Commissioner, and further information about John Robinson's background.

In the brief time that Pearsall had been stationed in Rabona, he had found only a small expatriate community and but few agriculture experts. Nevertheless, he had settled into the new life very well, and enjoyed being once again in an environment similar to that he had known in Africa. He welcomed the opportunity to work in a warm climate and in a situation where he was given far more responsibility than in the large, specialized departments he had been assigned to in England after his return from Africa. But it must be admitted that he was looking forward to Robinson's visit. He wanted to talk with the expert about the agricultural scene in New Zealand, which he had not had the opportunity to view at first hand.

Meanwhile, during mid-January in New Zealand, John Robinson received a final briefing from Michael Bennett, the External Aid Division (EAD) officer in charge of the Rabona Foreign Aid Program in the Ministry of Foreign Affairs. Bennett indicated to him that the government was ready to cooperate with financial aid for the Rabonan livestock scheme, subject to Robinson's recommendation justifying the expenditure. He gave Robinson a letter of introduction to the New Zealand High Commissioner in Rabona and the necessary travel documents.

Robinson arrived in Rabona during the third week of February 1972. He was met by Acting Director of Agriculture Pearsall, and the next day was introduced to the Minister of Agriculture, the Honorable T. H. Rangi. This meeting had a great impact on the New Zealand expert. Minister Rangi was most anxious to impress Robinson with the importance of the proposed livestock development scheme as far as the government was concerned. He made it clear that the sooner meat production was increased, the better it would be for the country. The minister acknowledged that Rabona had little expertise in this area and lacked the financial resources to undertake the venture alone. He told Robinson that all facilities of the Agriculture Department were at his disposal and that any assistance he required would be provided through the acting director's office.

A tour of the department's agricultural facility was arranged by Pearsall, who also accompanied the New Zealander on field visits to other parts of Rabona. The new experiences associated with this introduction to the Rabonan way of life greatly interested Robinson. He saw many areas where existing livestock practices could be improved.

Another member of the visitation group was Mete Tana, Regional Director for Crop Production, a native Rabonan who had completed a diploma in agriculture in Australia. Tana was highly regarded within the government, for he had demonstrated a sound understanding of the impact of Rabonan land tenure practices and social customs on agricultural development. He took the opportunity whenever possible to apprise Robinson of the problems likely to emerge in the government's effort to increase livestock production. Paramount among these were the acquisition of land and the need to cooperate with local landholding groups to ensure that they fully understand the potential benefits of the livestock development scheme. Mete Tana wanted to spend more time with Robinson to discuss local problems regarding livestock management. But apart from chance conversations during their visits to farm areas under consideration for future development, he was not able to elaborate on his ideas.

John Robinson spent a little over two weeks in Rabona. He briefly visited one other island in the archipelago, but otherwise limited his investigation to Rabona Island, the largest of the group and the most populated. He had occasion to speak with several Rabonans who farmed on a small scale and who each already owned a few head of cattle. These animals were grown primarily for family requirements, although some beef was produced for sale on the island. The New Zealander was shocked at the unsanitary methods employed locally for slaughtering cattle and for cutting up meat to be sold.

During the period of Robinson's visit, Kenneth Pearsall devoted nearly all of his time to assisting the livestock expert. An officer in the department had been assigned to obtain copies of reports and statistics required by Robinson. However, little had been written about livestock development in Rabona, and Robinson concluded that he would have to depend pretty much on his own observations for the recommendations he intended to make. Pearsall did not see a copy of the report by Matella and Talua. Because the investigation had been made in an unofficial capacity, the authors had prepared only four copies of the report. They gave two to Director Enoka and kept the others for themselves.

Robinson relied heavily on Pearsall's opinions. While this was reasonable in technical matters, it overlooked important needs and wants of Rabonans. Neither Pearsall nor Robinson recognized the depth of the problems relating to land tenure custom or the need to establish ready and complete communication with Rabonans about what was being contemplated in livestock production. They did not see, as Matella and Talua had, that any major livestock venture in Rabona would probably have to be based on the principle of grazing cattle under the trees on the coconut plantations. No other suitable land was available.

John Robinson prepared his final report after his return to New Zealand, basing it on notes made in Rabona. He had interviewed the Rabonan Minister of Agriculture on three occasions, two other cabinet ministers, four experts in the Agriculture Department, and six Rabonan landowners. He had visited 21 local farms and the department's experimental farm. Also he had looked into Rabona's slaughtering facilities, the government's beef subsidy and disease eradication schemes, and the islands' poultry and pig production.

Robinson's report was submitted to Michael Bennett at the Ministry of Foreign Affairs on March 22, 1972. It briefly outlined the method of investigation and described the existing programs for cattle improvement.

As already noted, Robinson was impressed with the technical knowledge of Acting Director of Agriculture Pearsall. He adopted the latter's suggestion that the best way to obtain quick results was to give top priority to expansion of the 300-acre (121.5 hectare) experimental farm operated by the Department of Agriculture. By utilizing these facilities, it was argued, a well-planned and organized beef ranch, for demonstration of pasture and cattle management with good quality breeding stock, could form the nucleus or base for later developmental schemes. To build on what already existed would be quicker than starting a new scheme from nothing.

The recommendations presented by Robinson were primarily concerned with this basic idea. Altogether, some twenty-two separate tasks were outlined for implementation within the overall project for a total cost of NZ$267,500 covering a three-year period (1972-1975).

Table 2.1 identifies these tasks and notes their estimated cost. The following paragraphs (keyed by number to the list in Table 2.1) briefly describe the tasks directly concerned with development of the cattle industry. Also included are several proposed tasks that deal with improve-

TABLE 2.1 – Summary of Proposed Project Tasks and Estimated Costs, Rabona Livestock Development Scheme, 1972-1975

	1972-1973	1973-1974	1974-1975	Total
1. Roadway and central race system	NZ$8,000	NZ$6,000	NZ$2,000	NZ$16,000
2. Fencing for pasture subdivision	4,900	2,000	3,000	9,900
3. Water supply	5,000	--	--	5,000
4. Cattle yards	2,000	--	--	2,000
5. Cattle supply	8,400	8,400	--	16,800
6. Pasture improvement	3,000	3,000	3,000	9,000
7. Farmer training in stocksmanship	2,000	2,000	2,000	6,000
8. Extension of cattle subsidy	10,000	10,000	10,000	30,000
9. Tuberculosis and brucellosis eradication	2,500	2,500	--	5,000
10. Mobile killing facility	10,000	--	--	10,000
11. Cold storage facilities	10,000	--	10,000	20,000
12. Abattoir at Rewi	15,000	--	--	15,000
13. Abbatoir staff training	1,000	1,000	1,000	3,000
14. Refrigerated delivery van	10,000	--	--	10,000
15. Artificial insemination facility	500	--	--	500
16. Animal quarantine center	--	5,000	--	5,000
17. Town milk supply dairyshed	12,000	--	--	12,000
18. Commercial poultry subsidy	4,000	1,500	1,500	7,000
19. Commercial pig subsidy	4,000	4,000	4,000	12,000
20. Research on pig and poultry feed	2,300	2,500	5,000	9,800
21. Supervision and financial control	1,500	1,000	1,000	3,500
22. Government abbatoir	--	30,000	30,000	60,000
Total Allocation	NZ$116,000	NZ$78,900	NZ$72,500	NZ$267,500

ment of Rabona's pig and poultry production, but these will not be elaborated here, since the focus of this case study is on cattle development.

Recommended Project Tasks

1. Improvement of the roadway and central race system on the department's experimental farm would enable all-weather use, even during the rainy season. This would permit greater utilization of the farm's facilities for training employees and groups of Rabonan farmers in livestock management as well as new and traditional crop production. It would also save labor as mechanized equipment could be used with greater effect. Two miles (3.2 kilometers) of access road and races (fenced lanes) would be paved with local materials. The Public Works Department would be requested to provide the necessary labor and equipment.

2. The fencing normally required for a beef cattle farm would subdivide 200 acres (81.0 hectares) of land to facilitate demonstrations of cattle and pasture management. Rabonan labor was judged capable of carrying out the work, but an experienced fencing contractor would have to be brought in from New Zealand as supervisor to ensure adequate standards in the work product. Construction of the 9 miles (14.5 kilometers) of fencing would necessitate importation from New Zealand of treated fence posts, barbed and plain wire, and electric fence units.

3. Construction of a satisfactory water supply and distribution network would enable cattle to be carried on the experimental farm at all times and thereby allow more opportunities for demonstration training. The building of troughs and installation of plastic pipe and an electric pump could be done by Rabonan labor if directed by an experienced local contractor.

4. New circular cattle yards with gravelled surface and concrete races, capable of holding 200 cattle, would incorporate a veterinary bail for confining animals undergoing treatment, a spraying lane, and weighing scales, for training Rabonans in improved livestock care. All of the work could be completed by departmental staff and local labor under expatriate supervision.

5. It was proposed to import 80 Polled Hereford heifers and ten bulls from New Zealand to establish a bull-breeding herd for long-term improvement of the local cattle industry, to assist the cattle subsidy scheme by providing local farmers with better quality stock, and to enhance operation of the tuberculosis and brucellosis eradication scheme (described in item 9, following).

6. Pasture improvement, regarded as fundamental to Rabonan livestock management, would be carried out over the three-year period to develop further 35 acres (14.2 hectares) of partially improved farmland and to establish a new pasture on an additional 165 acres (66.8 hectares). Both areas were part of the department's experimental farm. Guinea grass and siratro, both well-adapted forage grasses in the South Pacific, would be planted vegetatively in the customary Rabonan method. The pasture improvement plan would include subsidy of continuing research on various forage species,

planting methods, and grazing management in the interest of showing Rabonan farmers how to upgrade feeding of their cattle.

7. Since few Rabonans know how to work cattle in large numbers, it was considered essential that training in stockmanship be offered. In time, this could be done at the experimental farm. At the outset, however, some Rabonans should be allowed to get this experience at established ranches in another Pacific country, such as Fiji, where field conditions are comparable to those in Rabona. It was proposed that, during the three years of the project, from six to ten Rabonans be supported in this undertaking for up to six months each. Their travel fares, sustenance, and other allowances would be paid from the New Zealand grant.

8. Certain Rabonan farmers who already met most of the requirements for successful small-scale livestock management would be subsidized for critical needs on their own farms, such as improved water supply and distribution system, fencing materials, legume seed, and foundation stock. It was estimated that in each year of the project five local farmers could be subsidized.

9. The veterinary officer in Rabona was represented as conducting a well-ordered testing scheme designed to eradicate both tuberculosis and brucellosis from all herds in the country. He had estimated that complete testing of local cattle might turn up another 100 reactors, animals found to have one disease or the other. It was recommended that owners of known reactors be compensated at NZ$50 per head for their destruction in order to achieve disease-free herds in Rabona.

10. Robinson had observed that islanders usually butchered their beef cattle in the open, choosing a new site each time, so that if all of the meat were cooked and eaten the same day, the practice was reasonably hygienic. But this was not always true. He saw an urgent need for a mobile killing facility that could go from village to village to slaughter animals for individual owners and to inspect the meat for possible disease. The meat could then be put up for sale to local villagers immediately or be taken to the government meat market in town. He recommended that such a mobile facility be provided until sufficient demand justified building an abattoir on Rabona Island. In that event, the mobile unit could be transferred to Tapolo, largest of the outlying islands, to improve the situation there. The plan was seen as providing disease inspection, more protection from spoiled meat, and better utilization of butchered stock at a reasonable cost.

11. Refrigeration was unavailable in the outer islands of Rabona. At the time of Robinson's study, cattle were killed there in the same manner as described for the main island, and the meat had to be consumed on the day of the kill if spoilage were to be avoided. It was planned for the first year of the project to establish a government meat market with a cold storage facility on Tapolo Island, and to install another on Arangi Island the following year.

12. A nongovernment effort had already been made to build a small abattoir at Rewi, the Christian mission farm on Rabona Island, but inadequate

funding had prevented its completion. This killing facility had been intended primarily to service a first-rate piggery operated by the mission, but could be used for butchering beef as well. To complete the construction of this abattoir as a project task would lower the priority for a more extensive and costly government abattoir. The Agriculture Department would control the Rewi slaughterhouse to ensure adequate hygienic standards, but the mission would manage it.

13. If and when a government abattoir were established in Rabona, local staff with training and experience would be in demand. Meanwhile, the same capabilities were needed to operate the small abattoir at Rewi upon its completion. It was proposed that a few promising Rabonans be selected for training in New Zealand slaughterhouses and freezing plants, and be supported with project funds for travel and other allowances while overseas. Upon returning to Rabona, these individuals would receive on-the-job training under a qualified abattoir manager to advance their competence to the point of taking over the entire responsibility.

14. Robinson had discovered that no facility existed for delivering freshly slaughtered beef to needy outlying villages on Rabona Island. The same applied to the catches brought in by the government fishing boat. Provision of a refrigerated van from New Zealand would enable both needs to be served on an organized basis. The refrigerated vehicle would be useful for delivering fresh meat for sale to the existing government meat market from the small abbatoir at Rewi as well as from other places on the island.

15. The veterinary officer in Rabona planned to produce bulls by controlled mating of the stock imported from New Zealand, but he suggested to Robinson that at a later date artificial insemination (AI) might be resorted to as a means of introducing unrelated sires to build up the Rabona herds. A New Zealand Rotary Club had offered to provide stores of AI semen for use in Rabona, on condition that liquid nitrogen storage of the semen could be arranged for at the Veterinary Center. The modest sum of NZ$500 was proposed for this project task.

16. As the only livestock scheduled for introduction to Rabona would come from New Zealand and would, in effect, be in quarantine when settled on the department's experimental farm, a quarantine center as such was not a high-priority item. Nevertheless, quarantine regulations were being drafted, and a minimum sum was proposed to build the center in the project's second year.

17. Robinson had discovered a town milk supply dairy in Rabona, run by a church school with some 200 boys in residence, but the milk processing situation called for considerable improvement, for reasons of health and economics. The existing demand for milk, from the new hospital as well as from the mission, was estimated at 40 gallons (151.4 liters) daily. The project task in this case called for the Agriculture Department to install a proper processing shed and pasteurizing facility at the mission station, to be operated by the mission and to be made available for training and demonstration by the department. Further, visits to New Zealand by the

school's stock manager and agricultural teacher were recommended for the purpose of viewing town supply farms and milk treatment plants near Auckland.

18-20. Three project tasks will be noted here only briefly, for they fall outside the main thrust of this case study. These recommended tasks were to deal primarily with subsidized improvement or extension of existing attempts by Rabonans to establish the local pig and poultry industries and to produce cheaper feed, with the objectives of creating greater self-sufficiency among small farmers, substituting locally grown products for imported ones, and increasing employment opportunities.

21. The Department of Agriculture's commitment to supervise office work wherever needed for the project tasks would be prorated and recompensed from the New Zealand grant. In like manner, half-time of one clerk position, judged sufficient to handle financial control and progress reports, would be supported by the project.

22. This project task to construct a government abattoir was included in Robinson's original recommendations. It has already been mentioned that he had seen how the villagers in Rabona, by custom, slaughtered their livestock quite simply in the open. Any surplus meat cut up for sale was taken to the government meat market in town. The popular demand for marketed beef was expected to rise in future to a point that might require an estimated ten animals to be killed each week. At such time, an abattoir larger than the one at Rewi would be justified. Priority for this project task was downgraded, however, when Robinson decided to hold off until after the first year, when experience with the Rewi abattoir (item 12), the mobile killing facility (item 10), and the refrigerated delivery van (item 14) could be evaluated.

John Robinson's report was to be the basis for the document prepared for final review within the New Zealand government. In his view, there appeared to be no technical impediments to the recommendations made. Likewise, there seemed to be general agreement about the political, economic, and social values of the scheme. However, he had overlooked the social implications of land tenure and local farmer attitudes. The importance of keeping the Rabonan people fully informed about details of the plan had not been followed up. Although Mete Tana, the Rabonan specialist in crop production, had tried to keep the local leadership informed during Robinson's visits around the country, the people still did not have good information about the proposed development. They were also confused by their recollections of the investigation made by Roger Matella and Ariki Talua the preceding November, and the differences between what had been talked about then and the plan of action now favored by Robinson and Pearsall.

The New Zealander's report and the project design he offered did not really relate the targets set in the project tasks to the original objective. This was due in part to the fact that the goals as represented to Robinson at the start had been rather vague and to some degree contradictory. The EAD official in the New Zealand Ministry of Foreign Affairs, Michael Bennett, had been rather general, open ended, and more heedful of the long-term needs of Rabona. The Rabonan Minister of Agriculture, the Honorable T. H. Rangi, as a politician had been very specific and wanted immediate results, in the form of a dramatic increase in local beef production.   He was impatient with Robinson's approach, which seemed to postpone new land development and to restrict most of the project activity to the department's experimental farm.

Robinson seems to have been well aware of critical needs in the area of Rabonan manpower development.   While in Rabona, he learned to accept the fact that the pace of life was much slower, and that the experience and techniques relied on by Rabonans who were already working with livestock were geared closely to their traditional system.   Any future development of farms with large herds of cattle would inevitably demand adoption of new techniques and work habits and necessitate a major program of re-education. Unfortunately, Robinson did not, or could not, assess the extent and sort of training that would be appropriate to the situation.   This omission left some room for doubt about the ultimate success of the project.

John Robinson's proposal was the only one considered in New Zealand. The informal study done by Matella and Talua had never been made known to the Rabonan Minister of Agriculture nor to the New Zealand Ministry of Foreign Affairs.   Director of Agriculture Harvey Enoka was away on leave during the period when Robinson undertook his investigation, and Enoka had the only copies of the earlier report, other than those kept by the authors themselves, who were then studying in Australia.   While Robinson's plan fell within the provisions of the New Zealand government's foreign aid program and budget, it unfortunately did not tackle the main problem as viewed from the Rabonan perspective.

Project Appraisal

In New Zealand, John Robinson's report and proposals for livestock development in Rabona were endorsed and recommended for implementation by the officer in charge of the Rabona Foreign Aid Program, Michael Bennett, with a note that the entire presentation had been well received by the Acting Director of Agriculture in Rabona, Kenneth Pearsall.   In turn, the Pacific Regional Director of Foreign Affairs, Harold Newcombe, accepted his officer's judgment and forwarded the material to the Director of the External Aid Division (EAD), noting that the proposed budget could be met by development aid funds still allocated to Rabona, and that the project concept was accorded high priority by the Rabonan government.   The EAD director, for his part, was mainly concerned about whether the technical experts were in agreement and if the proposal fell within the scope of the Rabonan aid program.   He based his approval on the favorable evaluations made by his subordinates.   The Minister of Foreign Affairs concurred, as a matter of course, when assured of the project's feasibility and political desirability.

The formal proposal for bilateral aid, amounting to NZ$267,500 for the three-year period from September 1, 1972 to March 31, 1975 to improve the quality of Rabonan livestock and to provide certain related facilities, was finally presented to the New Zealand cabinet on June 12, 1972.

The proposal before the cabinet underwent several rather cursory appraisals. The Department of Agriculture, which had nominated Robinson for the study in the first place, supported the plan and offered to provide supervisory technical staff and whatever other support was needed to get the program underway. The treasury added its recommendation, subject to elimination of the project task (see Table 2.1, item 22) to build a government abattoir. Postponement of this NZ$60,000 job was advised until an abattoir of such size could be more fully utilized. The External Aid Division in the Ministry of Foreign Affairs noted that implementation of the project offered scope for private sector participation in New Zealand, through the requisition of cattle stock and the design and equipping of such facilities as the cold storage and town milk-supply plants. On the whole, however, EAD considered the development scheme to be unsuitable for execution solely by the private sector, and recommended that it be coordinated and supervised by the New Zealand Department of Agriculture. This was acceptable to the department. Cabinet approval followed, with general agreement that the entire project would be implemented along lines to be set down by the department.

The report by John Robinson seems to have been assessed in a rather disjointed manner. Overall, the proposal was evaluated primarily by Michael Bennett, the EAD officer, even though his knowledge of the Rabonan situation was minimal.   He was also in the ambiguous position of endorsing the work of a consultant whom he had selected and briefed. The Agriculture Department, which had nominated Robinson, was the only party with technical knowledge pertinent to the scheme, but it examined the merits of the proposition with only scanty understanding of the Rabonan scene. The Treasury investigation was concerned primarily with cost factors, i.e., that they were reasonable and that the total budget could be contained within the Rabonan aid allocation. Each of the principals involved in the cabinet review reflected a different commitment which, in each case, was rather narrowly defined. The decision to go ahead with the scheme was, in the final analysis based on the assurance that it fell within the broad policy set forth by New Zealand's Foreign Aid Committee and that it was politically and economically desirable in the country making the request.

Once the New Zealand government had committed itself to finance the project, the remaining questions to consider were who would participate in its direction and how would it be implemented. It now consisted of 21 project tasks with an estimated total expenditure of NZ$207,500, since the item for a government abbatoir had been deleted.

PHASE 2: SELECTION, APPROVAL, AND ACTIVATION

Selection of the Project Manager

The task of activating the project fell to the EAD officer in charge of the Rabona Foreign Aid Program. Upon receiving notification of the cabinet's approval, Bennett initiated two actions. First, he informed the New Zealand High Commissioner in Rabona and asked him to formally advise the Rabonan

Minister of Agriculture that the project was all set to go. Second, he contacted the New Zealand Agriculture Department's director and asked for his suggestions for prompt implementation. In response, the latter got in touch with John Robinson to inquire if the livestock specialist would be willing to carry on with the Rabonan venture. As Robinson had but recently retired from the department, it was anticipated that he might have the time required to direct the operation. In any case, all of the department's own officers were then fully committed to their regular duties.

After his two-week stay in Rabona, Robinson felt that he and his wife might well enjoy living and working there for two or three years. While he had but limited experience with livestock development in the tropics (having worked only in New Zealand's temperate climate), and was already past the age of retirement, he nonetheless agreed to accept the offer. The Ministry of Foreign Affairs was advised that the Agriculture Department would employ Robinson as director of the Rabonan project.

The choice of Robinson for this role was one that would have repercussions. He had proved to be competent in the posts held throughout his long service with the department. However, he had never borne responsibility for the overall management of a project. His experience in coordinating a relatively diverse group of activities was limited. Never had he worked for any period of time in the kind of climatic and cultural environments represented by Rabona. The complex communication linkages, the logistic problems, the management of island personnel, the coping with inevitable crises - all of these together meant that the project would not be an easy one for any expatriate to manage.

Organizational Linkages

The overall structure for managing the Rabona project was intended to allow participation from different quarters by personnel who would form a loosely organized team to oversee the project and to represent their respective agencies. The one individual who would be primarily responsible for reporting back to the New Zealand government, provider of the foreign aid funds, was Michael Bennett of EAD. He would also be Robinson's contact for any assistance the latter might require from the Ministry of Foreign Affairs. Similarly, within the Department of Agriculture, the Chief Advisory Officer for Farms, David Anderson, was appointed coordinator to work with Robinson on all matters needing attention in that department.

In Rabona, on the other hand, Robinson's principal contact would be the Director of Agriculture, Harvey Enoka, who by this time had returned from leave and had begun to pick up the threads of the projected livestock endeavor. Enoka was more than a little concerned about the way in which the proposal had been developed in his absence. He also felt that it would not really fill the need as envisioned by the Rabonan Government. However, the expatriate Kenneth Pearsall, now returned to his post as veterinary officer, was expected to continue to play a vital role because of his earlier relationship with Robinson, in which the latter had depended so completely on him in dealing with government staff and Rabonan farmers.

It has been accepted by all, as noted above, that prime responsibility for the undertaking rested with EAD in New Zealand. But from there on, the lines of communication and obligation were unclear. The loosely organized group of officials who carried various responsibilities for the project were able to function only because of the generally recognized methods of government operation and the established linkages between the offices concerned.

Actually, most of the action in New Zealand would take place in the Department of Agriculture. Robinson fortunately had developed a number of informal links within the department during the period of his prior employment. These would be useful for obtaining support and assistance. As mentioned, he was officially entitled to seek aid from David Anderson, Chief Advisory Officer for Farms, who had been named coordinator and was willing to assist Robinson when he could. But Anderson had to fit all work on the Rabona project into his normal workload, already a demanding one, for no provision had been made to relieve him with respect to the new responsibility. Robinson was never clear who had the final authority in relatively minor matters, such as selection of suppliers of materials or the specifications for personnel being recruited for the project.

How much authority he carried within the Rabonan Department of Agriculture was also never very clear to Robinson. Later, he would find it necessary to discuss almost every matter with either Harvey Enoka or Kenneth Pearsall so as to be certain of the department's approval and to avoid repercussions from subsequent misunderstanding. At times, the Minister of Agriculture was apt to intervene and ask for an explanation of some action taken.

Procedures regarding procurement and allocation of resource materials were left to be developed as the need arose. A formal set of procedures was never devised. It was generally agreed that progress reports would be submitted to EAD.

PHASE 3:   OPERATION, CONTROL, AND HANDOVER

Implementation and Control

As outlined in the previous section, the Rabona project was relatively complex, requiring as it did the coordination of two government departments in New Zealand and one in Rabona to implement some 21 separate project tasks. While adequate thought was given to planning the technical aspects of livestock development in Rabona, the attention directed toward manpower needs and management of the diverse project tasks left something to be desired. As will be explained, this oversight resulted in unexpected delays and cost overruns in the course of project implementation.

On-the-ground responsibility for the project and its component tasks rested with John Robinson as director. He was required to send monthly reports to Michael Bennett, the EAD officer in New Zealand, through the High Commissioner's office in Rabona. These reports were brief statements of progress which contained only little detail about the work completed and identified various problems as these developed. However, no provision was made for comparing monthly progress with project requirements as these were originally planned.

In Rabona, Robinson worked closely with the Director of Agriculture, Harvey Enoka. The latter was always willing to assist to the extent of his department's limited resources. Robinson did encounter some difficulty in relating to Enoka, because of differences in their cultural backgrounds as well as Robinson's own unfamiliarity with the Rabona administrative operation.

For example, clerical and accounting services were performed by two of the department's Rabonan employees who had been seconded to Robinson. Both of these individuals he found to be adequate in their performance of routine work, but in his opinion they lacked initiative, were reluctant to accept responsibility, and were lax about attention to details. As a consequence, he spent an inordinate part of his time supervising and instructing them. In general, he found it hard to communicate with Rabonans on the staff. His discussions with Kenneth Pearsall reinforced his own estimates of Rabonan abilities. Director Enoka, on the other hand, viewed the problem more correctly as one of language and culture rather than individual ability. He considered that Robinson, like Pearsall, still had much to learn about dealing with Rabonans. Both expatriates, in his opinion, were too inflexible in their desire to operate by management procedures they were used to, and not ready to make allowances for the new environment in which they found themselves.

The coordination of project activities suffered as Robinson continued to experience difficulties in relating to his work supervisors, Rabonans who had been assigned from the Agriculture Department to oversee small jobs in the project. He was not always specific in giving out orders, expecting the men to use their own initiative in working out the details. Their general lack of training, however, caused a reluctance on their part to make independent decisions. Robinson felt that he had to watch them closely, and in many cases he sought assistance from Director Enoka to resolve misunderstandings in this area. Furthermore, he was not satisfied with the progress reports received from them, and he spent much time undertaking onsite checks of his own.

General planning of the project had been based on Robinson's report and recommendations. Each of the project tasks was considered a separate entity, and the budget amount for each was the major constraint on its implementation. The day-to-day scheduling and detailed planning were extremely loose, however. The main problem was to coordinate the availability of skilled manpower with the procurement of materials and equipment so that costly delays might be prevented.

The allocation, procurement, and management of resources became a critical focus of concern in many of the project activities. The separation of task budgets established clear guidelines for allowable expenditures for each distinct task. The procurement of material resources was divided between the two countries. In Rabona, Robinson would place requisitions with the

Department of Agriculture for purchase and deliver of local goods to the designated project site. Overseas orders were sent, via the High Commissioner's office in Rabona, to Michael Bennett of EAD in New Zealand. He forwarded them to Agriculture, where the department's chief advisory officer for farms, David Anderson, received them and passed them on to the Purchasing Section. This segmentation of transmittals frequently gave rise to delays. On one occasion, for example, Bennett was away on leave and it was three weeks before the requisitions were sent on to Anderson. The main reason for using this system of communication was to take advantage of the special air freight delivery operating between the High Commissioner's office in Rabona and the Ministry of Foreign Affairs in New Zealand, thereby bypassing the normal but usually less dependable postal service. No serious problem existed with goods being lost or pilfered after receipt in Rabona, but at times the requisitioned materials were delivered to the wrong project site and remained there for days or even weeks before corrective action was taken.

There was little or no integration of work scheduling among the various project tasks. Each task proceeded more or less independently and at its own pace. A common fault in scheduling was that supplies to be used by laborers recruited for a given task were sometimes not delivered promptly. Consequently, the laborers could not be put to work, yet their employment remained a cost against the project. This condition became particularly critical when essential resources ordered from overseas suppliers failed to arrive by the appointed date. Such delays were due in part to a lack of advance planning but also, perhaps more significantly, to a failure to recognize the logistic problems for what they were in a developing country like Rabona.

As the project tasks moved along, revisions of the original plan became necessary to meet problems that arose in implementation. These problems usually resulted from the fact that the initial field survey by Robinson had been neither thorough nor realistic in regard to the actual conditions of Rabonan agricultural development. Unwanted delays and other impediments were dealt with on an ad hoc basis. There was no clear procedure for resolving breakdowns except by Robinson's own initiative and ingenuity. Plan revisions invariably meant increased expenditures of funds and labor to ensure a successful conclusion of the tasks in question.

Finally, in regard to the people of Rabona - that is, the small farmers who ultimately were expected to benefit by the whole project - little care was exercised by Robinson to keep them informed of what was going on and how it related to their interests in livestock development. They could not help but notice the increased activity at the experimental farm, for Rabona is not a large place. Many of them, laboring under the impression that what they saw was implementation of part of the Matella-Talua plan, recalled the extended discussions in the villages about grazing cattle under the coconut trees; but what they observed at the Agriculture farm did not seem to be going in that direction, and the lack of explanation left them in confusion.

Outcome of the Project Tasks

The operational, supervisory, and control aspects of the Rabonan livestock development project are best reviewed by briefly examining the outcome of each of the 21 project tasks. These were carried out between September 1972 and March 1975, and were essentially separate units in terms of objective, implementation, and budgetary constraint. Several of them may be characterized as fairly routine and posed no serious problems. But some of the more vital ones were subjected to frustrating delays and substantial cost increases, resulting, as often as not, from inadequacies of planning and management. Whatever the outcome, however, valuable lessons were learned from the experience. (See Table 2.1.)

Roadway and Central Race System (1). Several delays occurred in the effort to improve road and race (fenced lane) facilities on the Agriculture Department's experimental farm. The Public Works staff, working under Robinson's direction, were not able to complete the task in one operation as planned, owing to an unexpected shortage of essential equipment for leveling and paving the road. Thus, much of the work undertaken at the start was abandoned temporarily, and later had to be redone because of washouts resulting from heavy rains. Several sections also had to be rebuilt where road paving had been skipped. The original estimate that 2 miles (3.2 kilometers) of road construction was needed proved to inaccurate and a half mile (0.8 km) had to be added. Costs thereby rose more than NZ$5,000 or 31 percent over the amount budgeted.

Fencing for Pasture Subdivision (2). In this task to subdivide 200 acres (81.0 hectares) of land for beef cattle pasture, two basic faults appeared. One related to procurement of supplies and the other to availability of experienced staff and supervision. Local laborers were employed to clear the fence lines and dig the postholes, but they had to stop when shipment of the essential posts and wire ordered from New Zealand was delayed. Meanwhile, it was discovered that an additional 2 miles (3.2 km) of fence was required to ensure proper subdivision of the pasture. The workers were kept on for another two months with nothing to do, until it became evident that the materials would not arrive for some time. They were then assigned to other jobs.

When the task was reactivated, after the posts and wire and electric fence units became available, Robinson soon realized that the laborers lacked experience in this area. This caused him to set up on-the-job training to bring their work up to minimum standards. Shortly after, he decided that this was taking too much of his time, and besides the work was too strenuous for him. He sent an urgent request to the New Zealand Department of Agriculture to dispatch an experienced fencing contractor to Rabona as soon as possible to supervise the job. Fortunately, a man was located who would donate his services under the Volunteer Service Abroad program, asking only that his basic expenses be met by the project. With these modifications, the task in Rabona was finally completed but the project went six months overtime and costs were doubled.

Water Supply (3). The original proposal to improve the water supply and distribution system on the department's experimental farm had to be revised. Investigation showed that the existing deep well was in fact located on a neighboring property, whose owners threatened court action against the department for trespassing. Consequently, a new well was dug on the government property. The work throughout was done efficiently, and without further delay, with local labor directed by a private local contractor. Apart from the legal question, the only problem encountered was the necessity of constructing the new well, which increased the project cost by 40 percent.

Cattle Yards (4). Progress on this task was reasonably good, allowing completion within the scheduled time. It was necessary, however, to redesign part of the original plan. This doubled expenditures, owing to inadequate costing of items beforehand and to some delay in deliveries.

Cattle Supply (5). This project task was set up to provide bulls for herd improvement and to extend the holdings of local farmers under the department's subsidy program. Robinson's initial proposal for 80 Polled Herefords and ten bulls was later revised sharply upward. Veterinary Officer Pearsall, concerned that this number was vastly inadequate to achieve the objective, pursuaded Robinson to purchase an additional 180 head.

This placed a considerable strain on management of the entire organization. Expenditures for the project task increased by 483 percent, partly because cattle prices in New Zealand were higher than expected by the time the purchase was made. The cattle were acquired in late 1973 and early 1974, but, owing to inadequate advance booking of shipping space, could not be delivered to Rabona until November 1974. Meanwhile, grazing and other care of the stock had to be provided in New Zealand.

In Rabona, a further problem arose when the cattle finally arrived. It was planned to hold only 90 head of cattle on the experimental farm and to disperse the rest immediately to local farmers under the cattle subsidy scheme. However, not enough farmers were ready to take over the additional stock, and the farm's facilities were incapable of coping satisfactorily with the crisis thereby created.

Pasture Improvement (6). This project task moved slowly at first because development of new pasture was carried out by Rabonan vegetative methods of planting new grass. Robinson's experience with seed sowing methods was substituted, and by mid-June 1974 the experimental farm showed very good examples of new pasture. However, it took more time than expected to train local workers in the new methods.

After June 1974, the situation deteriorated rapidly when the new pastures had to be overstocked with cattle (as described in item 5). During the following season, very little could be done by way of pasture renewal or maintenance and the earlier achievements were nearly wiped out. This was a good example of how changes in the course of one project task had serious consequences for progress in a related one. Better planning and integration of tasks could have avoided such an outcome.

Farmer Training in Stockmanship (7). The plan was to support six to eight Rabonan farmers in stock management under tropical conditions on cattle ranches of a neighboring Pacific Island country. But cooperation from the country Robinson had in mind was not forthcoming. A training substitute was belatedly set up in the temperate climate of New Zealand. Only four

Rabonans were able to benefit by the experience because of the late start in implementing this task.

Extension of Cattle Subsidy (8).   Intended to provide needed materials, seed, and stock for selected farmers who had already demonstrated their capacity for successful livestock management on their own farms, this task fell somewhat short of the goal.   The primary reasons were faulty administration and a breakdown in communication with the field, mainly due to a shortage of extension personnel.   Judgments about the farmers' wants were not well founded, and the accounts for purchase of materials in New Zealand were flawed by clerical errors.

Tuberculosis and Brucellosis Eradiction (9).   This task was directed by Veterinary Officer Kenneth Pearsall.   His able management of the department's established test facility turned up a goodly number of diseased cattle, which were killed and their owners compensated from project funds, thus contributing significantly to the elimination of both diseases among Rabonan herds.

Mobile Killing Facility (10).   The original concept of a killing facility to be moved from village to village for use by local cattle farmers was abandoned in the first year of the project.   It proved to be unworkable because of scheduling problems and some reluctance by Rabonan farmers to change their custom of slaughtering stock, as described earlier.   Funds allocated for this task were then transferred to purchase a tractor in New Zealand and to construct a specially designed trailer for transporting cattle to the Rewi abattoir.   Some delay was caused by the altered plan, but it was expected that the new equipment would be reasonably successful in field trials.

Cold Storage Facilities (11).   Several factors contributed to unexpected delays in the task to establish meat storage and market facilities in the outer islands of Rabona.   On Tapolo Island, difficulties arose immediately concerning site selection and land acquisition.   Then, the fact that the island had no power source called for further study and plan revision.   Finally, the site chosen for the beef storage plant turned out to be also the center of an active fishing industry, and the proposed refrigeration facility had to be enlarged to satisfy the storage requirements for fish as well as beef.   The amended plan provided for an ice-making plant and two modified cold stores, which were purchased in New Zealand and eventually shipped to Rabona.   Total cost of this project task remained about as estimated.   No reference was made in the final report to an additional facility for Arangi Island, as had been proposed.

Abattoir at Rewi (12).   The plan to finish construction of the church mission abattoir at Rewi was realized after some delay.   Equipment was late in arriving from overseas.   But as the work was contracted out, Robinson was relieved of the worrisome problems of staffing and management which plagued him in most of the other project tasks.   The estimated cost was exceeded by only a small amount.

After completion of the plant, it was discovered that local farmer demand was not sufficient to make full use of the project's investment.   Although Rabona now had an abattoir of good standard for slaughtering both cattle and pigs, it was built too soon, and years would pass before its true worth could be realized.   Apparently no one had bothered at the start to match the projected growth rates of Rabona's cattle industry with the planned capacity of the plant.

Abattoir Staff Training (13). The task here was to train staff for the proposed government abattoir, but when the latter was deleted by the New Zealand reviewers, the priority for such training dropped and nothing was done. Later, however, it became evident that no local person was capable of managing the completed facility at Rewi. Therefore, a promising Rabonan was selected for six months' training in a New Zealand abattoir. Upon his return, even though this experience did not fully equip him for the job, he was appointed to manage the Rewi operation. Still later, project funds were allocated to train others in order to avoid total dependence on the lone Rabonan who now supervised the abattoir.

Refrigerated Delivery Van (14). The purchase of a van to transport meat from the abattoir to markets in outlying villages was a fairly simple matter, and the task proved reasonably successful. The original specifications had to be altered to provide a vehicle with four-wheel drive capacity to combat the poor road conditions in outlying farm areas. This change necessitated a 70 percent cost overrun. Breakdown of the van at one point required importation of spare parts from New Zealand, which held up the operation for several months.

Artificial Insemination Facility (15). This task was just a modest addition to the department's ongoing artificial insemination program administered by Veterinary Officer Pearsall. The requested facility for liquid nitrogen storage of cattle semen was provided without any problem.

Animal Quarantine Center (16). Agricultural officials in both Rabona and New Zealand agreed that establishing a quarantine center should be given low priority, considering that all livestock being brought to Rabona were coming from New Zealand. The allocation for this task, therefore, was left intact. The matter would be reviewed later when other project tasks became less urgent.

Town Milk Supply Dairyshed (17). The proposal to extend the facilities of the mission school's dairyshed suffered in implementation because of failure to identify clearly the technical equipment needed. Essential components, some of which had to be custom-built, were imported from New Zealand, and delays were encountered both in manufacture and in shipment of the items. Finally, in late 1975, the dairyshed was commissioned even though it still lacked certain operating features. The estimated cost for this project task increased over 65 percent.

Once in operation, the new facility was revealed to be uneconomic, as the public demand for pasteurized milk was not yet sufficient to ensure full production. Robinson recommended that New Zealand provide assistance for fuel and other costs until the situation improved. Still being comtemplated were the recruitment of an expatriate technician to help in the plant's operation, and the training in New Zealand of a promising Rabonan who could take over later.

Pig and Poultry Project Tasks (18-20). Since these tasks were incidental to the main concern of the livestock production project, that is, cattle, little need be said here except that project subsidies of the pig and poultry schemes produced positive results. The research into production of cheaper feed went rather slowly, however, because the required technical equipment was delivered very late.

Supervision and Financial Control (21). The budget estimate for this task, which concerned the entire project, had to be doubled. This was due to the slow work pace of the staff and the need to devise simplified record-keeping procedures. Actually, office supervision was only routine and did not exercise more than nominal control.

By the middle of 1975, most of the project tasks in New Zealand's bilateral aid program for livestock development in Rabona had been completed. Funds for the project, including the many cost overruns, were provided for the three-year period 1972-1975, and expatriate personnel from New Zealand had been employed under contract during that time. Completion of the project meant phasing out the activity of project director John Robinson, and transferring the various project tasks to the control and management of local personnel, mainly in the Rabonan Department of Agriculture.

Handover

No formal plan had been prepared by John Robinson for handing over control of the Rabonan livestock development project to the local administration. The general intent upon completion of the project was for the Rabonan Department of Agriculture to take over the operation. But when Robinson's work as director came to an end, it was already clear that no one in the department, or elsewhere in Rabona for that matter, was capable of assuming full responsibility for managing a continuation of the activities inaugurated under Robinson's supervision.

It became evident that an expatriate would have to be appointed to manage the undertaking after Robinson's departure. The latter, prior to leaving Rabona, had recommended to the New Zealand government that it continue foreign aid to Rabona by supporting a suitably experienced person to succeed him. The suggestion to bring in another expatriate, however, was not popular with Agriculture Department officials in Rabona. They considered the need for continued reliance on an outside expert to be a consequence of Robinson's failure to set up a proper program for training Rabonans as potential managers. Director Harvey Enoka, who was most concerned about this state of affairs, was convinced that it epitomized the poor planning and lack of foresight evident throughout the whole project. He was also critical on the grounds that the government's localization policy with respect to personnel was not being applied in this foreign aid project.

One reason for the failure to attend to the need for local manpower development was that everyone had been too busy solving the short-term problems which kept cropping up. This pressure prevented adequate consideration of the long-term requirements for future project management. In an attempt to forestall appointment of an expatriate manager, it was suggested that one of the two graduate students, Roger Matella or Ariki Talua, might be able to take over when they returned from their studies overseas. Director Enoka was not really certain in his own mind, however, that either of the two men had sufficient practical experience as yet to direct the livestock development plan as a whole.

The New Zealand government accepted Robinson's recommendation to continue support for an expatriate manager, and the Rabonan government agreed to this arrangement. Director Enoka then decided to appoint the two most qualified Rabonans in his department to understudy the new manager on a full time basis. It was estimated that expatriate management would be required for at least another two years.

PHASE 4: EVALUATION AND REFINEMENT

Evaluation of the livestock project by its sponsors ought to have included, as a minimum requirement, an analysis of what progress had been achieved toward the assigned objectives, also where the effort fell short of the target. No formal study of this kind was ever undertaken, however, either by New Zealand or Rabonan officials. Such a simple evaluation of relative achievement would, of course, still leave unanswered other important questions, such as whether or not the stated objectives were realistic, and whether, in view of other pressing developmental needs, Rabonan planners should have given the livestock project the top priority it received.

As a first step in evaluating some of the issues and outcomes of the project, it will be beneficial to review the overall objectives of the undertaking and to determine whether the method selected for implementation was, in the light of all available evidence, the best possible choice. In Rabona, decisions on priority needs for government projects were, in the last analysis, made by the political leadership. Although officials in the ministries (and, on occasion, outside consultants) produced the necessary information on which decisions were reached, the main role of these officers was to go along with the political judgments arrived at by the policy makers.

The livestock scheme, in fact, was initiated by economic planners in Rabona while they were exploring possibilities to reduce the country's considerable dependence on imported goods. On the face of it, the reduction of meat imports by developing a local livestock industry seemed to be a logical and technically feasible action toward achieving the desired long-term impact on the import problem. One governmental policy that would benefit such a scheme was the protection given to local industries by imposition of selective import restrictions and duties on overseas products. A local industry, once established, would be assured of a captive market for its product.

Agriculture officials in Rabona recognized that in the long run any livestock development would have to overcome two major problems. First, the country lacked the necessary manpower skills at all levels to sustain a livestock scheme of significant size. Second, any project, other than those on government-owned land, must meet the demands of local landowners in both social and economic terms if additional land were required for project use. In other words, the methods adopted for the care and feeding of cattle would have to meet local needs and conform to local conditions.

While the overall objective to develop a local cattle industry was generally acceptable, the timing and method of implementation were subjected to sharp criticism in some quarters. Harvey Enoka was outspoken in expressing his reservations to the Minister of Agriculture. However, when these doubts were minimized by his superior, he had no choice but to take responsibility for implementing a project with which he did not wholly agree.

The project design, as originally outlined by the government expert from New Zealand, was adopted, and the 21 project tasks were implemented with foreign aid funds provided by New Zealand. Completion of the project, however, did not bring attainment of the goal mandated by the Rabonan cabinet, that is, to develop a local livestock capacity that would render the country self-sufficient in beef production.

The project, in its implementation stage, encountered frequent delays, multiple cost overruns, and many other problems not anticipated. In spite of these difficulties and the failure to accomplish the original goal, it was recognized, both in Rabona and in New Zealand, that with further development and proper management the trial effort could indeed have a significant impact on national as well as local livestock production in Rabona. While the basis for herd expansion and improvement had been proved at the department's experimental farm, a need still existed to extend this knowledge and experience to Rabonans in the private sector who were prepared to invest some of their landholdings in livestock farming. This would require a number of followup projects, but no provision had been made for developmental activities in the future.

Many of the expected long-term benefits could have been achieved if more thought and imagination had been devoted to selecting the method of implementation. As previously described, two proposals had been drawn up, each of which dealt with the same problem but from a different viewpoint. One of these was the informal study conducted by the two Rabonan graduate students in agriculture. The other was the feasibility study carried out by John Robinson, recruited for the task from New Zealand. Evidence presented in this case study suggests that the ideas contained in the students' survey would, in fact, have provided a more realistic approach to achieving the desired long-term development.

The New Zealander's proposal, however, was the one that was implemented. It concentrated almost entirely on the expansion of existing government farm facilities. In contrast, the Rabonan students' proposal was oriented toward experimentation with natural resources in the countryside, for example, land areas for grazing cattle on plantations under the coconut trees. Their plan would have checked out a farming situation already familiar to Rabonans, the results of which could then be extended to other plantations in the island archipelago. A proposal of this sort would have brought private landowners into the project immediately and provided them with the essential learning experiences for the long-term development of a cattle industry.

Analysis of the manner in which this project was implemented highlights many of the issues that commonly arise during the course of development projects. A great percentage of the delays and cost overruns, for example, was due to inadequate planning in the early stages of the project and to the failure to conduct an in-depth study of the material needs and fiscal requirements of each of the 21 project tasks. In particular, many of the delays were caused simply by improper scheduling and clumsy procurement procedures in obtaining livestock, materials, and equipment from overseas.

Some understanding of the official attitude concerning the project's outcome may be gained from the final report which Robinson, as director, submitted to the New Zealand Ministry of Foreign Affairs. In this, he endeavored to identify the benefits that could be expected from implementation of the project's 21 tasks. He did not, however, attempt an overall assessment of project benefits in terms of the savings that could possibly be achieved in overseas spending as a consequence of increased meat production in Rabona. Cost overruns and delays were explained as the result of difficulties met in coordinating the necessary participation of various agencies in the two countries. Robinson parenthetically commented on problems he had encountered in working with what he regarded as inefficient, and at times uncooperative, government officials in Rabona, but he provided no details. Overall, he represented the project as having been executed in a satisfactory manner.

In Rabona, ill feeling about the project was evident within the Ministry of Agriculture. Some officials persisted in the attitude that the project had been imposed upon them by planners who lacked the technical understanding of livestock management in a tropical country like Rabona. The appointment of Robinson to direct the scheme was regarded as a poor choice. He was new to the tropics, and he was incapable of working closely with the local people. His lack of experience with management also meant that planning, scheduling, and control techniques were not employed in a professional manner. While the technical requirements of the Rabonan livestock development project were actually quite straightforward and should have been relatively easy to implement, Robinson's inattention to, or ignorance of, standard management practices not only resulted in unexpected delays and escalated costs but created an atmosphere of ill will between the two countries in what was to have been a cooperative relationship.

Recently, a review of foreign aid programs in developing Pacific countries was commissioned by the South Pacific Forum, a regular meeting of the leaders of governments of seven self-governing or independent island countries at which issues of common interest are discussed. (2) The task force appointed to make the study, after intensive exploration of the topic, came up with some general observations and many specific recommendations. A few of the latter, which seem to be particularly relevant to the Rabonan experience, are summarized here.

1. The provision of foreign aid and expatriate personnel cannot alone overcome the critical internal obstacles to development which afflect many Pacific countries, such as inadequate land tenure systems.

2. All Pacific countries need to develop their pool of local professional skills. Projects everywhere have suffered from the lack of local knowledge and experience on the part of agricultural and other professional people brought in from overseas.

3. Tighter selection and more intensive briefing should be introduced for expatriate personnel in foreign aid programs.

4. Local counterparts to expatriate personnel should not be specified in

aid planning unless they will be available and the organizational structure of the project makes sense with them in it.

This case study of a livestock development scheme in a tropical country, it should be noted, has documented a number of problems in planning and management which are not at all unique to the Rabonan situation, and which continue to characterize development projects in other parts of the South Pacific.

NOTES - Chapter 2

(1) On December 20, 1971, after the exchange rate had floated for several months, a new exchange rate of 0.82237 New Zealand dollars per United States dollar (1 NZ$ = 121.6 US cents) was introduced.

(2) More Effective Aid, A Report to the South Pacific Forum, published by the Forum's trade secretariat, the South Pacific Bureau for Economic Cooperation, in 1976 (SPEC (76) 11), 34 pp. Members of the task force which authored the study were His Lordship Bishop P. Finau (Tonga), chairman; C. Craw (New Zealand); Prof. R.G. Corcombe (Fiji); A.V. Hughes (Solomon Islands); L.R. Morgan (Papua New Guinea); M. Qionibaravi (Fiji); and R.G. Spratt (Australia).

3 The Way Abung Transmigration Project: Indonesia

Bintoro Tjokroamidjojo

PROJECT BACKGROUND

Within the context of Indonesia's national development effort, transmigration projects, or the resettlement of needy villagers to the Outer Islands, are a vital program. Here the primary goal of transmigration has been the reduction of Java's critically high population density. But another equally important reason has been the desired economic development of the "Land Beyond," those sparsely settled outlying islands which surround Java. The continuing program of assisted migration is one part of the total endeavor by the Republic of Indonesia to achieve nation building.

Socioeconomic Rationale of Transmigration Projects

Two urgent national objectives throughout the past century have been the moderation of Indonesia's alarming rate of population growth and the lightening of the burden of population density, especially in the islands of Java and Bali. The transmigration program, conceived within the framework of national development policies, has aimed at improving the people's welfare by 1) providing some relief from population pressures in Java, and 2) promoting agricultural development of the thinly settled Outer Islands by the movement of migrant families from overcrowded rural Java. In recent years, as national policy under the Republican regime has changed, the planning of transmigration projects has come to be viewed less from the standpoint of easing pressure in heavily populated parts of Indonesia, and more in the hope of augmenting the labor force in less populated areas. Transmigration activities have thereby emerged as an integral feature of Indonesia's new regionally oriented development policies. The past predominance of demographic concerns has shifted slightly to embrace a more directly economic approach. From a sociopolitical viewpoint, the transmigration program facilitates and enhances those integrative trends sought after in the overriding task of nation building. (1)

The extent of the overall problem is partially reflected in the fact that Indonesia's population in 1971 amounted to nearly 120,000,000. Of that number, 66 percent (more than 78,000,000 people) lived in Java and nearby Bali, which together make up only seven percent of the nation's total land area. The density of population in Java alone was 565 persons per square kilometer. This may be compared with densities in other islands of the archipelago, such as 377 in Bali, 38 in Sumatra, 37 in Sulawesi (Celebes), nine in Kalimantan (Borneo), and two in Irian Jaya (West New Guinea).

These figures demonstrate that in 1971, the great mass of the Indonesian people continued to be dependent on agriculture for their principal livelihood. The situation in the rural areas of Java and Bali had deteriorated rapidly, owing to the ever smaller amounts of arable land available to farming households threatened by acute population pressures. In the 1970s, the number of Indonesians was expected to increase at an annual rate of about 2.4 percent. With opportunities dwindling in agriculture and age-old village industries, unemployment in Java and Bali was widespread. On the other hand, it was clearly evident that in the Outer Islands, which were only sparsely populated, economic development was severely hampered by the insufficient labor force and lack of overhead capital for social needs.

Development of all regions in Indonesia is a priority consideration in national planning. Since 1960, regional plans based on surveys of development potential and identification of poles of growth have received serious attention. For this reason, moves to transplant people, either spontaneously or by formal government assistance, are linked importantly to improvement programs and projects everywhere in Indonesia. The stated objectives could conceivably be met whenever implementation proceeded from planning that was firmly rooted in a strong rationale.

In actuality, transmigration programs in Indonesia have served rather directly the main purpose of improving the living standards of peasants from Java and Bali. During the 1950s, and in the previous colonial period, transmigration meant the transplanting of villagers from the crowded areas of central Indonesia to Sumatra and other islands in order to preserve their way of life and agricultural productivity. Spontaneous, or voluntary, migration was motivated by employment opportunities both in planned colonization and in contract labor recruitment for commercial plantations. There were no significant signs of integration between the migrants and the local peoples among whom they settled, however. As early as 1964, Keyfitz and Nitisastro suggested an emphasis on "community planning" in the implementation of transmigration projects. (2) In any case, resettlement served a very significant function in regional development.

According to a study made in 1976 by a World Bank team, (3) some difficulty was encountered in estimating the extent of improved social welfare among the transmigrants. Nevertheless, this research did indicate that the income of resettled persons had increased in comparison with their former earnings, although it was still below the average per capita income for all Indonesians.

In general, Indonesian transmigrants may be classified into three principal groups, reflecting the degree and nature of government assistance received.

1. Transmigrants fully sponsored by the government as participants in a planned project. (The government in this instance is responsible for all costs of transport to and settlement in the destination area);

2. Transmigrants receiving only partial aid from the government. (The latter provides land on which to live and grow crops, but the settlers bear the cost of travel from their place of origin);

3. Transmigrants formerly employed on plantation estates (upon termination of labor contracts, they settle entirely at their own expense on land acquired in the vicinity of a transmigration project).

Support components made available to eligible transmigrants by the government may be specified in more detail, as follows: (4)

1. The cost of transportation;

2. Allotment of a plot of land, amounting to 1.0 hectare during the colonial period, 1.5 hectares in the 1950s and after, and 2.0 hectares beginning about 1969). (Some of this land was intended for residential use and dry field cultivation but the larger part, in a ratio of three-to-one, was for growing wet rice or cash crops);

3. Simple agricultural tools and implements;

4. The cost of building materials and living expenses until all or some of the crops were harvested. (Variations of this provision existed, including the bawon system to be described in the next section).

The willingness of people to migrate presented no great problem. The number of applications exceeded the openings to be filled, by a ratio of 10 to 1. The primary motivations underlying their readiness to move included poverty, exploitation by landowners, and debt evasion. Their goal was usually expressed as the desire for economic security and ownership of their own land.

Generally, local people in the Outer Islands were willing to accept the new arrivals from Java and Bali because of certain direct as well as indirect benefits received, such as increased funds for local public works and services. Some lands, however, were alienated by the government from communal holdings of the local populations. These lands were allotted to the transmigrants with initial rights of use, and could be converted after five years into proprietary rights. In actuality, the transfer of land under these titles to the settlers was not always smoothly achieved.

The Way Abung Transmigration Project as a Case Study

This case study focuses attention upon a particular set of experiences in the management of a transmigration development project: to provide new knowledge of, and insight into, the accomplishments gained and the difficulties encountered, and to identify areas for further improvement in the field of project management. A transmigration project analysis has the added advantage of being representative of Indonesian social, political, and economic conditions.

The transmigration project at Way Abung, carried out between 1969 and 1974, followed a complete cycle of implementation, beginning with project preparation and proceeding to migrant recruitment, resettlement, coordination of project activities during the relocation period, and the final transfer of project responsibilities to normal administration. In 1975, surveys were conducted to evaluate the results of the undertaking in order to improve future policy measures in the planning and implementation of similar activities.

Migration to Way Abung actually started in 1965, but in 1969 a new project was launched to move a new group of settlers to that location. The next five years demonstrated clearly that management not only involves planning techniques, economic appraisals, and feasibility analyses, but also must be concerned with the overriding problems of institutional relationships and their coordination, institution building, and decision making. Noneconomic issues, especially in the social sector, must be taken into account at every stage of planning and implementing a project such as the one sited at Way Abung. In developing countries such as Indonesia, a society undergoing transition, the movement of people from one region to another, and the consequent alterations in specific life patterns require the special attention of those engaged in public policy implementation and project management.

HISTORICAL BACKGROUND: COLONIZATION AND TRANSMIGRATION

As far back as the early nineteenth century, the conceptualization phase of the transmigration process in Indonesia had begun. Sir Thomas Stamford Raffles, then Lieutenant Governor during the British interregnum in Java from 1811 to 1816, and Du Bus de Gisignies, Governor General of the Netherlands Indies from 1826 to 1830, both foresaw the possibility of Java becoming dangerously overcrowded. They suggested as a relief measure the feasibility of colonizing selected areas of the Outer Islands with Indonesian migrants from Java. (5) Throughout the colonial period, such planned movements of people were usually referred to as colonization. Following the Japanese occupation and the war of independence in the 1940s, interisland migration was resumed in 1950 under the name of transmigration.

Experiments with Colonization, 1905-1931

The period from 1905 to 1931 may be characterized generally as one of trial and error or, in other words, of experimentation with resettlement. In spite of the British and Dutch concern expressed earlier, it was not until 1902 that any serious consideration was given to resolving the problem of Java's overpopulation by recourse to colonization programs. In that year, the government initiated studies preparatory to moving large numbers of people from Java to the Outer Islands. H. G. Heyting, a Dutch administrator in Sukabumi Regency in West Java, was assigned to look into the matter. In a few years, he became the first government official to administer the colonization of Javanese in Sumatra. In that role, he was responsible to the Indies government's Department of Internal Administration. Gedong Tataan in South Lampung, South Sumatra, was the first location selected for colonization. (6) Justification for choosing this site is evident when one considers its nearness to the capital city of Lampung, at the very southernmost tip of Sumatra and thus the point closest to Java.

In November 1905, Heyting finally settled the first group of colonists in Gedong Tataan. In that action, the desa (village) of Bagelen was founded by 155 families from densely overpopulated Kedu Regency in Central Java. By the end of 1921, when the government launched another colonization scheme in Lampung, which later became known as Wonosobo, the number of settlers in the many villages of Gedong Tataan colony had increased to 19,251 persons. (7)

As mentioned earlier, the concept of planned colonization had indisputable validity in its goal of ameliorating certain socioeconomic conditions. The problem that arose was rather one of feasibility in operational terms. Land for resettlement purposes had first to be cleared and reclaimed, and the complex systems of irrigation channels called for unusual skills in engineering design and construction. Finally, large numbers of settlers had to be cared for while being transported from densely populated areas in Central Java to the locations prepared for them in Sumatra.

During the period from 1905 to 1931, organized colonization efforts faced heavy competition from the plantation estates' recruitment of labor in Java, mainly for North Sumatra. In carrying out its mission of transplantation, the colonial government had to bear a substantial financial burden. By comparison, the cost of contract labor for the estates was already incorporated within the cost structure of the commercial enterprises and usually comprised only a small percentage of the total operational expense.

The government also encountered other difficulties in carrying out its program, a few of which are mentioned here. Inadequate preparatory surveys frequently resulted in the selection of land for cultivation that was poor in soil qualities. The actual clearing of land, usually left to the settlers themselves, proved to be inefficient and uneconomical, for Javanese peasants had long ago lost their capability to clear forested regions, as was practiced by Sumatrans in ladang (dry field) type of swidden farming. Many generations had passed since the jungles of Java had been transformed into irrigated rice fields in which the contemporary Javanese were accustomed to work. Furthermore, epidemics in the resettled areas were prevalent, especially of malaria, and this weakened the productive capacity of colonists through chronic ill health. (8)

Expansion and Stabilization of the Colonization Program, 1932-1941

The second period in the implementation of transplantation programs in Indonesia started in 1932 and ended in 1941, after which the Japanese occupied the Indies during the Second World War. In 1932, the government's colonization effort was revised considerably, mainly under the active direction of a Dutch national named Junius, administrator of the Lampung region, and his assistant, J. Van der Zwaal.

During this period, the government continued as before to bear the costs of recruiting and transporting the colonists and of providing them with land for residence and cultivation. However, a radically new system was introduced which had the effect of shifting the government's responsibility for much of the initial settlement cost to the shoulders of older established settlers. This system was named bawon in reference to a Javanese custom whereby helpers in a family's rice harvest were given a share of the crop in return for their work. As the bawon institution was applied in the Lampung colonies, the living expenses of new migrants were actually met by the older settlers. The sponsored movement of people from Java was timed to coincide with the harvest of croplands already under cultivation in Sumatra. Newcomers were then able to earn enough by way of bawon to carry them through the preparatory period until their own first rice crop was ready to cut. After that, the novices were considered capable of depending on their own resources without further government assistance.

Other distinguishing features of this second period included the opening up of new settlement areas, more careful and comprehensive surveys for deciding on suitable locations, more discriminating recruitment of migrants, and general improvement of all planning and other preparatory steps for launching new colonies. Much of this change resulted from the formation in 1937 of the Central Commission for Migration and Colonization of Indonesians (9) by Governor General S. Stachouwer, who had been appointed the previous year. This commission was directed to centralize supervision of all agricultural colonization involving Indonesian people. The first secretary and administrator of the new agency was C. C. J. Maassen, Adviser on Agrarian Affairs in the Department of the Interior, who was already well experienced in administering colonization projects.

Among the improvements brought about by the Commission's actions, as indicated, was the setting up of better criteria for choosing prospective colonists. This was certainly a most important consideration for assuring the successful implementation of future colonization projects. A set of rules to guide officials responsible for recruiting migrants from Java included, among others, the following: (10)

1. Good farmers (for obvious reasons).

2. Strong and healthy people (able to withstand hardship),

3. Young people (reduce future population rise in Java),

4. Family groups (for social control in new settling),

5. <u>Not</u> families with many youngsters (hard on working parents),

6. <u>Not</u> pregnant women (little help to their husbands),

7. <u>Not</u> former estate workers (tend to be malcontents),

8. <u>Not</u> bachelors (likely lovers of other men's wives),

9. Encourage a whole village to move (then disregard all others rules for selection).

In addition to the constant pressure of socioeconomic conditions in Java, the Ethical Policy (11) pursued by the Netherlands Indies government lent support to the concept and reality of organized colonization as a means of improving the welfare of the common people in rural areas. The principal problems encountered during this prewar period were the lack of efficient irrigation facilities in the colonies, the marketing of products resulting from the settlers' labor, and the social isolation experienced by migrants within the host region. Especially in the 1930s, the economic depression caused much suffering among Indonesians still living in Java. To publicize the benefits to be gained from participation in the colonization program, the government published and distributed leaflets and produced and exhibited films describing what had already been accomplished. By the end of 1941, a total of 173,959 colonists from Java had been resettled in Lampung. (12)

After the 1940s, planned colonization activity experienced not only a sharp cutback but, in fact, almost completely stopped. The Second World War, the Japanese occupation, and the Indonesian struggle for independence against the Dutch made further resettlement on an organized basis impossible until the late 1940s.

Government-Sponsored Transmigration, 1950-1974

In the short period from 1947 to 1950, when Indonesia was in the midst of maintaining its political independence, the Republican government gave considerable attention to the resumption of organized resettlement of people from Java to the Outer Islands. Such movement of Indonesians was now called transmigration, instead of colonization as it had been under the Netherlands colonial administration. Responsibility for planning and developing specific programs passed from one ministry to another for a time therefore did not have a very good chance for achieving implementation. In 1947, the Economic Brain Trust, under the chairmanship of then Vice-President Mohammad Hatta, studied various possibilities for organizing and carrying out new programs of transmigration. In 1948, the charge was handed on to the Ministry of Labor and Social Affairs.

Not until 1950, when Indonesia had regained its sovereignty and the country's situation was considered to be relatively stable, did transmigration planning finally become operative. A special office was created, known as the Transmigration Service. At first it was placed within the Ministry of Community Development, but later it was transferred to the Ministry of

Social Affairs. The first director of the Transmigration Service was Suratno Sastroamidjojo. Branch offices were opened in both Java and Sumatra. In 1951, Ir. A.H.O. Tambunan was appointed to head the service. (13) These two officials must be regarded as pioneers in recognition of their achievements in reviving organized resettlement of Indonesians during the early years of the Republic. The number of families resettled under government-sponsored arrangements from 1952 to 1973 was estimated to be approximately 100,000.

Transmigration activities in Indonesia from 1950 to 1974 may be usefully classified into four different phases, according to the operational emphasis in each.

Phase 1, 1950-1955

During this time, organized transmigration efforts were truly revived. Planning was undertaken, new policies were formulated, organizational requirements were defined, and surveys of various aspects of transmigration were initiated.

In 1951, a special advisory committee was formed to assist in the implementation of transmigration projects. Its membership, representing as it did various ministries, was intended to be a forum for achieving better coordination of the many activities relating to transmigration in which different government agencies had become involved. Djanuismadi, a senior official in the Ministry of Home Affairs, chaired this committee. Tambunan, head of the Transmigration Service, served as secretary.

Another agency created in this period was JAPETA, a public corporation responsible for land clearance. Land surveys were conducted by the Land Survey and Land Use office. Land allotted to transmigrants was increased to 2.0 hectares.

Planning of transmigration programs was done mainly by the Transmigration Service, the results of which came to be referred to as the Tambunan Plan, named after the service's director. Close coordination was maintained between that office and the National Planning Bureau. At this time, the bureau was engaged in formulating a Five-Year Development Plan (1956-1960), which was concerned largely with priorities for expenditures in the public sector to stimulate the country's economic development.

In one year (1952) during this first phase, 3,855 families or a total of 17,605 persons were resettled from Java to the Outer Islands by the Transmigration Service.

Phase 2, 1956-1965

During these years, management of Indonesia's internal migration program continued to be the responsibility of the Transmigration Service. Tambunan, its director, was succeeded in turn by Messrs. R. M. Notowidjojo, R. Surjodibroto, and Mayor Suwarto. Other government and semigovernment agencies, such as the Bureau for National Reconstruction (BRN) and the Corps of National Reserve (CTN), were given assignments to organize the resettlement of persons such as those who had served in the Indonesian army.

Political changes which tended to divert attention from directing the national economy, also the security disturbances occurring throughout Indonesia, contributed to the government's inability to deal satisfactorily with the task of large-scale transmigration. It was already evident, however, that the main problem in managing the resettlement programs was the inefficiency and ineffectiveness of working relations among the several departments charged with supporting implementation of those programs.

Professor Widjojo Nitisastro, noted Indonesian economist, wrote about this weakness of the transmigration program at this time:

. . . the main problem seemed to be the organization rather than the financing of the program. Resettlement is a many-sided venture. While the government assumed a central role in every aspect of resettlement, there was for years no definite delineation of responsibilities of the different government agencies with regard to the scheme. The Department of Transmigration set up in 1950 never had sole responsibility for the entire undertaking--in the sense that a "regional development authority" might have had. Furthermore, its coordination with other agencies such as those responsible for the building of roads and irrigation works was far from satisfactory. This organizational deficiency resulted in bottlenecks and wasteful duplications.

He went on to point out the serious consequences of this situation, among which were:

. . . shortage of irrigation works and transportation facilities. Since most of the settlements were designed on the basis of wet cultivation, proper irrigation played a decisive role. Transportation facilities were insufficient not only between Java and the other islands, but also locally between new and older settlements and between the newly settled areas and the more populous areas of the same region. There were instances where settlements had to be abandoned because deficiencies in initial soil surveys led to an erroneous choice of the areas. In other cases, settlers moved to other areas because inadequate water supplies resulted in meager crops. On the other hand, there were settlements with abundant food crops that the settlers were not able to sell because of the lack of proper marketing facilities. (14)

The validity of these statements is supported by all the facts. They set forth the extent of deficiencies that demanded improvement if the management of the transmigration program were to be more effective in the years ahead.

Phase 3, 1966-1968

During this period, a new style of self-help transmigration (Transmigrasi Swakarya Gaya Baru) was encouraged. Such migrants were also referred to as "spontaneous," meaning those who paid their own passage to the settlement area and thereafter received the same government aid as regular migrants until they became settled.

Under the new system, each family was accorded the following rights and facilities:

1. Two hectares of land, part of which (0.25 hectares) was cleared and available for residential use;

2. Six kilograms of nails for building a house;

3. The necessities of life to the extent of 40.5 kilograms of rice per family head each month for six months;

4. Use of general facilities, such as office (and housing for those in charge), policlinic, storehouse, and elementary school.

Spontaneous transmigrants were placed in locations near settlements of regular colonists. Since they had to build their own houses, they were accommodated in the dwellings of established settlers, or in transient dormitories provided for the purpose, until their own houses were completed.

New areas in the Outer Islands were opened up for cultivation by transmigrants. Among others, this included the Way Abung area in Lampung, South Sumatra. The task of overseeing the resettlement program was charged to the Directorate General for Transmigration in the Department (Ministry) of Transmigration and Cooperatives. The Director General at this time was Brigadier General Soebiantoro.

Phase 4, 1969-1974

The year 1969 saw the beginning of REPELITA I, the First Five-Year Development Plan (Rencana Pembangunan Lima Tahun) launched under the new regime headed by President Suharto. REPELITA I was designed to raise the living standards of Indonesians by increasing the production of food and other consumer goods and by improving the conditions of health, sanitation, education, housing, labor, and public welfare in general. Part of this national development plan, and one of the primary elements in Indonesia's attempt to solve its population problem, was the program for resettling people from the densely populated regions to those land areas which possessed a high development potential but only a low man/land ratio. Hence, an economic motive was also strongly evident for the development of all of Indonesia as a nation.

During this period of planned development, responsibility for the task of resettlement remained in the office of the Directorate General for Transmigration, still directed by Soebiantoro, now a major general. This office was located in the Department of Manpower, Transmigration, and Cooperatives, an organizational arrangement designed to coordinate both population and manpower policies within a single ministry. The department was headed by Minister Subroto, whose dedication assured much attention to the government program in transmigration. His analysis of the rationale for resettlement was stated in a study entitled "Strategy of Transmigration and Cooperatives within the Frame of the National Strategy." (15)

The Way Abung Transmigration Project

Resettlement in the Way Abung area actually started in 1965. In that year, 1,200 families were transported from Java within the framework of the new-style spontaneous transmigration program noted in the preceding section. Those settlers have since become local citizens of the area and no longer fall within the jurisdiction of the Directorate General of Trans-migration. A more concerted effort was launched in 1965, with new groups of settlers brought into Way Abung until 1974. This represents the period of the project described here.

The project area covers 20,350 hectares in North Lampung Regency of Lampung Province in South Sumatra. It is divided into three parts: Way Abung I, Way Abung II, and Way Abung III (A and B sections). Each consists of 22 units, or villages of 450 to 700 families. During the five years from 1969 to 1974, about 10,950 families were resettled in Way Abung. These originated primarily in the provinces of East Java, Central Java, and West Java and the special territory of Jogjakarta. Most of them were ethnically East Javanese. This number constituted about 80 percent of the total now living in Way Abung. Some transmigrants arrived after March 1974, the end of the project period. (16) Still remaining under the care of the Transmigration Service are 12,369 families, or approximately 60,000 individuals.

As noted earlier, spontaneous transmigrants such as those participating in the Way Abung project had to bear all travel costs from their point of origin, but they did receive government aid after arrival in the settlement area. This category was distinguished from that of general transmigrants, who were sponsored by the government and thus eligible for aid in all aspects of resettlement, including travel. There were still others who migrated on their own initiative to locations near the project area and who became local citizens outside the care of the Directorate General for Transmigration. Spontaneous transmigrants were allotted two hectares of land, one quarter of which was for residence purposes and the remainder divided between dry field and wet rice field or use for a second crop. Way Abung settlers, in government-approved practice, had a right after five years to attain pro-prietary title in this land.

The conditions surrounding the Way Abung project could be regarded as generally favorable. First, the location was close to the main transportation network linking Java to Lampung in South Sumatra. Second, the area consisted of agricultural land where water for irrigation could be obtained with relative ease from either rivers or groundwater sources. Note might be made, however, of some problems of land use, including the maintenance of soil fertility which in recent years had tended to decline. Third, experience showed that relationships between migrants and the local people were reasonably satisfactory.

Nonetheless, the settlers faced a number of problems. Based on studies conducted later, it must be acknowledged that certain transmigration policies and program practices needed reformulation and improvement. One example may be cited here. Even though the project area was adjacent to the main highway system, the roads linking it with the many villages were badly in need of development or repair. The poor character of these roads unfavorably affected conditions for marketing the goods produced by the settlers. The prices offered for exported commodities, including cash crops such as cassava, were extremely low and assured little or no profit to the settlers because of the high cost component for transportation. The principal crops grown in Way Abung were rice, corn, beans, vegetables, and cassava. The first two were primary staples for local consumption and only cassava was produced for export.

In this connection, it should be added that during the period 1969-1974 the project administration did not give sufficient attention to providing animal livestock, either for direct consumption, market production, or for help in cultivating the land. Of necessity, therefore, field labor had to be carried out manually.

PHASE I: PLANNING, APPRAISAL, AND DESIGN

Project Formulation and National Development Policy

This case study focuses on the planning and implementation of a resettlement project in Way Abung between the fiscal years 1969-70 and 1973-74. As explained earlier, resettlement in that area of South Sumatra had started several years before, in 1965, and migration activity has continued since 1974. After 1974, however, efforts were made to improve substantially the project's management. With assistance from the World Bank, it was then possible to conduct a basic evaluative survey and to obtain financial support for realization of recommended changes.

Let us briefly review the conception of the Way Abung project idea and its identification in 1964 as a new venture in transmigration history.

The principal aims of transmigration (and of colonization earlier) from the beginning of this century in Indonesia have been reviewed and identified. The Way Abung project became a significant part of that effort as conceived within the context of objectives then prevailing in the Republic. More specifically, the goals of the Indonesian transmigration program were a direct reflection of development policies promulgated in the First Five-Year Development Plan (REPELITA I) inaugurated in fiscal year 1969-70. For this reason, identification and definition of the activities in Way Abung were planned to integrate the project with development projections at the national level. During the project's first year, that objective had not been entirely achieved, although the intent of the administrators was apparent.

For the Way Abung project, then, the initial planning stage involved setting up specific objectives and targets. The rationale of Way Abung as a transmigration undertaking was identified and formulated. Answers were sought to such questions as whether conditions of the region would be favorable for resettlement, how many hectares of land could be opened up, how many transmigrants could be settled in the area, and what time span would be suitable for the project's implementation.

The idea of establishing a resettlement project in Way Abung was first suggested in 1964, based on findings from research conducted by the Transmigration Service. A special investigation of soil conditions was carried out by the Office of Land Survey. Areal surveys were also made. Officials who were behind the proposal included Pagar Alam, Governor of Lampung Province, and A. J. Situmorang and Maat Judolaksono, administrators in the Lampung Regional Branch of the Transmigration Service. Later, the idea was reviewed by the Bureau of Planning. Others from the Service who were involved in the process of project formulation were Aksono Andono and Soentoro.

Some of the main reasons supporting the proposal for a transmigration project in Way Abung were:

1. Land from local community holdings had been alienated by the government for such a purpose in 1962.

2. Part of the area's 30,000 hectares had been surveyed; local people had only 10 percent of the land under cultivation at that time.

3. Transportation links with the outside were relatively good; for example, Way Abung was only 24 kilometers from Kotabumi, the district capital, and 135 kilometers from Tanjung Karang, the provincial capital.

4. Within the area certain kinds of timber were available that could be used as building material by transmigrants.

5. Water sources were fairly accessible, although a later survey did reveal that groundwater reserves were not sufficient for wet rice culture and that irrigation would be required.

The project gained further impetus from the new style of self-help transmigration (Transmigrasi Swakarya Gaya Baru), explained earlier. Newly arrived migrants, having paid for their own travel from Java, would receive a living allowance for six months and assistance in building their houses, in addition to the standard allotment of land for cultivation and residence. Officials of the service, however, introduced a new self-help feature at this point, namely, that migrants would have to clear their lands themselves. One reason for this change was that JAPETA, the public authority previously holding that responsibility, had become inoperative. The first swakarya transmigrants were resettled from Java to Lampung (and also to Kalimantan) in 1965.

At this preliminary stage of project development, one of the main problems was the transportation of people from Java to their destination sites. Poor shipping facilities for some time necessitated the setting up of holding terminals in some port cities, such as Jakarta and Surabaya. The size of the standard land allotment during this period proved later to be too small; studies showed that 2.0 hectares of land were insufficient to realize the goal of increased income for transmigrants through farming. Still another problem arose when some of the land that had been cleared for settlers' use was reoccupied by local people who claimed prior rights in traditional use.

Identification of Project Components

Within the context of project formulation, certain components that represent activities and problems of transmigration need to be identified and their interrelationships taken into account. Components that concerned the planners of transmigration projects in Indonesia and, more specifically, in Way Abung were:

1. Recruitment of transmigrants in their places of origin,

2. Preparation for their relocation and holding at port terminals,

3. Transportation from places of origin, through terminals, to destination areas,

4. Surveys of land in the resettlement area,

5. Clearing the land and preparation of plots for cultivation,

6. Construction of a land transportation system, including main road, village roads, field roads, and bridges,

7. Construction of private housing and public buildings,

8. Reception of transmigrants in the new settlements,

9. Construction of secondary and tertiary irrigation, including groundwater wells and river water conduits,

10. Guidance from extension service agents in subsistence agriculture and cultivation of marketable products,

11. Provision of farm equipment and irrigation pumps,

12. Provision of means of transport,

13. Construction and maintenance of social service facilities, including schools, policlinics, and prayer houses,

14. Development of other income-producing activities besides farming,

15. Promotion of cooperatives related to marketing, transportation, and distribution of consumer goods,

16. Breeding of livestock, especially of cattle for help in cultivating the land, for consumption, and for the market,

17. Establishment of financial facilities, such as credit unions, especially within the framework of BIMAS (Bimbingan Masal Swasembada Bahan Makanan, or Mass Guidance for Self-Sufficiency in Food),

18. Legal processing of land rights: government alienation of community lands under customary law; granting of rights of use and cultivation, and later of proprietary rights, to transmigrants,

19. Regional administration and maintenance of security. (17)

Many of these components and their interrelationships were not given sufficient consideration in the formulation of the Way Abung project. Some attention was paid to sustaining a dialogue among the agencies involved, but the most serious problem continued to be the lack of an integrated approach toward linking the various interests represented. The success of this type of project depended very much upon the consistency of effort and the effectiveness of cooperation to be achieved.

The rationale for the Way Abung project, as it began in 1969, was basically a continuation of what had been formulated earlier. One important difference, however, was that the previous requirement for settlers to clear their own land in the swakarya (self-help) system was abandoned. The responsibility for all land clearance was assumed by the Directorate General for Transmigration.

From Project Design to Approval

In the planning stage, identification and formulation of any project is properly followed by development of design specifications, which are then appraised together with an assessment of budgetary needs. The proposed plan, processed through whatever formal procedures may be in force, is finally subjected to review for approval, the prerequisite for implementation.

The Way Abung transmigration project for fiscal year 1969-70, and for the following four years, was designed to agree with the scheme of the general transmigration program as stipulated in REPELITA I, Indonesia's First Five-Year Development Plan instituted in that year. Transmigration policy as outlined in the national plan reflected the government's effort to achieve a more even distribution of population throughout Indonesia. It was also viewed as a direct response to the critical need for manpower in regional development among the islands beyond Java. REPELITA I required that in programming transmigration activities the government should undertake appropriate research studies both in the projected resettlement areas and in the migrants' places of origin.

The project design for Way Abung, as required for all government development projects, was presented in two special formats for official review. One was called Daftar Usulan Projek (DUP), or Project Proposal Plan. The other was known as Daftar Isian Projek (DIP), or Project Content Plan. Both forms were used in the annual planning and budgeting process in Indonesia to aid the coordination of project programming and budgeting control.

The DUP, as the Project Proposal Plan was commonly called, was essentially a description of the project and a statement of justification and feasibility. The DIP, or Project Content Plan, specifically identified all of the relevant activities designed to achieve the targets or product goals in each fiscal year. Actually, the DIP not only cited the product goals to be accomplished in a given year; it also outlined the project objective within a longer time perspective, and each activity was allocated a place within a detailed time plan. In addition, the DIP listed specific expenditures needed to implement the project and provided an accompanying schedule of disbursements.

The completed project forms were evaluated and appraised. When approved, they became guides that were binding on administrators in implementation details and cost expenditures.

A Project within a Project

Very unfortunate was the fact that the Way Abung project during 1969–1974 was only one part of the larger Lampung (Province) Transmigration Project. This constituted a very critical weakness, because no separate project design existed to support management control of the Way Abung "subproject."

In general, the Project Content Form (DIP) was prepared within whatever department was concerned and was submitted by the director general who was responsible. In the case of the Lampung Province project, the DIP was drawn up and presented by the Director General for Transmigration in the Department of Manpower, Transmigration, and Cooperatives. The project form was then analyzed in joint consultation by BAPPENAS (the National Development Planning Agency) and the Directorate General of Budgeting in the Department of Finance. Based on a decree by the president, (18) approval was required from both BAPPENAS and the Department of Finance before the necessary authority could be issued to the department charged with implementing the project or any part of it. This standard procedure was established to insure consistency of project evaluation within the scope of the overall national development plan.

The Project Proposal Form (DUP) and the Project Content Form (DIP) for the Lampung Transmigration Project were both composed by Soentoro and Aksan Andono, officials in the Directorate General for Transmigration. The two documents were subsequently analyzed by Ngadimun, an officer in the National Development Planning Agency, and by Soemarno in the Directorate General for Budgeting. After further consideration and agreement by their respective superiors, namely, Sujoto of BAPPENAS and Almatsier of the Budgeting office, the DIP as the activating plan (19) was presented for final approval by the two organizations. Authorization was issued for each year of the Lampung Province undertaking (including the Way Abung subproject, for the five years of REPELITA I) after the DIP for that year had been approved. (20) The Lampung Transmigration Project started in 1969-70 and was planned for completion in 1973-74.

The main features of the 1969-70 Project Content Form (DIP) for the Lampung project may be summarized as follows:

1. Opening and preparing areas for settlement,

2. Preparation of basic housing facilities,

3. Resettlement of transmigrants,

4. Building or rehabilitation of irrigation facilities,

5. Provision of seeds, pesticides, and fertilizers,

6. Administration of land titles.

Besides these programmed activities, consideration was also given to provision of agricultural implements and to establishment of social facilities

in health and primary education for a designated period. Targets were estimated for all project components. The budget allocation for the entire
Lampung project for 1970-71 amounted to Rp17 million. (21) The project
manager was also head of the Transmigration Provincial Office located at
Tanjung Karang; he was assisted by the project's treasurer.

Activity components for the Way Abung subproject were not readily
discernible in the DIP for the Lampung Transmigration Project. It was not
until 1975-76 that Way Abung was designated as a separate operation with its
own DIP plan. The district officer of the Way Abung subproject received
funding and facilities in accordance with what had been requested and
approved for Way Abung within the DIP for the Lampung project. These
allocations were decided on by the Lampung project manager as head of the
Transmigration Office for Lampung Province. Transmigrants to be settled at
Way Abung in 1969-70 numbered 1,802 families or 7,834 persons, and for the
whole five-year development period totaled 10,950 families or 49,247 persons.

Other Planning Considerations

In the course of time, continual improvement was sought in the forms as
well as the procedures utilized in programming and budgeting, with the DIP
constituting always the core of the entire process. Such modifications at the
national level inevitably had a favorable effect on planning for the
transmigration project in Lampung Province.

In preparing the Lampung project plan for 1969-70, sophisticated
techniques such as cost-benefit analysis were not employed. (22) This did not
mean that benefits viewed from the aspect of national development, such as
the improved welfare of transmigrants, were not taken into account nor that
the calculation of standard costs of transportation and placement of the
settlers was overlooked. Consideration was given to such critical factors as
consistency and scale of priority. Recommendations from studies conducted
earlier were carefully assessed and incorporated in the resettlement scheme.

It should now be evident that project appraisal was influenced economically by the pressures of population in certain parts of Java and Bali, by the
national concern for regional development, and by the possibilities for
establishing new markets. Technically, assessment took into account land
conditions, agricultural potential, water resources, and timber reserves for
construction use. The social relations between settlers and local people and
the opportunities for social ability also had to be evaluated, and in financial
matters, there was always the obligation to examine the adequacy of funding
within the constraints of a limited budget.

An important aspect of the planning stage was the effort made to insure
that needed sources of financing would come primarily from the project
budget. During appraisal of the DIP, this matter was duly considered. For
purposes of devising the project design, criteria commonly applied to
estimate expenditures were employed: for example, unit costs for certain
types of housing and unit costs for transporting migrants to the settlement
areas. Because of the constraints of limited resources in this country, the
utilization of proper planning and assessment techniques will continue to be
essential to the programming and budgeting process in Indonesia.

PHASE 2: SELECTION, APPROVAL, AND ACTIVATION

Organization and Staffing

Events described in the previous section flowed easily into the organizational activity to be related here. There was no clear distinction between these stages in the actual exercise of project planning and management in Indonesia. The primary concern at this point was to set up an institutional and procedural infrastructure for resource mobilization and utilization.

The preparation and approval of the Project Content Form (DIP) and the instructions on procedures to be followed in implementing the budget constituted the preconditions for activating the Transmigration Project. Standard procedures - including, for example, contracting, tenders, and a reporting system - were all set forth in the budget implementation instructions. Each year the feedback from lessons of experience in managing the project would be utilized to improve the effectiveness of those instructions. Such a continuous improvement did not necessarily mean, however, that administrative measures then in force were either sufficient or satisfactory. They still showed many weaknesses, especially in 1969-70, when the new subproject in Lampung Province was initiated.

For the Way Abung subproject, the problem was even more serious, because its organizational plan was not represented by a separate Project Content Form. As has been explained, provisions for that activity were included within the DIP for the whole transmigration operation to be carried out in Lampung Province. With that in mind, the organization and staffing of the Lampung Transmigration Project, as well as the Way Abung subproject, may be outlined for 1969-70 as follows.

Overall responsibility for organizing transmigration in Indonesia resided in the office of the Director General for Transmigration in the Department of Manpower, Transmigration, and Cooperatives. The Directorate General for Transmigration, with headquarters in Jakarta, was divided into four divisions, namely, the Directorates of Research and Preparation, Land Reclamation, Mobilization and Settlement, and Guidance and Development. In those provinces where migrants had originated or where they had settled, the Director General was represented by Provincial Directorates of Transmigration. Each of these was headed by a Provincial Director (see Figs. 3.1 and 3.2).

Each Provincial Directorate was divided into four sections, namely, the Offices of Research and Preparation, Land Reclamation, Settlement, and Guidance and Development (see Fig. 3.3). For those districts identified more directly with migrant origin and settlement, and regarded by the Director General as sufficiently important, Regency (District) Offices were maintained (see Fig. 3.4). Each of these was administered by a District Officer.

The Way Abung subproject during the period from 1969 to 1974 was directed by the local district officer, who reported to the Lampung Provincial Director of Transmigration. The latter was also the project manager for the

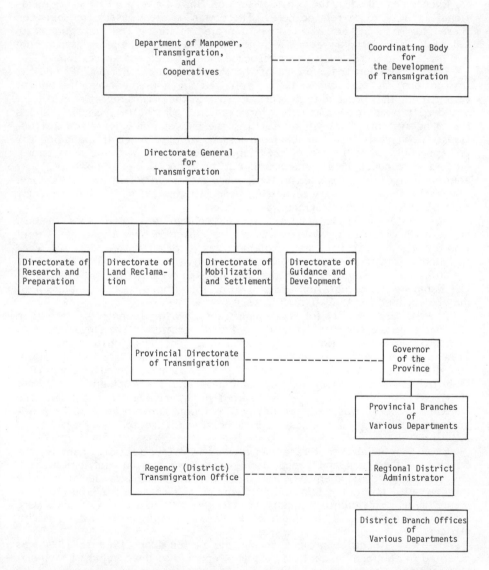

FIGURE 3.1   Organizational Structure of the Indonesian Transmigration Program, 1969/70

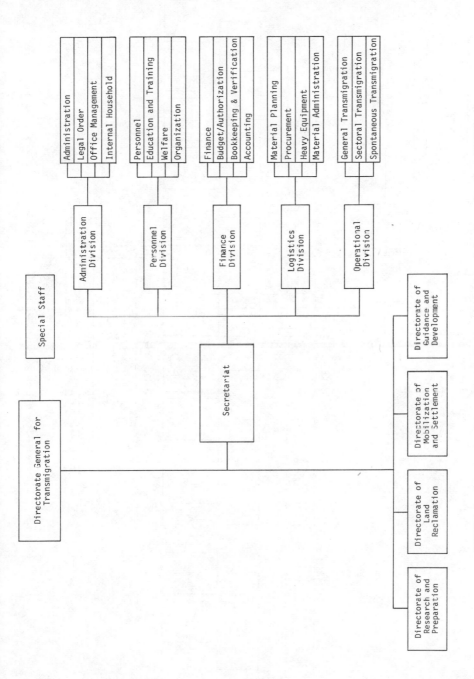

FIGURE 3.2   Organizational Structure of the Directorate General for Transmigration, 1969/70

71

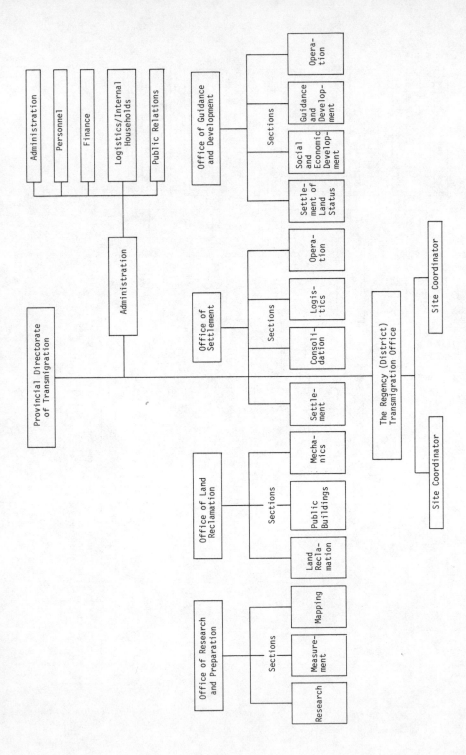

FIGURE 3.3 Organizational Structure of the Provincial Directorate of Transmigration, 1969/70

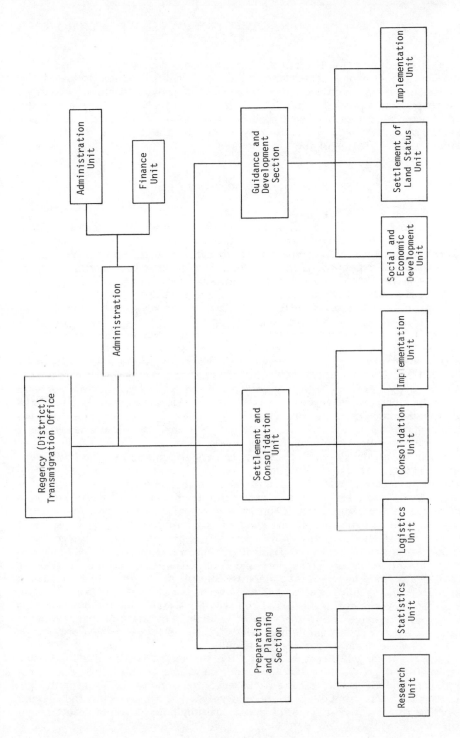

FIGURE 3.4 Organizational Structure of the Regency (District) Transmigration Office, 1969/70

73

Lampung Transmigration Project and was therefore doubly responsible for the Way Abung operation. The district officer for Way Abung followed the instructions he received from his superior, the provincial director/project manager, which depended on the latter's judgment of what was needed for the Way Abung subproject. A treasurer was appointed for the Lampung Transmigration Project; he was responsible to the project manager for financial administration of the resettlement.

Coordination of Participating Agencies

It should be noted that in implementing the Indonesian transmigration program, including the Lampung Project, a number of government agencies and institutions directed activities that were designed to support the realization of national expectations in this area. A most serious problem, however, became the need for creating and maintaining harmonious relations among the various contributing programs so that the substantive task of resettlement could be carried out effectively and efficiently. The problem was basically one of proper coordination.

For this purpose, an interdepartmental group was established at the national level, called Badan Pengembangan Transmigrasi (literally, "Body for the Development of Transmigration"). Its primary function was actually more coordination than development. The chairman of the new forum was the Minister of Manpower, Transmigration, and Cooperatives. Its membership included, among others, representatives from the Department of Public Works and Electric Power, Interior, Communications, Agriculture, Health, and Education, as well as from BAPPENAS (National Development Planning Agency) and the People's Bank (Bank Rakyat).

Attempts at developing concerted efforts and integrated policies were fairly successful at the national level, owing to the work of the Coordinating Body for the Development of Transmigration, but similar attempts did not materialize satisfactorily at the provincial level and they were even less productive at the project site. Thus, the governor of Lampung Province was supposed to be responsible for the conduct of transmigration activities within his territory. Close cooperation was normally expected between the governor and the Provincial Director of Transmigration in Lampung. The latter had to rely on the governor for support and cooperation from the heads of other Lampung Province agencies who were responsible for sectors like irrigation, education, and public health. The governor did have the authority to coordinate government activities at the provincial level, but the outcome was not always a positive one in the view of resettlement site managers. In most cases, decisions about implementation on the site of either project or subproject were made by provincial officials.

Clearly, then, while responsibility for the execution of the Indonesian transmigration program rested with the Department of Manpower, Transmigration, and Cooperatives and its Directorate General for Transmigration, the Republic was compelled to rely largely on the provincial and district governments for day-to-day policy and actual implementation of resettlement projects.

Functions of the Directorate General for Transmigration

It will be useful to elaborate on the functions of the Directorate General for Transmigration and its principal organizational components, namely, the four directorates and the secretariat. The structure of this national agency, which maintained headquarters in Jakarta, has been indicated in Fig. 3.2. The main functions and tasks of its several offices are set forth as follows.

Directorate General for Transmigration. The agency's overall responsibilities were apportioned among its four directorates. Information about the meaning and objectives of transmigration was transmitted to Indonesians, mainly in the more populated areas of Java and Bali, in order to attract their interest as potential migrants who would be willing to resettle in the Outer Islands. Land was acquired and developed in the destination areas. Preparatory measures were undertaken in the settlements to accommodate the needs of migrants after they arrived. Transportation was provided and organized from places of origin to places of settlement.

Directorate of Research and Preparation. This division collected and processed informational data and conducted research studies relevant to transmigration. It formulated administrative and operational plans for resettlement based on policies which had been outlined by the Director General. It carried out mapping surveys and drew up designs for settlement area facilities. It maintained files of statistical data, inventories, and other documentation concerning all activities of the Directorate General.

Directorate of Land Reclamation. This division was responsible for all preparatory measures relating to land clearance. It managed the construction of housing and other physical infrastructure, and arranged for the acquisition and maintenance of mechanical equipment used in the destination areas.

Directorate of Mobilization and Settlement. This division was charged with the task of mobilizing and settling the transmigrants. It transported them from their places of origin to the destination areas, and provided them with all essential supplies. It administered the consolidation of new settlements, and provided facilities for general health maintenance.

Directorate of Guidance and Development. This division promoted the general development of transmigration projects. It also provided for the social and economic needs of the migrant community. It attended to the resolution of problems relating to the land rights of settlers. It undertook preparatory measures in the transfer of administration of transmigration projects to local governments after three years.

Secretariat. This office assisted the director general in all matters. It undertook evaluations, made estimates, and formulated plans for monitoring the personnel, material, and financial administration of the Directorate General. It drafted the annual budget of the Directorate General. It organized data on various problems, made recommendations, and submitted reports to the director general. It prepared for the provision of general policy implementation. It exercised general supervision and facilitated staff coordination relating to the execution of tasks assigned to the several Directorates.

Administration in the Settlement Area

It was indicated earlier that general policy and implementation of the Indonesian transmigration programs as managed by the Directorate General for Transmigration were dependent to a very large degree on the administrators at provincial and regency (district) levels for what actually transpired in the settlement area.

The organizational structure of the Provincial Directorate of Transmigration as it pertained to Lampung Province is presented in Fig. 3.3. The relationship of this office to the governor of Lampung Province on the one hand, and to the Regency (District) Transmigration Office and the Way Abung subproject on the other, has also been noted. The organizational structure of the Regency (District) Transmigration Office is displayed in Fig. 3.4, and its relationship with the Way Abung subproject is charted in Fig. 3.5.

PHASE 3: OPERATION, CONTROL, AND HANDOVER

Management Problems in Project Implementation

As mentioned, management of resettlement activity at Way Abung was the responsibility of the provincial transmigration director, in close cooperation with the governor of Lampung Province, according to the Project Content Form (DIP) approved for the more comprehensive Lampung Transmigration Project. But the day-to-day administration in Way Abung rested with the regency, or district transmigration officer, who was charged with the task of directly supervising implementation of the subproject in that area.

Way Abung Project Site Management

In actual practice, as noted earlier, the district officer could only implement the direction or execute the instructions transmitted to him by the provincial director. The scope of activities conducted by the Way Abung chief depended essentially on financial allotments and provisions in kind which were decided on at the provincial level. But the nature of his relationship with the provincial director and the strength of his attitude about making suggestions and proposals based on his own appraisal of real and felt needs of the settlers also affected the management of the project.

In the period from 1969 to 1974, the project site was divided into two areas, Way Abung I and Way Abung II. Each was administered by an area coordinator under the supervision of the district officer. The coordinator for Area I was located in Tata Karya, one of six constituent village units. In Area II, the coordinator's office was in Pulung Kencana, one of 14 villages in that division.

Each village unit consisted of a number of hamlets. Each hamlet was made up of ten neighborhoods, and each of the latter normally comprised ten families. Every village unit was superintended by a village headman and his

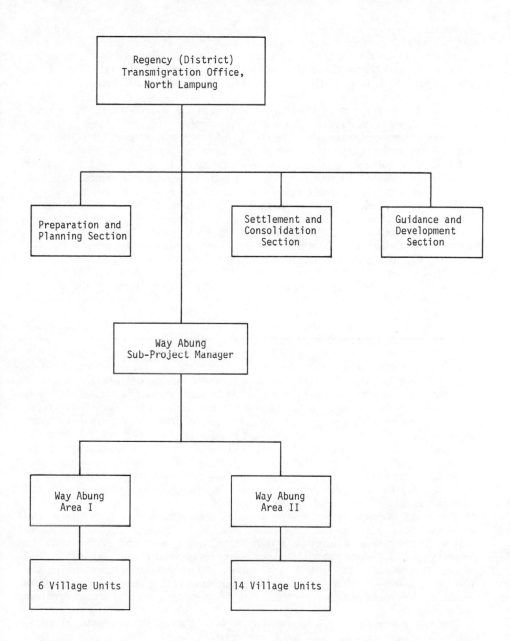

FIGURE 3.5   Organizational Structure of the Way Abung Project 1973/74

assistants.   He was charged with general development of the village.
Associations for the same purpose were set up at the hamlet and
neighborhoods levels.   Each neighborhood association ideally had ten family
heads as its membership, but the number actually depended on the size of the
population group, as was the case also with the hamlet associations (see Fig.
3.6).

After the first year of the Way Abung project, a provisional village administration was established in each village, consisting of village headman,
secretary, treasurer, security officers, a religious official, and a committee
that dealt with matters of marriage, divorce, and reconciliation.   A
committee of village development was created to promote development
activities generally. Village social groups and farmers' associations were also
formed to work cooperatively in areas of social and economic growth.

The project manager, as director of the Transmigration Office in Lampung
Province, was located in Tanjung Karang, the provincial capital. The two
area coordinators at Way Abung had nothing to do with the Lampung Transmigration DIP (Project Content Form). They were merely responsible for
carrying out the task of implementation in their respective areas.   The
provincial director, in composing the DUP (Project Proposal Form), had
obtained all necessary data from the area coordinators through the district
officer, so that he was supposed to know the people's needs in those
areas. (23)

Leadership and Coordination Needs

Some impressions gained from the comparative study of management in
various transmigration projects indicate that leadership orientation is one of
the most important variables in project administration. (24) Consider that
there are two types of project managers. The first is the traditional type,
who operates according to regulations and follows instructions received from
his superiors. The other is the developmental type, who is more creative and
innovative. He attempts not only to meet day-to-day requirements of the
settlement project, but also to promote a more viable and dynamic
community that can become an integral part of the larger regional community. Judging from the experience of Way Abung, the management of that
project was less of the developmental type.

The main problem in implementation at Way Abung was to establish and
maintain a concerted effort in direct response to changing project requirements at the site. While the provincial director was concerned with the
overall coordination of activities, such as recruitment of migrants, movement
to the destination area, initial settlement, and provision of care during the
first few years, the district officer was compelled to give immediate
attention to management problems as they arose in the transmigration
community.

Responsibility for land reclamation at Way Abung, for example, properly
fell within the jurisdiction of the Directorate of Land Clearance, which had a
branch office in Lampung Province under the Provincial Directorate of
Transmigration. But, in fact, clearance of land at the project site had to be
accomplished by contracting out the work to private enterprise.

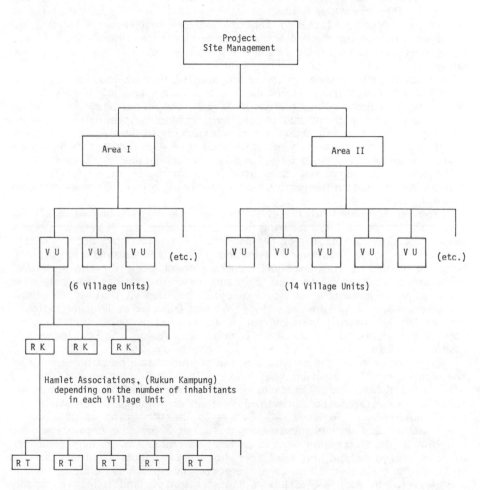

FIGURE 3.6   Village, Hamlet, and Neighborhood Relationships, Way Abung Project

This and many other cases proved that weakness in implementation and resultant output was caused by a lack of coordination. Thus, when the settlers were ready to cultivate the land, the construction of irrigation channels had not yet been completed. According to the Department of Public Works, Way Abung was not an area with high priority for irrigation cultivation. Further, the agricultural services extended to settlers were not well suited to the quality of the land, nor to the method of dry farming required. The network of roads that was built in Way Abung, although not at all complex in design, failed to meet the settlers' requirements. Cattle had not been provided for the project; consequently the plowing of the land was being done manually, which meant a lowered productivity of the migrants' labors.

Not an immediate problem at the project site, nonetheless a threat to the resettlement program as a whole, was the inadequacy of transportation facilities from the populous regions in Java to destination areas in Sumatra. Spontaneous transmigrants had to stop over in holding terminals in Jakarta, causing demoralizing delays and considerably adding to their financial burden, for they received no government assistance until they arrived in the Outer Island settlements. According to a study conducted by University of Indonesia social scientists, this situation contributed significantly to a reduced motivation on the part of Indonesians being recruited for spontaneous transmigration. (25)

From such lessons as these, it can be stated that one of the most important leverages for improving management output at Way Abung was a better coordination of project components. For an overall picture of the relationships to be maintained in implementing the transmigration project, refer to Table 3.1 for a schematic arrangement depicting the matrix of relevant activities, subactivities, and agencies or institutions responsible for their accomplishment. It was expected, in theory, that 11 of these components would be considered by Provincial Director of Transmigration in performing his overall management functions. The same generalization applied even more to the district officer at Way Abung who held immediate responsibility for all aspects of the project operation. (26)

While problems of implementation thus stemmed to a certain degree from the weakness of coordination, they also resulted from other causes, some of which are indicated here. In planning, more emphasis had been placed on the relief of demographic pressures in Java than on regional development and social improvement in Sumatra. Delays in the processing of government financial aid and disbursements contributed to a lowered capacity of the program to absorb transmigrants in destination areas. Government clearance of land lagged behind the need for allocation of plots to newly arrived settlers, and the latter did not have the necessary equipment to clear the land themselves. In addition, official administration of land titles was unduly cumbersome.

Credit facilities were supposed to be extended through the People's Bank (Bank Rakyat Indonesia) as part of the BIMAS program, but did not materialize as expected. BIMAS (Bimbingan Masal Swasembada Bahan Makanan, or Mass Guidance for Self-Sufficiency in Food) was a government program established in 1965 to increase rice production through Extension

TABLE 3.1   Institutional Relations and Responsibilities, Way Abung Project

Activities	Subactivities	Agencies/Institutions
Recruitment of migrants, preparation for movement		Dir. Gen. for Transmigration Provincial Government
Transportation and holding terminal in Jakarta		Dir. Gen. for Transportation; Dept. of Communications
Soil Studies; research		Soil Research Institute; Dir. Gen. for Agrarian Affairs
Land alienation from community lands		Dir. Gen. for Agrarian Affairs
Land clearance and development		Dir. Gen. for Transportation
Basic facilities	Housing; water; roads; etc.	Dir. Gen. for Transportation; Dir. Gen. for Road Construction; contractors.
Irrigation	Primary; secondary; tertiary	Dir. Gen. for Irrigation Dept. of Home Affairs
Settlement of migrants		Dir. Gen. for Transportation; Provincial Government
Agriculture and extension service	Food and other crops; marketable commodities	Dir. Gen. for Transportation; Dept. of Agriculture; People's Bank; Dir. Gen. for Cooperatives
Social facilities	Elementary and secondary schools; health center; mosque	Dir. Gen. for Transportation; Dept. of Education; Dept. of Health; Dept. of Religious Affairs; community
Land rights	Right of use and cultivation; proprietary right	Dir. Gen. for Agrarian Affairs
Marketing and home industry		Dir. Gen. for Transportation Dept. of Trade; Dir. Gen. for Cooperatives; People's Bank
Farm and other equipment	Farm and other equipment; transport means for marketable produce	Dir. Gen. for Transportation; Dir. Gen. for Cooperatives; People's Bank
Development of cooperatives		Dir. Gen. for Cooperatives
Cattle and other animals		Dir. Gen. for Transportation; Dept. of Agriculture; People's Bank
Administration and security		Dir. Gen. for Transportation; Provincial Government

Service assistance in improved seed, more use of fertilizers and pesticides, expanded irrigation, and provision of credit facilities for purchasing agricultural aids on a crop repayment plan.

Another problem calling for serious attention was the marketing of migrant-produced goods and the pricing of imported consumer products. The existing terms of trade were not at all favorable to the settlers. A principal reason for this was the poor condition of roads linking the settlement villages with the market centers. The local trucking business was monopolized by a certain commercial firm which succeeded in maintaining very high shipping charges for both exported and imported merchandise. According to a study by the World Bank, the transportation cost component in pricing ran as high as 60 percent. (27)

Measures of Project Performance

Supervision, monitoring, and control constitute a very important aspect of project management. At Way Abung, these functions were carried out in accordance with standards stipulated in the Project Content Form (DIP) for the Lampung transmigration operation. The project manager (Provincial Director of Transmigration) was obligated to submit quarterly reports on the physical progress and financial expenditures of the project. (28) These reports were forwarded to the Department of Manpower, Transmigration, and Cooperatives (through the Directorate General for Transmigration) as well as to BAPPENAS (National Development Planning Agency) and the Directorate General for Budgeting. It should be acknowledged, however, that the reporting system lacked elements pertinent to problem-solving and followup activities. Besides, the performance benchmarks did not provide much direction for effective monitoring and control. At present, the reporting system is undergoing review and improvement.

In addition, field supervisory missions were carried out by staff from the Directorate General for Transmigration. Those activities were identified as requiring followup action were then reported to the Department of Manpower, Transmigration, and Cooperatives, or were forwarded to the Coordinating Body for the Development of Transmigration for consideration. At the project site level, the district officer for Way Abung in consultation with the Provincial Director for Transmigration exercised supervision and control more directly but without management procedures to support them in these functions. They were, however, encouraged in the utilization of network analysis.

In the period from 1969 to 1974, a number of significant accomplishments issued from the Way Abung subproject among which some are mentioned here as representative.

In the villages scattered throughout Areas I and II, a total of 49,247 persons, including 10,950 family heads, had been resettled. (29) Land which had been cleared and opened for cultivation amounted to 13,687 hectares.

In the public health sector, Area I had a Type B Health Center established at Tata Karya and a clinic at Bumirestu. Area II operated a Type B Health Center at Daya Murni, five Policlinics at Margomulyo, Mulyosari, Chandra Kencana, Pulung Kencana, and Panaragan, and a clinic at Dayasakti. Medical personnel to manage these facilities included four nurses, thirteen nurse assistants, one midwife, and three midwife assistants. This force was also aided by 49 traditional midwives.

Twelve Village Unit Cooperatives (Koperasi Unit Desa, or KUD) had been organized by the end of the project period. Before the establishment of KUD, five cooperatives had been in operation at Tata Karya and Purbasakti in Area I, and at Mulyosari, Margomulyo, and Dayasakti in Area II.

Considerable activity was generated in the public education sector. By 1974, there were 83 elementary school classrooms. Thirty of these were of permanent construction and 53 were only temporary. The teachers for these schools numbered 152 and supervised a total of 5,544 pupils who were distributed through six years of elementary or primary schooling as follows:

2,734 (first grade)

1,327 (second grade)

719 (third grade)

461 (fourth grade)

204 (fifth grade)

99 (sixth grade)

At the secondary education level, there was one general high school, located at Mulyosari, which had 30 students and ten teachers. In addition, secondary education in economic subjects was offered in a school at Tata Karya, also with 30 students and ten teachers, and in agricultural subjects in a school at Dayasakti with 15 students and eight teachers.

The BIMAS program for self-sufficiency in food production has already been mentioned. Land utilized for rice cultivation at Way Abung as part of that operation amounted to 1,075 hectares and involved 2,108 settlers. Additionally, 269 migrant farmers in the same program raised other crops on 280 hectares of land. Transmigrants from 1969 to 1974 also received supplemental aid from the World Food Program (WFP 715). These food stores were allocated to them in lieu of payment for doing such work as dredging irrigation channels, rehabilitating the roads, and controlling soil erosion.

Four village units at Way Abung, comprising about 2,000 families, were integrated in 1974-75 with the regency, or district, administration. As these communities had been founded in 1965, this meant that they were under the supervision of the Directorate General for Transmigration for a total of nine years, four more than regulations then in force normally permitted.

Statutory Changes Affecting Implementation

In 1972, a very important development took place which, although it had no marked influence on the course of the Way Abung subproject, would affect the implementation of the national transmigration program in years to come. Statute No. 3, 1972, concerning the Basic Stipulations for Transmigration, gave to the Department (Ministry) of Manpower, Transmigration, and Cooperatives more leverage and authority than it had possessed before in the implementation of resettlement projects.

The general policy aim of the statute was to conduct both general and spontaneous transmigration in the most efficient manner in order to achieve improvement of migrants' living standards, to extend regional development more evenly throughout Indonesia, and to ensure a more balanced distribution of population, to utilize more effectively the natural resources and manpower of the Republic, to promote national unity and integration, and to strengthen national defense and security.

The costs of all transmigration activities sponsored by the government would come from the state budget, and would be apportioned according to the various requirements of resettlement. Transmigration areas would be determined by presidential decree, as the authority and responsibility for various settlement activities inevitably involved a number of different government departments and agencies. Authority for further execution of the program would be delegated to the Department of Manpower, Transmigration, and Cooperatives with the understanding that the Department of Home Affairs would participate closely.

Determination of destination areas would henceforth be based on the following criteria:

1. Uninhabited or only sparsely populated regions,

2. Sufficiency of land to permit agricultural production on a wide scale,

3. Opportunities for expanded employment and better livelihood on the part of transmigrants,

4. Importance to the national security,

5. Other considerations that might be viewed as important by the government.

The End and a Beginning

Transfer to Normal Administration

According to the stipulations of Republican law or administrative decrees concerning transmigration, settlers were maintained under the care and guidance of the Directorate General for Transmigration for five years. After that period, the task was taken over by the provincial governor in a transfer to normal administration.

Upon completion of the transmigration project, or any portion of it, transfer proceeded in the following manner. In the first instance, a technical team was appointed to prepare for the changeover (it also evaluated the project). The team was composed of representatives from the participating departments and was chaired by the provincial governor. Consideration was given to economic and social qualifications for termination of the migrant community, according to guidelines previously established by the Directorate General for Transmigration, such as the following:

1. The project, or any part of it, must be managed for at least five years.

2. Each family head must have possession of a house for himself and his family.

3. The legal security of land (either farm or nonfarm) allocated to the family head must be established in accordance with decrees issued by the Director General for Agrarian Affairs (No. 3, 1967) and the Minister of Manpower, Transmigration, and Cooperatives (No. 18, 1971).

4. The infrastructure and facilities of the village gave satisfactory assurance of a settled life and the promise of further growth in conformance with developmental stages based on the principle of self-help.

5. Eligible families must form an orderly and legally established community unit with designated land boundaries and a provisional form of village administration.

The next step was the actual transfer of responsibility from the Department of Manpower, Transmigration, and Cooperatives to the Department of Home Affairs. Eligible village units in the Way Abung project would then be integrated within the regional (regency) government. While this procedure applied to village units that had been established by the Directorate of Transmigration five years earlier, in actual practice the time was sometimes extended to nine years for migrant communities founded in 1965, when Way Abung was first opened up. Furthermore, transfer did not mean that all members of a given village were necessarily involved in the move at the same time. Some settlers who joined the village unit later continued under the responsibility of the Directorate of Transmigration until they had completed their official five-year residence.

In fact, the changeover to routine administration also occurred at different times depending on the sector of activity scheduled for transfer. For example, administration of agricultural extension services was normalized after plots of land had been under cultivation for only two years. In the case of health centers, the operational costs were carried past the five-year period by the Transmigration office until the Department of Health was allocated funds sufficient to maintain the centers under regional government. Elementary schools, on the other hand, were transferred to the regional government's care at the same time that the project as a whole was handed over.

Some further description of village and district administrative relationships is necessary at this point. As noted earlier, each migrant community in the Way Abung project was managed by a headman of the village unit. But village administration when subordinated to the regional government after transfer was performed by a village chief. There is a distinct difference between the headman of a village unit, as an official under the Directorate General for Transmigration, and the village chief as a functionary of the regional government. The former had been responsible for the Way Abung project manager, who at the same time was head of the regency transmigration office, whereas the village chief now answered directly to the head of the regency (district) government.

During the period of the Way Abung project (1969-1974), the village administration of new settlement communities was set up under the guidance of the Directorate General for Transmigration. The head of a village unit and his assistants were elected by members of the community, but the successful candidates had to be acceptable to and approved by the transmigration office. Since 1974, establishment of village administration, as well as the election of village officials, has been subject to joint review by the Minister of Home Affairs and the Minister of Manpower, Transmigration, and Cooperatives. Village administrators are still elected by the transmigration community, but they must now be approved by the regional government. Their status continues to be provisional, as the instruments of a village still in process of preparation.

Land proved to be a principal problem in the transfer of responsibility from the Directorate General for Transmigration to the provincial government. It often happened that the official grant of two hectares of land to a family head was not yet entirely under cultivation at the time of transfer. There were several reasons for this. The transmigrant may have been unable to farm all of his land because of the limits of his own working capacity and not being in a financial position to employ others to assist him. Or, the land allotted to him may have been located at some considerable distance from his house so that, not having been cleared because of difficulties presented by the distance involved, it remained in a forested condition. There were also instances where the land was found to be still occupied by others when a settler wanted to clear off the forest, even though the land had been designated for his use in the settlement project.

A related problem existed in regard to the proprietary rights of settlers to land they had cleared and cultivated for five years. Especially subject to dispute was land that had been alienated by the government from local communal holdings in the years before REPELITA I (and the associated Way Abung project) got underway in 1969-70. The local people, who had prior communal rights in the land, challenged this alienation on the basis of their traditional ties with the land. The government's acquisition of these disputed lands had been based on a "letter of decision" negotiated with the local clan that was linked by custom with the area. Since that time, the final transfer of land to the settlers has been strengthened by the requirement of a letter signed by the governor (Head of Level I Region) (30) and disposed of finally by the Minister of Home Affairs.

The regional government and the Directorate General for Transmigration had long held different views about criteria for determining projects eligible for transfer to normal administration. Such conflicts of interpretation have been resolved by a joint decree on the regulation of resettlement projects issued by the Minister of Home Affairs and the Minister of Manpower, Transmigration, and Cooperatives

The fact remains, however, that in a transmigration area where the settlement of migrants had proceeded in stages over the past years, there continued to exist side by side the local people who were indigenous to the area and the settlers who had become local citizens, both groups coming under the regular regency (district) administration, and those settlers who were still regulated by the district transmigration office and had yet to be transferred to the jurisdiction of the regional government.

PHASE 4: EVALUATION AND REFINEMENT

Evaluation of Way Abung

An evaluation of the Way Abung resettlement project during the final years of implementation of REPELITA I (First Five-Year Development Program in Indonesia) was presented in the provincial transmigration director's annual report for 1974-75. (31) The progress of project implementation was also recounted in quarterly reports submitted by the project manager to his superior, the provincial director.

During the final stage of implementation, the Way Abung subproject of the Lampung Transmigration Project showed signs of a declining trend, judging from such indicators as the lesser number of migrants who were resettled in Way Abung. However, viewed in terms of its potential, the Way Abung activity did seem to provide definite possibilities for subsequent expansion. For that reason, intensive research was conducted toward that end. (32) The primary objectives were to investigate the causes of apparent decline during the project's last years, and to identify possible bases for its rehabilitation, such as the new transmigration project being launched at Baturaja in the north of Lampung Province adjacent to Way Abung.

These studies, besides analyzing weaknesses in project management, constructively reviewed new policy recommendations for rehabilitation which displayed a fundamentally different approach to transmigration. For example, alternatives were considered to the official grant of two hectares of land to each migrant family, because two hectares were judged to be insufficient to improve the living conditions of settlers. Some recent proposals, based on cost-benefit studies, have suggested increasing these land allotments to five hectares. Further, the idea was put forward that transmigration might be profitably directed toward the development of rubber plantations as well as the cultivation of consumer crops already emphasized.

From the viewpoint of management theory, a more integrated approach to project planning and implementation is called for here. A principal strategy would be to plan project budgeting in a more consistent manner when funding comes from various sources and involves different agencies. In the case of Way Abung, the planning of research and evaluation studies was linked with an effort to attract multilateral funding as an additional resource that could enable the performance of such activities as might be required to rehabilitate and improve the project in a followup effort.

Reorganization of Transmigration Management Structures

During the period of final evaluation, and partly as an outcome of the surveys conducted at Way Abung, two very important developments took place that would affect future implementation of the Indonesian transmigration program.

Both were the issuance of presidential decrees. The first (No. 44, 1974) specified a new organizational structure for all government offices, including the Directorate General for Transmigration. The other (No. 45, 1974) detailed the restructuring of administrative and secretariat functions in the Directorate General for Transmigration (see Fig. 3.7). This provided for a Secretariat, a staff Directorate of Training, Research, and Evaluation, and four operational Directorates, namely, Planning and Programming, Preparation and Implementation, Recruitment and Placement, and Development and Guidance. Each provincial directorate of transmigration, also referred to as the representative's office, duplicated the headquarters structure except for the staff function (Training, Research, and Evaluation). Fig. 3.8 shows this structure as it existed in the receiving and settlement areas.

Another presidential decree (No. 29, 1974) provided the organizational structure for external linkages and for internal coordination at national, provincial, and district levels in implementing the Indonesian Transmigration and Rural Development Program (see Fig. 3.9).

Summary and Conclusions

From the foregoing analysis of the Way Abung transmigration project, certain lessons can be learned that will be useful for improving management practice by means of policy recommendations and measures.

In the initial stage of planning any project, some perception of the dynamics of development is required. The project should have an identifiable function and role within the macroframework of the larger development program of which it is a part - in the present instance, Indonesian transmigration. It should also contribute to the attainment of objectives conceptualized more generally in the context of regional and national development. The social and economic benefits of the directed activity should be readily discernible.

Another important factor is the readiness of decision makers to accept the worth of a proposed operation, as measured by their participation in the complex process of policy analysis and formulation. The same willingness should be evidenced in the actions of other agencies involved, when their support is required for achieving the project's goals.

In the next stage of the project cycle, design and appraisal, planning should be considered from an integrated viewpoint. The various elements of activities functioning to support the project's product-goals should be programmed in harmony if they have to be performed by several different agencies. The working relationships among participating agencies have to be clearly delineated. The experience of planning in Indonesia has shown that consistency and coordination in project implementation are more likely to be assured if first the budgetary components of project activities are woven into a harmonious pattern. The primary task of coordination will then be effectively achieved through this control of budgetary resources.

Planning can be more effective if all components are integrally reflected within a single project form, such as the DIP (Daftar Isian Projek) already

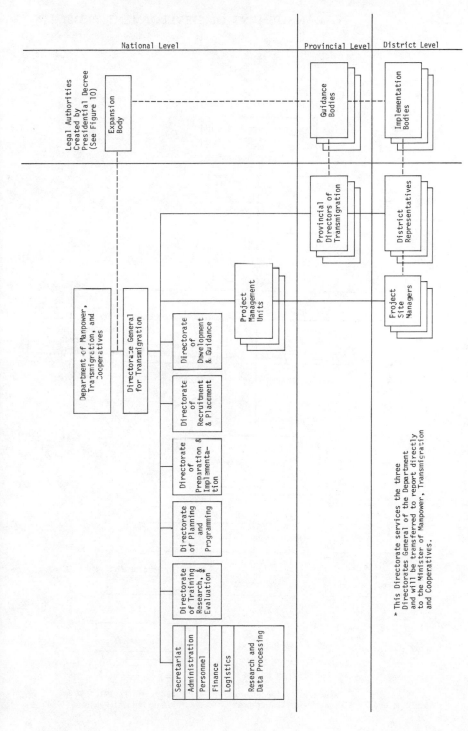

FIGURE 3.7 Organizational Structure of the Directorate General for Transmigration, Transmigration and Rural Development Program, 1974

National Level   Provincial Level   District Level

Legal Authorities Created by Presidential Decree (See Figure 10)

Expansion Body

Guidance Bodies

Implementation Bodies

Department of Manpower, Transmigration, and Cooperatives

Directorate General for Transmigration

Directorate of Development & Guidance

Directorate of Recruitment & Placement

Directorate of Preparation & Implementation

Directorate of Planning and Programming

Directorate of Training Research, & Evaluation*

Secretariat
Administration
Personnel
Finance
Logistics
Research and Data Processing

Project Management Units

Provincial Directors of Transmigration

District Representatives

Project Site Managers

*This Directorate services the three Directorates General of the Department and will be transferred to report directly to the Minister of Manpower, Transmigration and Cooperatives.

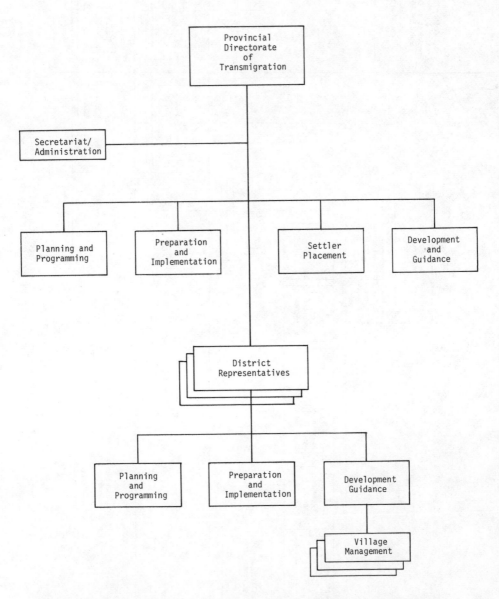

FIGURE 3.8 Organizational Structure of the Provincial Directorates of Transmigration
     in Receiving and Settlement Areas, Transmigration and Rural Development Progra⟩ , 1974.

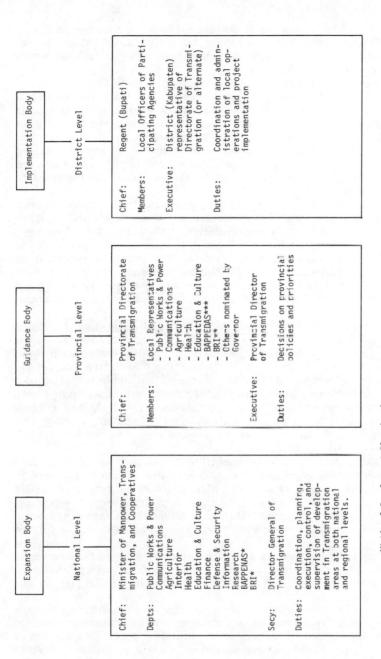

Expansion Body

National Level

Chief: Minister of Manpower, Transmigration, and Cooperatives

Depts: Public Works & Power
Communications
Agriculture
Interior
Health
Education & Culture
Finance
Defense & Security
Information
Research
BAPPENAS*
BRI*

Secy: Director General of Transmigration

Duties: Coordination, planning, execution, control, and supervision of development in Transmigration areas at both national and regional levels.

Guidance Body

Provincial Level

Chief: Provincial Directorate of Transmigration

Members: Local Representatives
- Public Works & Power
- Communications
- Agriculture
- Health
- Education & Culture
- BAPPEDAS***
- BRI**
- Others nominated by Governor

Executive: Provincial Director of Transmigration

Duties: Decisions on provincial policies and priorities

Implementation Body

District Level

Chief: Regent (Bupati)

Members: Local Officers of Participating Agencies

Executive: District (Kabupaten) representative of Directorate of Transmigration (or alternate)

Duties: Coordination and administration of local operations and project implementation

*National Development Planning Agency

**Bank Rakyat Indonesia (Indonesian People's Bank)

***Regional Planning Units of the Provincial Government

FIGURE 3.9   Coordinating Bodies for the Transmigration and Rural Development Program, 1974 (Created by the Presidential Decree, No. 29, 1974)

described.   Appraisal may then be undertaken from the vantage points of economics, technical feasibility, marketing potential, financial costs, resource availability, social conditions, cultural impact, organizational structure, and management practice.

If possible, cost-benefit analysis should be employed in determining the criteria for sound project implementation as seen from alternative positions. Appraisal techniques for application in special fields are now being developed to facilitate planning and implementation.   Considering the scarcity of qualified experts in a country such as Indonesia, such techniques are frequently best applied through the medium of technical assistance provided by a donor country.   Encouraging the use of these techniques is all the more important when we recall the scarcity of local resources and the need to maximize their utilization.

In Indonesia, the national system of planning and implementation has been characterized by one very significant feature.   The appraisal and ultimate approval of a project are the joint responsibility of the National Development Planning Agency and the Directorate General for Budgeting.   The planning agency, for its part, undertakes to review the project's potential in contributing to macrodevelopment as defined by nationally recognized needs and priorities.   The budgeting office, on the other hand, views the proposal with an appreciation for the constraints imposed by possibly limited financial resources.

In the next stage of project organization and implementation, the focus and degree of coordination pose a very critical problem.   Coordination at the project management level should be endorsed by and integrated with those forums or bodies maintained at higher levels for more effective interaction, so that a concerted effort can be realized in the actual implementation of a project.   Physical activities at the project site need to be coordinated with the disbursement or expenditure of project funds.   The budget allocation process should always be in accord with official stipulations.   Budgeting procedures must be continuously improved toward providing more flexibility without relinquishing fiscal control.

Monitoring and control of project operations constitute an essential part of the entire management process.   At present, the practices followed in Indonesia to support these functions still require refinement.   Basic procedures that have yet to be incorporated include effective reporting, benchmarking, problem solving, and followup.   The quarterly reporting system now employed in Indonesia is being subjected to continual revision for further improvement.

In project management, there is a significant difference to be observed in the performance of a traditional type of leadership compared to that of a developmental type.   Any program of managerial training should give serious consideration to this factor.

The final stage of the project cycle ordinarily involves handing over or transferring responsibility to normal government administration or, in some cases, to public enterprises or corporations.   Standing orders in the form of established procedures should be made sufficiently clear so that a vacuum of authority or wastage of physical output from the project may be avoided. Evaluation of the completed activity can provide useful information in formulating policy recommendations and measures for improved management of the project in the event that it is continued or expanded, or for application to the implementation of still other projects.

Strategies for Managing Development Projects

As a way of summarizing the principal lessons learned from the Way Abung transmigration project, the following strategies for managing development projects are outlined for further consideration.

1. The formulation of project goals and targets should take into full account the feasibility of operational plans in anticipation of their implementation. The setting of objectives should also be done in conformity with national development plans in force at the time.

2. The organizational structure of a project should provide for all activating elements of onsite management. Coordination of the various project components performs a very vital function, because a project generally depends on a package of integrated activities for its successful completion.

3. Managing a project involves the expert mobilization and utilization of varied resources - human, natural, material, and financial - all within a pattern of harmonious relationships. Administrative systems, comprising procedures and other essential components, should be developed to provide the requisite infrastructure to accomplish the project goal.

4. The function of leadership should be oriented toward the development type, that is, being innovative and creative. A project that contributes to the national development of an emerging country such as Indonesia is, by its very nature, a vital ingredient in the comprehensive effort of planned social change.

5. The linkages between management and its clientele should be monitored continually to maintain maximum communication and interaction. In a transmigration project, the successful attainment of project objectives will depend ultimately on the motivations and attitudes of the various client groups, namely, the potential migrants in Java, the actual settlers in Sumatra, and the local populations in the settlement areas.

NOTES - Chapter 3

(1) Sri-Edi Swasono, "The Land Beyond, Transmigration and Development in Indonesia" (unpublished paper for a seminar on transmigration; Jakarta: Faculty of Economics, University of Indonesia, 1969), p. 129.

(2) Nathan Keyfitz and Widjojo Nitisastro, Soal Penduduk dan Pem Pembangunan Indonesia (Population Problems and Development in Indonesia) (Jakarta: P.T. Pembangunan, 1964), p. 132.

(3) World Bank (Team Report), "Appraisal of a Transmigration and Rural Development Project" (unpublished paper; Jakarta: April 8, 1976), p. 57.

(4) Among others, Keyfitz and Nitisastro, p. 129.

(5) Sri-Edi Swasono, "The Land Beyond, Transmigration and Development in Indonesia" (unpublished paper for a seminar on transmigration; Jakarta: Faculty of Economics, University of Indonesia, 1969), p. 10.

(6) Amral Sjamsu, Dari Kolonisasi ke Transmigrasi 1905-1955 (From Colonization to Transmigration) (Djakarta: Djambatan, 1960), pp. 4-5.

(7) For a detailed account of colonization activities in 1905-1931, see Karl J. Pelzer, Pioneer Settlement in the Asiatic Tropics (New York: Institute of Pacific Relations, 1945), pp. 191-199.

(8) Widjojo Nitisastro, Population Trends in Indonesia (Ithaca: Cornell University Press, 1970), pp. 89-90.

(9) Nathan Keyfitz and Widjojo Nitisastro, Soal Penduduk dan Pembangunan Indonesia (Population Problems and Development in Indonesia) (Jakarta: P.T. Pembangunan, 1964), p. 122

(10) Keyfitz and Nitisastro, pp. 122-123.

(11) This was a policy trend which prevailed after 1900 among Dutch politicians, recommending provision of better education and social services to the Indonesian people in acknowledgement of the riches exploited by Dutch interests in the Indies almost continuously since the late eighteenth century.

(12) Sjamsu, p. 9.

(13) Sjamsu, pp. 78-79.

(14) Nitisastro, Population Trends, pp. 129-130.

(15) Prof. Dr. Subroto, "Strategi Transmigrasi dan Koperasi dalam rangka Strategi Nasional" (Strategy of Transmigration and Cooperatives within the Frame of National Strategy) (unpublished report; Jakarta: March 1972).

(16) In 1969, the Indonesia government changed its fiscal year from the calendar year to the 12-month period extending from April 1 to March 31.

(17) Adapted from, among others, N.D. Abdul Hameed, "Transmigration Economy of Way Abung" (unpublished paper; Jakarta: World Bank, February 15, 1975).

(18) The Presidential Decision on the Implementation of the Budget of Revenues and Expenditures is promulgated following the enactment of the annual Budget Law. The following are Presidential Decisions to implement the Budget Laws:

Fiscal Years	Annual Budget Law	Presidential Decision
1969-70	No. 2	No. 33
1970-71	No. 5	No. 25
1971-72	No. 5	No. 14
1972-73	No. 1	No. 48
1973-74	No. 3	No. 11
1974-75	No. 2	No. 17
1975-76	No. 1	No. 7
1976-77	No. 1	No. 14

It should be added that provisions in the Presidential Decisions on the Implementation of the Budget of Revenues and Expenditures have been improved year by year.

(19) The completion of the DUP form can be regarded as an exercise in project planning. Only the DIP document needs approval from superiors of BAPPENAS and the Budgeting Office. Approval of the DIP implies approval of the implementation of the concerned project plan.

(20) The fiscal years started on April 1, but approval of the DIP was usually late.

(21) Indonesia in 1969 had a flexible exchange system in which the floating value of the rupiah was determined eventually by marked demand and supply. In early 1969, the rates of offer and demand revolved around Rp326 and Rp333 per US$1.00. The present rate of exchange revolves around Rp415 and Rp420 per US$1.00.

(22) Planning techniques based on cost-benefit analysis, however, together with shadow pricing, were applied in evaluating the Way Abung Trans-migration Project of 1969-1974, and also in planning its revision and expansion from 1976-77 onward. A process of planning and replanning was in fact adopted.

(23) Not until REPELITA II (the Second Five-Year Development Program, instituted in 1974-75) was it determined that the project coordinator together with the project treasurer, would reside at the project site. Following this stipulation, all management problems at Way Abung were dealt with directly and resolved at the project site. The provincial director (now titled the Lampung Province Representative of the Director General for Transmigration) retained general responsibility for supervising and coordinating all of the projects within his jurisdiction.

(24) From an interview with Much. Iljas of the Directorate General for Transmigration.

(25) Djoko Santoso and Ali Wardhana, eds., Some Aspects of Spontaneous Transmigration in Indonesia (Jakarta: Institute for Economic and Social Research, Djakarta School of Economics, University of Indonesia, 1957), p. 428.

(26) Not until 1974 was coordination of transmigration activities improved, by the issuance of Presidential Decree No. 29.

(27) World Bank (Team Report), "Appraisal of a Transmigration and Rural Development Project" (unpublished paper; Jakarta: April 8, 1976), p. 57.

(28) The Quarterly Progress Report Form was employed in Indonesia to implement the project planning, programming, budgeting, and evaluation cycle.

(29) In the previous four years, dating from 1965 when Way Abung first accepted transmigrants, an additional 6,511 persons, including 1,552 family heads, had already been resettled in the area.

(30) "Province" is the name for a territory headed by the governor in the frame of government decentralization. The governor is the highest representative of the central government in the province. "Level I Region" denotes a territory administered by the head of Level I Region in the frame of autonomous government. The terms "Province" and "Level I Region," in fact, refer to the same administrative territory. The governor is also the head of Level I Region. As governor, he coordinates the activities of departments of the central government in the province. As head of Level I Region, he administers the office of the autonomous regional government. The governor/head of Level I Region is appointed by the president on recommendation of the regional House of Representatives.

(31) Directorate of Transmigration, Lampung Province, "Annual Report, Fiscal Year 1974/75" (Tanjung Karang, 1975).

(32) Among others, two important studies that evaluated the Way Abung project and recommended followup action for the future are N.D. Abdul Hameed, "Transmigration Economy of Way Abung" (unpublished paper; Jakarta: World Bank, February 15, 1975), and World Bank (Team Report), "Appraisal of a Transmigration and Rural Development Project" (unpublished paper; Jakarta: April 8, 1976).

4 Laguna Rural Social Development Project: Philippines

Ernesto Garilao

PROJECT BACKGROUND

Rural Social Development

The Philippine Rural Reconstruction Movement (PRRM) was organized in 1952. Its employment of rural reconstruction as a method originated with the Ting Hsien experiment in China during the 1930s. The China experiment was eventually made known to Asian leaders in the early 1950s, who recognized that the program as developed in China might be useful in their own countries. Similarly, the people and organizations supporting the movement felt that the rural reconstruction philosophy, strategies, and approaches might be adapted to the development of farm communities in rural areas of other countries.

The first organized attempt to apply this method took place in the Philippines, where it was anchored to a fourfold program emphasizing livelihood, education, health and self-government. The new Philippine movement (PRRM) became a catalyst in the rural development of the country. It was a forerunner of the government post of Presidential Assistant on Community Development, which has since been abolished, having been incorporated into the new Department of Local Government and Community Development. PRRM was also instrumental in passage of the Barrio Council Law in 1955.

The success of the Philippine movement illustrated that the basic philosophy, approaches, and techniques evolved in China could be adapted to another developing country with a different cultural tradition. Supporters of the concept, encouraged by the results PRRM had achieved and wanting to help launch comparable social development movements in other countries, formed the International Institute for Rural Reconstruction (IIRR). Although incorporated in the United States, this new organization was based in the Philippines because of its close working relationship with PRRM. IIRR has

97

since aided in establishing rural reconstruction movements in Colombia, Guatemala, and Thailand and has provided training for personnel from those countries.

PRRM received substantial foreign funding, but it wanted to mobilize local resources to achieve a greater measure of self-determination. Efforts were made to raise local funds, primarily through grants and donations from the government, private organizations, and business corporations. Later on, the barrio sponsorship program was initiated, wherein a donor agreed to support PRRM operations in one barrio for a minimum of two or three years. As PRRM grew older, however, there were not a few critics who raised questions concerning the effectiveness of the movement's methods and approaches. These questions were not faced head-on by PRRM until after the election in 1971 of Eduardo Canlas* as the organization's new president.

This case study will report how Canlas sought the financial assistance of a local foundation, Philippine Business for Social Progress (PBSP), to cooperate in a new program that would redirect PRRM's own activities and refine its traditional methods and approaches. PBSP was destined to play a critical role in the future of PRRM. Organized in December 1970 by a number of Philippine business companies, PBSP was intended to provide financial and technical assistance for existing efforts in social development. PBSP has the financial resources to do so; it was funded by member-company corporations who pledged one percent of their income (before taxes) to the cause of social development. Sixty percent of this pledged income went to support the foundation's own activities and the remaining 40 percent was reserved for the contributing member-company to expend on its own social development projects.

PBSP, though new to this field of social endeavor, was interested in experimenting with a rural social development prototype. PRRM, on the other hand, was an experienced organization with a strong interest in enriching and updating its traditional methods and approaches. What PRRM lacked, however, was funding. The Laguna Rural Social Development Prototype, to be funded by PBSP and managed by PRRM, would serve as a marriage of convenience for achieving the goals of both organizations.

The Problem

The Philippine Rural Rural Reconstruction Movement (PRRM) had been organized, as noted previously, to promote the development of rural areas by responding to four major problems - poverty, ignorance, disease, and civic inertia. In consideration of these problems, it had conceived a fourfold program directed at improving livelihood, education, health and self-government.

By 1971, PRRM found itself facing two major problems within its own

---

* All names of persons involved in the Laguna Project have been disguised in this case study for reasons of personal privacy and confidentiality.

organization.   One was the lack of funds to sustain adequately its field
operations program.   The other was a serious question about the relevance
and effectiveness of the approaches it had been utilizing to meet the needs of
assisted communities.   Traditionally, its major financial support had come
from the International Institute for Rural Reconstruction. The PRRM board
of trustees, however, had decided to attain a more independent policy
direction and financial posture, and was desirous of phasing out further
financial assistance from the International Institute for its innovative
program explorations. The PRRM board saw an opportunity to avail itself of
grant aid from a private foundation, Philippine Business for Social Progress
(PBSP), which also was interested in innovative approaches to social
development. The PRRM board foresaw the possibility that the two groups,
motivated by similar objectives, might achieve great mutual benefit by
working together on a pilot project aimed at creating a rural social
development prototype adapted to the Philippine environment.

The Project

The rural social development project eventually undertaken in joint
venture by PBSP, the funding agency, and PRRM, the implementing
organization, was located in Laguna, not far to the southeast of Manila. The
project was intended to test a development scheme using a community
organization approach for achieving attitudes and social organization competency among residents of some 50 barrios, sufficient to assure effective
leadership in social and economic institutions that could meet existing
community needs. If the scheme were validated, it could be replicated in
other similar communities in the Philippines.

This case study of the Laguna Project demonstrates the processes utilized
in planning and implementing the program, and describes the interaction
between funding agency and implementing organization, as well as the
problems and different perceptions of the two organizations which emerged in
the course of the project. It further illustrates the obstacles and difficulties
involved in initiating program changes that are not fully understood by, nor
have the full support of, the project organization's rank and file.

Laguna Profile

Laguna Province is situated to the southeast of Manila on the island of
Luzon. It is bounded on the east and south by Quezon and on the west by
Batangas and Cavite Provinces. To the north lies a portion of Rizal Province
and a lake, Laguna de Bay. The terrain of Laguna Province consists mainly of
rolling plains that extend along the eastern, southern, and western shores of
Laguna de Bay.

As of 1970, the year before the Laguna Project was launched, the
province's population stood at 699,736. (1) With a land area of 1,760 square

kilometers, its density was about 39 persons per square kilometer, a ratio over three times greater than the national average. The extent of urbanization was quite high. Half of the population resided in areas classified as "urban," compared with only 32 percent for the nation as a whole.

Laguna had a proportionately high youthful population (14 years and younger), computed at 45 percent. The rate for those able to read and write was also high, that is, 86 percent of the population six years and older. Tagalog was the principal dialect, but 48 percent of the province also spoke English. Of those 25 years of age or older, 64 percent had finished elementary school, 14 percent high school, and 10 percent had earned a college degree, but 11 percent had attended no grade at all. Religion was predominantly Roman Catholic (88 percent).

Of the 1970 population ten years and older, only 48 percent were economically active or employable; of this number (484,192), 93 percent did have gainful employment. Laguna had widely diversified industries. For example, of all workers with some experience, 36 percent were engaged in farming, fishing, hunting or logging, with coconut plantations and rice farms predominating in the agricultural category. Manufacturing - that is, occupations involving craftsmen and production process workers - accounted for 21 percent, and rapid urbanization was expected to escalate this rate. Other categories included services (18 percent), commerce (12 percent), transportation and communication (6 percent), and construction (5 percent), plus a small miscellany of other occupations.

Laguna Province was administered by a governor who, together with a vice-governor and a three-man provincial board, was elected every four years. The province was divided into 29 municipalities and one city. These political units had elected mayors, vice-mayors, and councillors. Each city and municipality was further divided into barrio units headed by a barrio captain and a barrio council, all elected.

This was the political situation until martial law was declared in 1972. It has been gradually modified since then. A large part of Laguna Province has been incorporated into Metropolitan Manila, a new political division headed by a governor. The political offices of vice-governor and vice-mayor were abolished. The old provincial boards have been replaced by new legislative assemblies, the Provincial Assembly (Sanggunian Panlalawigan) and the Municipal Council (Sanggunian Bayan).

In sum, Laguna is a rapidly urbanizing province, and is traditionally, culturally, economically, and politically sensitive to the changes being effected in the metropolitan Manila area. It has the reputation of being progressive, receptive to change, and open to experimentation. Politically, before 1972, it more often sided with the opposition than with the majority party.

Before the start of operations in Laguna, PRRM conducted a study of 50 barrios in eight towns and the city as part of the planning activities for the proposed 50 barrio social development project. The results of that survey were interpreted as positive. Favorable attitudes of the respondents were reported in all areas of cooperation, economic development, education, health, and family planning.

PHASE 1: PLANNING, APPRAISAL, AND DESIGN

Concept and Identification of the Project

On March 11, 1971, Eduardo Canlas was promoted from executive vice president to president by the board of trustees of the Philippine Rural Reconstruction Movement (PRRM). As president, he immediately had to attend to two major problems. The first was identification of new funding sources to sustain the organization and its field operations. The second was reassessment and redefinition of priorities in its programs.

Although fund raising was a primary function of the PRRM board of trustees, the funds raised were not adequate to continue operations at the present level. Many corporate donors were not renewing their sponsorship of programs in the barrios for the following year, and the problem was compounded by the necessity to reassign personnel from the terminated barrio projects. Funds from the International Institute for Rural Reconstruction (IIRR), a traditional source of aid, were being phased out by the PRRM board's decision to achieve more independence in direction of policy and to minimize reliance on foreign funding.

There was also the problem of effectiveness and relevance of the organization's programs. Not a few who were knowledgeable about these operations had raised doubts and questions about the effectiveness of the program for rural reconstruction, for many of the assisted barrios had subsequently failed to sustain program activities on their own once the assigned rural reconstruction workers had been pulled out.

Shortly after assuming the presidency in March 1971, Canlas wrote to Dr. Richard Lee, president of the International Institute for Rural Reconstruction, for some modification of its continuing financial assistance. He asked that the yearly ₱200,000, (3) which had been earmarked by the Institute for new senior PRRM personnel, be used temporarily for operations. Dr. Lee agreed, in his reply of April 7, that of that amount only ₱100,000 would be allotted for new senior personnel, as originally conceived, and the other half could "be used for helping PRRM meet its financial emergencies." In the same letter, Lee expressed his disappointment that "very little new money has been raised" to sustain PRRM operations, but he was hopeful that the newly elected chairman of the PRRM Board of Trustees, former Senator Jose Gonzalez, "will want to exert his level best, together with other conscientious board members like (Andres) Montecastro, Jr., and (Jose) Suarez, to raise the needed funds for the PRRM."

Canlas, at the same time, addressed himself to the second problem. In early April, he and a small core of the PRRM staff, together with some outside sympathizers, conducted a weekend strategy session on possible new directions for the organization. A concrete outcome of this activity was a working paper, "PRRM: Its Nature and Functions," which would become the first conceptual framework from which the future Laguna project would evolve. The framework emphasized training, research, and direct service orientation in characterizing the organization's approach to rural reconstruction. Its project methods and techniques should lead to development of positive changes in the people's attitudes and behavior, as well as in the community's social and economic structures. These changes would then be reflected in subsequent projects and activities planned and implemented by the community itself. While projects might be used as vehicles for development, they should not become ends in themselves. This concept emphasized the "people-and-process" orientation in the social development approach. Finally, because of its limited resources, PRRM would program assistance for a limited period only, to a point at which the community would have attained self-sufficiency. After that, the project personnel would be withdrawn from the community.

One participant in the weekend startegy session was Clara Sison, a bureau director in the Department of Social Welfare, whom Canlas had invited to join the PRRM organization as training director. Sison, however, had an application pending with Philippine Business for Social Progress (PBSP), a foundation recently organized by local business companies to promote social development. Since PBSP was still in an initial operational phase, Sison felt that she could play a vital role within the PBSP organization by assisting other, similarly oriented groups to secure help in their development efforts.

The concept on which PBSP was founded was formulated initially by the Association for Social Action (ASA), of which Canlas was president. The idea had been merely to raise funds, thereby freeing social development organizations from this time-consuming function. However, as other groups were invited to participate and as more organizers became involved, the objectives and priorities of PBSP turned out differently than had been originally planned. Furthermore, that organization in time presented some disadvantages to PRRM, as many of the latter's corporate contributors and sponsors were failing to renew their contributions for the reason that they were now contributing to the foundation's activities.

Canlas, disturbed by this development, outlined the problem to one of his own trustees, Bernard Du, who had been elected as a member of the PBSP executive committee. Du, in turn, informed the PBSP management of Canlas's dilemma, and a meeting was held on April 14, attended by Du, Canlas, David de los Santos, and Marcelo Perez, the last two being PBSP executive director and associate director respectively.

The meeting was timely, as PBSP itself was working to create a rural development prototype using the social development approach, a theoretical concept employing methods and techniques proved effective in business management and adapted for application in social development programs. The meeting produced substantial results for PRRM, because PBSP was receptive to assisting it financially in exploring innovative approaches to rural development. Canlas thought the most important agreement reached was that "PRRM and PBSP would together work on the plan and specifications of the project in order to make it truly the best considering the objectives and resources both of PBSP and PRRM." (3) The project he had in mind would be managed by PRRM and funded by PBSP; at the same time it would serve as the rural social development prototype which the latter group was also interested in validating.

On June 17, 1971 Canlas and the PRRM board of trustees submitted the formal proposal to PBSP, requesting financial support for the project in question for at least three years, from the start of project planning to termination of the field operation. The stated purpose of the project was "to determine and to demonstrate the conditions requisite to making a social development program successfully operating in a rural community." The plan of technical assistance to the project community would involve three phases, depending on the level of development needs in the community.

Two days after submission of the proposal, the PBSP executive committee approved it in principle but requested that a budget for the planning phase be submitted for review. The staffs of both organizations worked on cost estimates and a project timetable. On July 15, they submitted the cost estimates for Phase I, the planning phase, together with a justification for Pampanga, a province north of Manila, as the site for the proposed project.

The choice of Pampanga was unanimous among the PRRM technical and field operations staff. Pampanga Province was a land reform area, and the proposed project located there could conceivably be integrated with ongoing government efforts, thus increasing the chances of success for the land reform program. PRRM had assessed its existing operations in Pampanga as among its more successful, due to the people's receptivity and cooperation. However, certain sections of the province were heavily infiltrated by local communists, the Huks. Armed encounters between the Huks and government troops were not uncommon. The peace-and-order situation, though highly publicized, had not affected the activities of PRRM rural reconstruction workers in the field. Although the proposed project would include 50 barrios in three towns, the diffused effect might well extend to the whole province.

Although Pampanga was proposed because of its land reform angle, the PBSP executive committee decided otherwise. On July 16, it disapproved selection of any land reform area. It emphasized instead the desirable "representativeness" of a project site that would ensure application of project results, based on a 50 barrio prototype, to other similar groupings in the Philippines.

PRRM then shifted the project site to Laguna Province, where the major agricultural crop, coconut, offered greater potential for long-term efforts at industrialization. Furthermore, Laguna was believed to have a higher "success potential." It was closer to Manila, and was therefore advanced in infrastructure development, and it had a better peace-and-order situation. In terms of its "representativeness," Laguna was a Tagalog-speaking province, and within its area of influence would be other Tagalog-speaking provinces in central and southern Luzon with an estimated total population of 12 million people.

The revised proposal, with Laguna as the project site, was submitted for assessment by the PBSP staff and forwarded to the PBSP executive committee for decision on August 20. The proposal asked for a grant of ₱143,522 to finance study research and preoperating costs of the project planning phase for seven months. The general objective of the planning phase was identified as follows:

To construct a theoretical scheme of assistance to rural communities based on the principle of self-determination, for purposes of testing and validation in the field over a period of three years, duly accompanied by research documentation and evaluation, with the end in view of developing a rural social development prototype model according to the social development approach.

The proposal likewise identified the specific objectives to be accomplished for the same period.

Canlas was hopeful that the program would be approved. In his letter to Dr. Lee on July 5, he wrote "... it should be somewhat heartening to note that we do have friends at the very highest and most sensitive levels of PBSP." Three of his own trustees, Bernard Du, Jaime Villa, and Jose Suarez, were either executive committee members or trustees of the PBSP organization. PBSP's new executive director, Roberto Isidro, had served as alternate member of the PRRM board for many years. PBSP President Antonio Ruiz had been a close associate of Canlas in college. "And most important," Canlas continued, "the next four and most important people on the management and project evaluation staff are all old friends: Marcel (Marcelo) Perez, Claring (Clara) Sison, Nina (Cristina) Manuel, and Cely (Celia) Leopoldo.   This is why I am confident that the utmost that can be granted will be granted to us."

Canlas's confidence was sustained. On August 20, PBSP approved a grant of ₱143,500 for the program planning phase. This was only ₱22 less than had been requested by PRRM.

The Planning Phase

Approval of funding for the planning phase was retroactive to June 1 and would end December 31, 1971. As with its other assisted programs, Philippine Business for Social Progress (PBSP) entered into a memorandum of agreement with the Philippine Rural Reconstruction Movement (PRRM) to formalize the terms and conditions binding the two organizations in the proposed project. During this period, PRRM as the implementing group was to develop and finalize the project's conceptual and evaluative framework. Specifically, the theoretical scheme of assistance had to be completed, the developmental approaches concretized, and the concept of barrio self-help defined. Also to be worked out were the implementation of preoperating activities, which included identification of project site, conduct of community studies, feasibility studies for income-generating projects, recruitment and training of project workers, and pretesting of points of entry in the barrios by the field operations staff.

The findings of these activities would have to be consolidated and finalized into the "Integrated Development Plan," to be submitted to the funding agency for approval by the end of the planning phase.   The development plan in turn would serve as the framework and guide for project implementation.

At the time of project approval, the conceptual framework had already been concretized by PRRM senior staff members, and subsequent efforts were concentrated on preparation and implementation of preoperational activities and the design of an evaluation scheme.

Theoretical Scheme of Assistance

The principle of self-determination on the part of assisted communities was identified as basic in the development plan. In line with this principle, plans of action were viewed as evolving from the people's own identification and understanding of their needs and their awareness of the resources available for meeting these felt needs.

Because it was felt that community organization was the approach that best appreciates the principle of self-determination, the planners decided that the rural worker should basically be a community organizer playing the roles of guide, enabler, catalyzer, expert, analyst, organizer, consultant, liaison, mediator, and advocate, as demanded by varying circumstances, in order to nurture developmental attitudes among the barrio residents. This implied that requests for assistance would be initiated by each barrio, and that PRRM and its field workers would be welcomed in the barrios.

It is in this light that PRRM's fourfold program and its community organization approach may be viewed as mutually enriching each other. As now constituted, PRRM has technical assistants and extension workers trained in the fourfold programs whose task goals are directed at the basic problems common to developing peoples everywhere, namely:

1. Livelihood - to increase farmers' production and effective income, directed at poverty.

2. Education - to enhance literacy and culture, directed at ignorance.

3. Health - to improve family health and environmental sanitation, directed at disease.

4. Self-government - to strengthen the political and dynamic structures of each barrio, directed at civic inertia.

These task goals should promote the process goals of development, and thus serve chiefly as a structural checklist against which to determine whether or not a community-wide program is well balanced.

The theoretical scheme of assistance contained in the PRRM approach to community development is illustrated in Fig. 4.1.

Because PRRM was concerned with total human and community development, it must deal with all three of these aspects. They would have to be treated almost simultaneously, but the modification of skills and attitudes would be given primary attention. Structures and projects must depend upon the people's own perception of their needs and their recognition of the resources at hand to accommodate these needs.

Stages in the Plan of Assistance

PRRM's general plan of assistance to the barrios involved three stages. Each stage reflected the emphasis required by the state of development of the particular community. But this did not negate the interrrelationship, at each stage, of attitudes and skills, social and economic structures, and projects as outlined in Fig. 4.1.

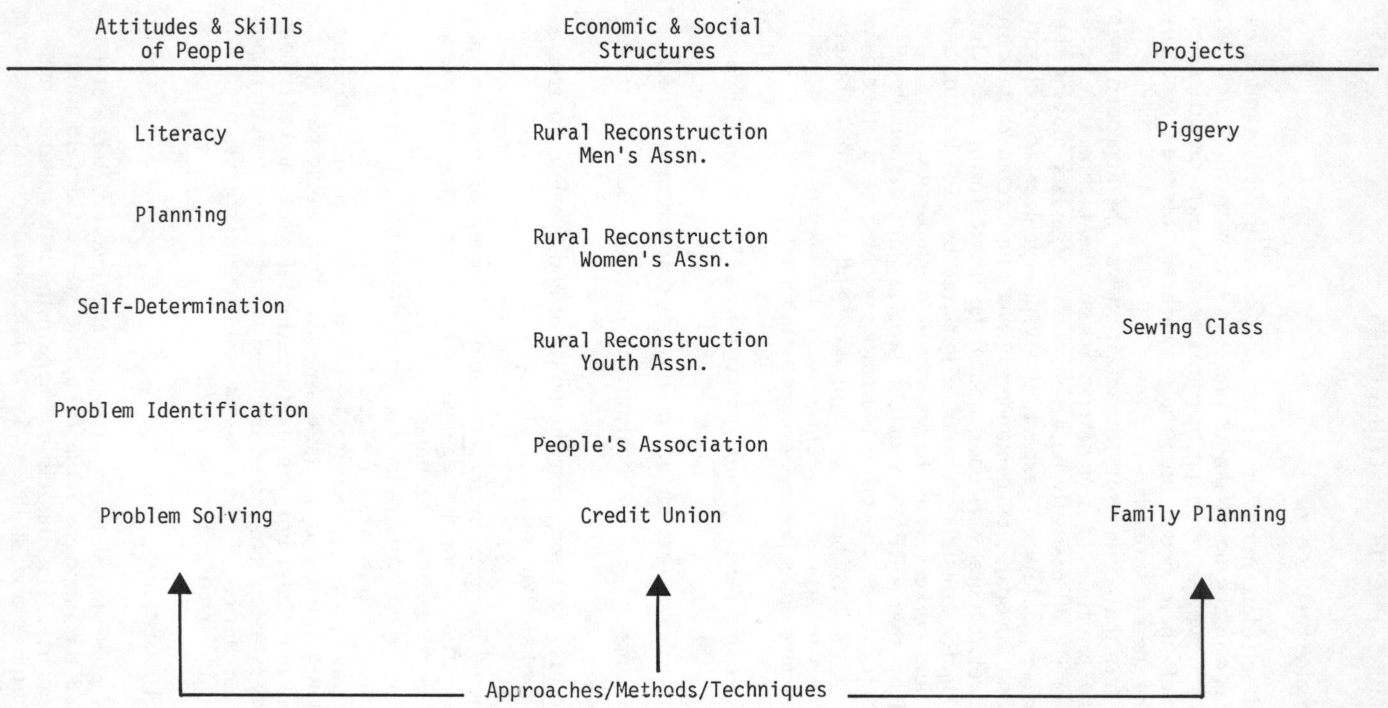

FIGURE 4.1 Aspects of Development

Attitudes & Skills of People

Literacy

Planning

Self-Determination

Problem Identification

Problem Solving

Economic & Social Structures

Rural Reconstruction Men's Assn.

Rural Reconstruction Women's Assn.

Rural Reconstruction Youth Assn.

People's Association

Credit Union

Approaches/Methods/Techniques

Projects

Piggery

Sewing Class

Family Planning

The first stage was concerned with encouragement of new and positive attitudes in the individual man and woman living in the barrio, whereby they would be receptive to changes in their own private lives as well as to changes in their lives as members of the community. This stage, essentially psychological or behavioral, would provide the foundation for all subsequent human development efforts.

In the second stage, certain economic and social structures would be formed within the community, institutionalizing the progress achieved during the first stage. The new social structures would function, for example, as community associations and barrio councils, through which members of the community would be able to interact in organized sectors. The economic structures envisioned were credit unions, consumer cooperatives, buying clubs, farmers' associations, and rural industry cooperatives.

The third stage would be directed toward creating social and economic structures at the interbarrio level, either municipal, provincial, or regional, where economy and efficiency of scale could be achieved, integrating activities that might otherwise remain restricted within the boundaries of the barrio. Examples of these structures include provincial federations of buying clubs; cooperatives or farmers' associations; a federation of barrio councils; a provincial cooperative bank; and others.

Range of PRRM Objectives

Direct assistance to the barrios by PRRM had to be confined to a limited period of time because its resources were limited. The PRRM development workers, therefore, would be phased out at some propitious point in the development sequence, and their responsibilities and functions assumed and continued by the barrio leaders who had been trained to take over.

Figure 4.2 is an attempt to portray the range of PRRM objectives in barrio development.

Each horizontal line represents the unending course of barrio development. Point A is that point of barrio development toward which PRRM, through the field activities of its Rural Reconstruction Workers (RRWs), seeks to assist the barrio and its people. At this point, it is expected that the field workers (RRWs) have inculcated in the barrio folk such skills and attitudes as are relevant to their development, and have introduced such structures and projects at the barrio level as will enable the community to propel itself toward ever fuller development. When Point A is reached, the barrio can be considered to have attained the start of self-propulsion. At that time the PRRM field workers should be withdrawn.

The vertical columns, touching at least two barrios, represent a further stage of development, that is, cooperation between or among barrios in larger developmental structures and projects operating in various fields. It is assumed that these structures and projects are being undertaken by the barrios on their own initiative, the latter having imbibed proper attitudes and developed sufficient skills as indicated by their progress to Point A. These more inclusive structures, because of their size and complexity, require more sophisticated expertise for their successful establishment. Therefore, PRRM assistance at this stage would be provided through more advanced training by

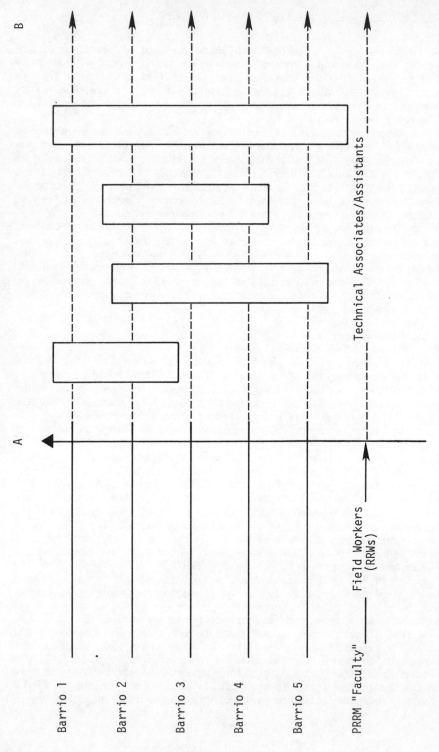

FIGURE 4.2   Range of Development Objectives

its faculty of technical associates and assistants, who would not only have more experience as community workers but would also then be equipped with additional technical skills to assist with interbarrio development.

Structure, Organization, and Personnel

The organizational structure adopted for the Laguna Project operations emphasized the matrix relationship among key management personnel (see Fig. 4.3). This was judged to be the system which best recognized the principles of community organization. At the senior staff level, the matrix involved the PRRM president and the heads of training, research, and field operations. At the project level, it linked the program coordinator, the area coordinator, the municipal (or team) coordinators, and the community organizer (or rural reconstruction worker). The position linking the two groups was occupied by Aurora Paz who functioned as both research director and program coordinator.

As program coordinator, Paz was responsible for seeing that the operations staff implemented the scheme of assistance according to specifications. As research director, she was to guide the Laguna Research Secretariat in implementing the research and evaluation design of the rural social development prototype.

The project operations staff, on the other hand, was headed by the area coordinator, who was directly responsible for the field implementation of the scheme of assistance. He would prepare the field plans jointly with each municipal coordinator, in consultation with the program coordinator. The area coordinator would need to be skilled in community organization supervision and advance program planning.

Directly under the area coordinator were three municipal coordinators, each of whom was directly responsible for the formulation and implementation of the field plan in his own section. Under each municipal coordinator were the rural reconstruction workers (RRWs) who, as community organizers, were responsible for initial formulation of the barrio development plans and their implementation, following approval by the municipal coordinator.

The operations staff was supported by technical assistants who would provide consultancy services in such areas as agriculture, cooperatives, health, and literacy education. Evaluation of PRRM project personnel would be made twice a year.

PHASE 2: SELECTION, APPROVAL, AND ACTIVATION

Identification of the Project Barrios

After the PBSP executive committee had decided in favor of Laguna as the project site, in its August 1971 approval of the planning phase proposal, the PRRM field staff prepared ocular survey guidelines for preselection of the required 50 barrio communities. Each barrio would have to have a population of at least 500, be strategically located and accessible by public

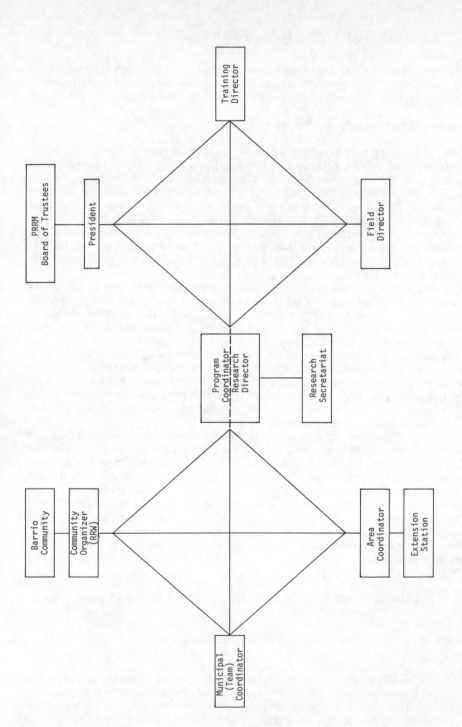

FIGURE 4.3 Organizational Structure for the Laguna Project

transportation, and have a favorable law-and-order situation. The majority of its population must be permanent residents. Its elected officials must welcome PRRM assistance, and the scope of the PRRM field program in education, health, self-government, and livelihood must be feasible in the barrio. Finally, no other agency with similar development services was to be extensively involved in the barrio.

A barrio, once tentatively identified, was not finally selected until a PRRM team had conducted a community dialogue with at least 15 residents, including elected officials of the barrio. This community dialogue focused upon the problem areas, the felt needs of residents, and existing organizational activities in the barrio. The nature and functions of the PRRM organization were discussed, as were also the possible kinds of assistance that PRRM could extend to the barrio. Only after the barrio had accepted the PRRM offer of assistance was it included in the 50 barrio project.

Pretesting the Points of Entry

A rural reconstruction worker (RRW) was then assigned to the barrio, and his first task was to conduct a preliminary community survey. This activity served two functions. First, it introduced the worker to each of the families in the barrio. Second, it informed the worker about the expressed needs and problems of the community and acquainted him with opportunities around which the barrio might be reorganized. When the RRW had integrated himself in the community, he conducted a motivational campaign by organizing the people to respond to a single identified problem. This activity was referred to as "pretesting the point of entry" into the barrio by the field worker. The RRW, however, was cautioned by his supervisor that the activity thus selected must be a need truly felt by the community, and not identified from the worker's point of view and imposed upon the people.

All these steps had to be accomplished during the planning phase so that findings from the preoperation activities could be incorporated into the final development scheme.

Recruitment and Training of Project Staff

Since the planning phase involved field activities, rural reconstruction workers had to be recruited and trained. One major decision made by PRRM was to not recruit new workers, but to select the "best workers from the Nueva Ecija and other area operations" and assign them to the Laguna Project. This was a decision necessitated by practical considerations. President Canlas had to find new assignments for field workers whose barrio programs had not been renewed because of failure of sponsors to continue funding. Hiring new, additional personnel for Laguna would also aggravate the financial status of the PRRM organization. Furthermore, since the personnel to be selected were regarded as the best of the regular PRRM field staff, the assumption was that they would perform better than newly recruited workers.

The PBSP leadership, however, had initial reservations about this reliance on old PRRM employees in a project whose conceptual scheme and operating procedures were different from those employed in previous PRRM projects. The main question centered on whether the old PRRM workers could make the necessary modifications in their approach to barrio development. Canlas reassured PBSP management that only the best of the PRRM workers would be selected and that they would receive training in the new approach. He defended his position convincingly, and the PBSP management finally went along with the proposed alternative.

A two-week in-service training program for PRRM staffers reassigned to the Laguna Project was started on September 27, 1971. The first week was devoted to project orientation and briefing. This covered an overview of the program planning phase, a socioeconomic profile of Laguna, a renewed emphasis on the PRRM fourfold program, methods and techniques for conducting motivational activities, procedures for participant observation and household surveys, and matters of administration and new policy governing the Laguna operations.

The second week was primarily occupied with participation in "creativity sessions," whose objective was "to develop the creativity of the participants so as to enhance their skills as community organizers." These sessions were conducted by the Philippine Educational Theater Association. Sixty hours in all were devoted to sessions on such topics as creative theater, body movement, creative improvisation, vocal exercises, and so on.

Fielding of Personnel

The assignment of PRRM workers to the field in early November 1971 was poorly timed. This month was dominated by the national elections. The workers' arrival in the Laguna barrios and the conduct of initial activities were misunderstood by many of the local residents. Questions were raised about whether the RRWs were employed by the government, whether they were representing a particular candidate, or whether this was just a pre-election gimmick to be discontinued afterward.

Feedback of this situation was immediately relayed by PRRM to the PBSP leadership when certain modifications in the planning phase schedule were found to be necessary. A review meeting attended by executives from both organizations was held on November 15, and a modified sequence of activities for the planning process in each barrio was drawn up and mutually agreed upon.

After the barrio surveys had been completed, it was planned that community dialogues would again be conducted, based on the findings of those surveys. With the results of the community dialogues in hand, planning activities for individual barrios could be initiated. Because of the elections, however, the community dialogues and the motivational campaigns would not be started until the elections were over. The RRWs would then undertake their motivational campaigns and pretest their points of entry without waiting for completion of the barrio development plans. It was agreed, nevertheless, that these plans would surely be completed by February 29, 1972, and the various responsibilities for preparation and consolidation of the plans were delineated.

PBSP and PRRM also agreed that the RRWs should be given more intensive training in the community organization approach, owing to PBSP staff observations that the initial training received in September and October had not been adequate. The additional training was scheduled for January 16 to February 26, 1972.

In the same meeting, the initial budget of ₱143,500 for the planning phase, approved in August 1971, was reduced to ₱134,201.10, for the earlier budget was observed to have been higher than required.

Extension of the Planning Phase Schedule

In January 1972, the PBSP management reported to the PBSP executive committee that all activities scheduled for the PRRM planning phase in the Laguna Project had been completed, except for those which had been postponed to avoid the misconceptions provoked during an election year. Because of that delay, the PBSP executive committee approved extension of the program planning phase to February 29, 1972. The cost of the two months' extension would be absorbed by the revised budget.

During the remaining two months, the preoperation field activities, the motivational campaigns, and the pretesting of points of entry would be continued. The individual barrio development plans were to be submitted by February 29, together with the research and evaluation design of the program.

The innovative community organization (CO) approach had been mutually agreed to by the two organizations as fundamental to the PRRM development plan. The initial field performance of the RRWs had not been favorable. They had the tendency to follow traditional PRRM methods and approaches, a characteristic observed by the PRRM staff itself. The additional month-long CO orientation training was held in Nieves, Nueva Ecija, in January and February, as scheduled. Seven sessions were conducted on CO concepts and principles, techniques, processes, recording, program planning and strategies, worker roles, conflict management, and council organization.

Although these sessions provided the Laguna Project staff with a basic orientation in community organization, the training was still considered by PBSP leadership as not being intensive enough, considering that it ordinarily took at least four months of training in CO theories, concepts, and supervised field work before a trainee could acquire the basic CO knowledge and skills. To remedy this situation, PRRM sent the Laguna Project's area coordinator and three municipal coordinators to the Kaunlaran Multi-Purpose Training Center for the approved four-month course. Since these coordinators were expected to serve as line supervisors, PBSP insisted that they should complete the basic CO training course so that they would be adequately equipped to supervise the work of RRWs in the field.

PHASE 3: OPERATION, CONTROL, AND HANDOVER

Implementation: Year I

On April 14, 1972, the staff of PBSP, on the basis of program planning results submitted by PRRM, recommended approval to the PBSP executive committee for a grant of ₽462,110.30 for Laguna Project Year I operations budget, retroactive to March till December 1972. The PBSP executive committee responded by acting favorably on the recommendation. It also approved, in principle, the funding of feasible income-generating activities in Laguna as might be identified in the future.

When project operations formally started in Laguna Province in March 1972, the project's line supervisors were still in residence at the four-month community organization (CO) training course at Kaunlaran Multi-Purpose Training Center. Of the four who attended, one failed the course and was reassigned. The area coordinator, Robert Reyes, was unable to complete the course due to the pressure of field operations responsibilities.

Training and Assessment at Kaunlaran

By July 1, 1972 about half of the original PRRM staff of 24 field workers assigned to activities at the barrio level had either resigned or requested transfers to other PRRM projects. These were the rural reconstruction workers (RRWs), "who were not able to adjust and function within the modified scheme of assistance which had been evolved in the project." The resignations and the requests for transfer confirmed the earlier reservations by PBSP concerning the capability of the old PRRM workers to adapt and integrate with the new scheme of development assistance. Their actions also attested to the inadequacy of the preoperations training they had earlier received.

To attend to these limitations, PBSP recommended that the remaining RRWs and the newly recruited workers be trained at the Kaunlaran Center before they were sent into the field. PRRM accepted the recommendation, and in August and September, 25 field operations personnel and four researchers from the Laguna Project attended the CO training program. Of the 25 RRWs and new recruits for training, Kaunlaran failed ten. Of these, one resigned but the other nine were retained or, in the case of the recruits, were newly hired by PRRM, in spite of their poor training performance as evaluated by the training center staff.

The Kaunlaran training requirement became a source of major conflict between PRRM and PBSP and the Kaunlaran Center. PRRM management could not fully accept the negative evaluations submitted by Kaunlaran staffers for some of the PRRM workers. Several reasons were given for this objection. The training was presented in English and, as PRRM workers had observed, was highly conceptual and academic. Most of the readings and case studies used were Western-oriented and were not compatible with the workers' prior field experiences. PRRM workers who lacked a good command of written and oral English failed to impress the Kaunlaran staff as promising workers. The PRRM management disputed this observation, as many of these "questionable" workers were known to have established rapport easily with assisted communities and to have mobilized the latter in support of PRRM field projects.

However, PBSP sustained the Kaunlaran recommendations, for the center had been established primarily to serve PBSP as the training operation for its own CO workers. In spite of the negative assessments made at Kaunlaran and the reservations about PRRM workers held by PBSP, the PRRM management stood firm and retained its workers who had been evaluated negatively.

Internal Problems of PRRM Management

The Kaunlaran problem was further aggravated by the resignation of the project's area coordinator Robert Reyes, effective September 30, 1972. In an interview with a PBSP project officer, Reyes expressed difficulties he had encountered as area head, charging interference from the PRRM program coordinator in regard to operations. Furthermore, he claimed, the matrix emphasis in the relationships of senior staffers was creating too much confusion in the field. He saw no alternative but to resign, and to accept an invitation from the International Institute for Rural Reconstruction to join its staff.

The results of that interview were reported to the PBSP management, which had been viewing all of these resignations with serious concern. Since Laguna was a prototype project involving substantial funding, PBSP decided to assign another project officer from its own staff, Joaquin Castro, to monitor the Laguna operation. Of all the PBSP officers at this time, Castro seemed the most qualified. He had both practical experience and formal training in management, and he was quick in grasping the CO concepts and philosophy.

While PBSP interpreted the Reyes resignation as reflecting serious problems in PRRM management, it did not foresee, nor was it informed about, implications of the resignation for PRRM as an organization. There were several factors operative in this regard. Reyes had previously been a PRRM technical assistant for cooperatives and was recommended by PRRM field director Antonio Morales for promotion to head the Laguna area operations. In this capacity, Reyes was given relative leeway to operate independently, although he was required to report regularly to the field director. His field reports at first were assessed as adequate.

Later, PRRM program coordinator Aurora Paz recalled that on several occasions during the early months of operations Morales had begun to warn the senior staff about Reyes's performance in his new post, but this had been dismissed as Morales's way of downgrading Reyes. The picture changed, however, when PBSP expressed serious concern about the fast turnover of Laguna field personnel. PRRM management was forced to scrutinize the Laguna operations more carefully, and in the process Reyes's weak project leadership was exposed. The senior staff was thereby compelled to monitor constantly the performances of both the project operations staff and the area coordinator. Aurora Paz, as program coordinator, was responsible for ensuring that the conceptual scheme of assistance was being implemented. Reyes only viewed this as interference which caused undue confusion in the field.

PRRM President Canlas, however, saw the area coordinator's resignation in another context. He expressed his own position on the matter, in rather strong terms, in a letter of October 24, 1972, to Dr. Lee, president of the International Institute for Rural Reconstruction (IIRR):

> . . . it is distasteful to me to even bring up again, or probe into the matter of IIRR's having negotiated with our personnel for positions in IIRR. The case of Robert Reyes brought to light what up till then remained concealed, though suspected . . . . In the final analysis, no matter the reasonings in-between, harm was done to PRRM by the defections of some of our personnel to, and the reception of some of our personnel by, IIRR. Considering all the handicaps and problems that we were already facing, this certainly came from an unexpected sector and thus represents the most unkindest cut of all.

If Canlas reacted strongly to the Reyes resignation, it was with good reason. The Laguna Project was encountering opposition from within PRRM, specifically from personnel working in its operations at Nueva Ecija, with tacit support from certain quarters within IIRR, which had long been associated financially with those PRRM activities. The Nueva Ecija personnel resented Laguna, because they viewed it as the pet project of Canlas and the PRRM senior staff. Laguna was being funded adequately, by the special grant from PBSP, whereas Nueva Ecija was not. Salary rates at Laguna were higher. Workers from Nueva Ecija had been recruited for Laguna because they were the "best among the PRRM workers." The personnel at Nueva Ecija also felt that Canlas, in spending much more time on the Laguna Project, was neglecting Nueva Ecija, especially in securing necessary funds to stabilize the latter operations.

Laguna, as viewed by Canlas and the senior staff, represented a new PRRM approach to social development. If proven effective there, it would be adopted in all other PRRM operations. This possibility was disputed by the PRRM old-timers, who could see no difference between the two approaches. Finally, resentment by the older workers was directed against Canlas and the senior staff; it was felt that the president had no direct experience in service at the grassroots level and that all of the senior staff were newcomers in the PRRM organization.

To compound the problem, Canlas was having policy differences with IIRR, formerly closely associated with PRRM. Although now a separate organization, IIRR and its president Dr. Lee still enjoyed the primary loyalty of many workers at Nueva Ecija. Canlas knew that the workers' opposition to himself was mounting, and saw in the Reyes resignation an act of sabotage.

Pending identification of a new area coordinator for Laguna, the PRRM management temporarily assigned its administrative director to that post for the month of October. But PBSP leadership pressed for immediate appointment of a new area head. As it would take some time before a qualified replacement could be identified and hired, Maj. Mario Ramos (ret.),

PRRM operations head at that time, volunteered to direct the Laguna Project. Ramos had joined PRRM in November 1971 as a member of the senior staff. He had retired in 1962 as an army major and had since received his MBA degree from the University of the Philippines. Before joining PRRM, he had been extensively involved in management of various business companies. It had originally been Ramos's suggestion that the matrix relationship among key management personnel be adopted for use in the Laguna Project.

On November 15, 1972, however, the matrix organizational structure at Laguna was abandoned. A new line organizational structure was set up which made the area coordinator primarily responsible for project operations and required him to report directly to the PRRM president. The area coordinator was renamed "social laboratory manager" to emphasize the "laboratory" approach or the "experimental" character of the project. Duties and functions of all operations management and staff personnel were also redefined and clarified, as shown in Fig. 4.4.

Castro as PBSP monitor and Ramos as PRRM operations manager at Laguna made a good working combination. Castro was both perceptive and incisive, and as a management specialist he did not feel comfortable with the situation at Laguna. He increased the time he spent on field monitoring of the project, and he discussed his insights and recommendations with Ramos. The latter, possibly because of his own background in management con- sultancy felt that PBSP was a client with every right to expect satisfaction. He considered it his obligation to accept the PBSP recommendations because the foundation was funding the project.

Ramos had his work priorities well defined. First, the barrio research surveys had to be tabulated and analyzed. Castro had discovered that these surveys, although completed in the field during the planning phase, had not been entirely processed; if they were already tabulated, the results had not yet been analyzed. Second, the individual barrio development plans, originally scheduled for completion by February 29, 1972, still had to be finished and made operative. Castro recommended to Ramos that the processing of the barrio development plans be started immediately. They should be completed before March 1, 1973, in time for the start of Year II operations.

Castro recalled sometime later, in an internal memo dated October 14, 1973, that "it is quite unthinkable that operations of the magnitude of Laguna which require funding of no less than P 1 million as planned by PRRM started with no operating plans to guide operations in Laguna but such was the case."

PRRM Retrenchment and the December Manifesto

PRRM had previously agreed with PBSP to conduct a periodic evaluation of its RRWs. The December 1972 evaluation showed that of the 27 RRWs whose performance was reviewed, only 13 were assessed favorably. The remaining 14 RRWs received judgments ranging from "slightly below standard" to "very poor." Of this latter group, the four who had been evaluated as "very poor" were terminated. Of the other ten, one resigned voluntarily, and the rest were placed on two-month probation.

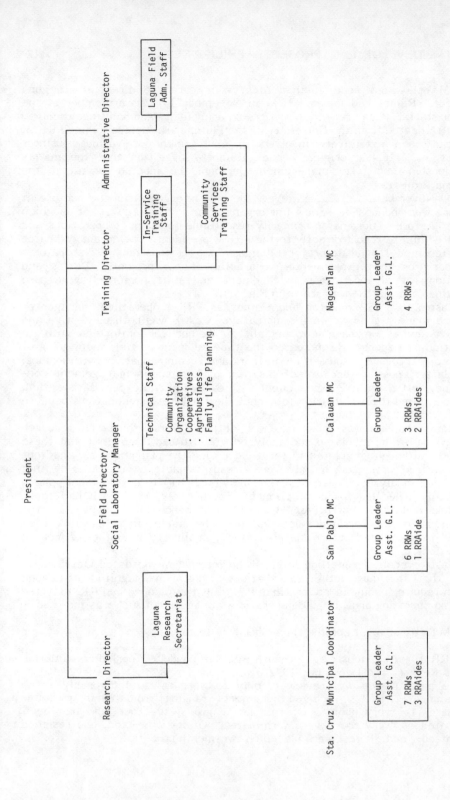

FIGURE 4.4   New Project Management Structure, November 1972

The PRRM decision to place the nine workers on probation was disputed by PBSP, the latter preferring that the workers be terminated because they had failed to meet PRRM standards of performance. The senior staff of PRRM pleaded their case. A compromise was suggested by Ramos, according to which he would provide direct supervision over these workers. They were to be informed of their two-month probationary status, after which their performance would again be evaluated. Ramos would then recommend whether their services should be terminated or continued. PBSP reluctantly agreed to this compromise.

PRRM had good reason to resist termination of those workers whose performance might be improved if given the necessary support. Since March 1971, funding had continued to be a critical problem. Approval of the Laguna Project by PBSP had momentarily eased the general situation, for it allowed the better PRRM workers to be placed in a stabilized project for the following three years. However, the other funds coming in were not sufficient to sustain PRRM operations indefinitely. The declaration of martial law in September 1972 and the initial uncertainty which followed became a critical factor.

The PRRM board of trustees decided to adopt a policy of retrenchment, as further contributions from business companies would be slowed until after the new government had stabilized. The board instructed Canlas to formulate a retrenchment program wherein operations would be reduced to a scale that PRRM income could reasonably support. The new policy was implemented by an official memorandum issued on December 4, 1972. Fifty percent of PRRM personnel at Nueva Ecija were to be terminated, which would seriously curtail operations in that area. It is important to note here that the retrenchment policy did not affect the Laguna operation, for the latter was secure with separate PBSP funding.

The management memo created an organizational crisis. It provoked immediately a manifesto asking for the resignation of President Canlas, signed by 104 PRRM workers and addressed to the PRRM Board of Trustees. The manifesto was signed not only by the workers who had been terminated but by those who remained on the payroll at Nueva Ecija. It also included the names of 14 workers from the Laguna Project.

Canlas was not surprised that the retrenchment memo was opposed by the staff at Nueva Ecija, but neither he nor the senior staff had expected the opposition to result in a manifesto demanding the president's resignation. To complicate matters further, the signatories had included workers from Laguna, who would not be affected by the retrenchment move. The December manifesto certainly proved one point, and that was the consolidation of worker opposition against Canlas, the senior staff, and the innovative project in Laguna. Groups within PRRM who had either policy or personal differences with Canlas and his senior staff had united on one issue - his resignation.

The PRRM board of trustees sustained and supported Canlas. It did, however, create a special committee headed by former PRRM president Jose Gonzalez to look into the Nueva Ecija situation.

PRRM Review of Project Operations, March-December, 1972

On January 9, 1973, the PBSP management secured approval from the PBSP executive committee for financial assistance in the amount of ₽85,020 for the Laguna Project for January and February 1973, to cover the last two months of Year I implementation.

Because PRRM had undergone decisive changes in its policies, organizational structure, personnel staffing, and administrative procedures from March 1 to December 31, the PBSP staff in an assessment of PRRM's present capability came to three major conclusions:

1. First, PRRM had demonstrated flexibility, in its policy-making processes as well as in its supportive operational organization, to meet the unique work conditions required for the PBSP Laguna prototype. The shift from purely project-oriented activities to a scheme of assistance integrating the PRRM fourfold program with the community organization method had entailed a painful adjustment on the part of the PRRM organization, resulting in high personnel turnovers and the institution of new management procedures.

2. Second, PRRM had followed up on the necessary changes and showed promise of stabilizing as well as a willingness to keep an open mind about change if required to do so.

3. Finally, the PRRM management still enjoyed the full support of its board of trustees and executive committee.

For the last ten months of 1972, PRRM activities in the barrios had been centered on leadership training sessions, cooperatives seminars, and adult education classes. Skills-training classes were conducted in tailoring, dressmaking and hair science. Classes for farmers were given in rice production, green revolution, animal production, mushroom culture, and vinegar making. Health projects were initiated, covering such subjects as construction of toilet bowls, feeding programs, and family planning. PRRM workers also assisted the communities in their beautification programs. Social organizations, such as women's associations, youth clubs, and adult organizations, were reported to be operative in most of the project barrios.

On the other hand, the communities' economic needs were not being attended to effectively. No economic feasibility studies had been completed; consequently no economic projects were initiated. Some new economic structures, however, were reported to have been organized, specifically, credit unions in 12 barrios and farmers' associations in six.

Survey Report by the Asian Social Institute

The positive efforts of social laboratory manager Ramos toward improving the Laguna management operations would shortly be overshadowed by a baseline study report submitted by the Asian Social Institute (ASI) in January 1973. (4) The survey was based on data collected earlier in the year, from May to June 1972. But it did reveal, from an outside organization's viewpoint, the reactions of the target barrio communities to the PRRM project. ASI did qualify its observations by noting that, at the time when data were gathered, the RRWs had been in the barrios for, at most, only five months. This period of activity, it was acknowledged, was perhaps not sufficiently long to expect stabilization of PRRM operations.

On the positive side, three barrios reported that their expectations of PRRM were being met, due primarily to the active operation of home industries in the area. Barrio residents who were engaged in mushroom culture, initiated by PRRM workers, appreciated the projects because their incomes had been augmented thereby. Many barrio communities had adapted to the toilet bowls which the workers had taught them to make.

But the ASI study reported at great length about other, negative reactions of the barrios on how the project was being implemented:

An overwhelming majority of the barrios are disappointed with their experiences of the organization's operations. While at the start, people had high hopes for the aid and guidance they may receive, now they are simply frustrated and barely interested in future projects. Some barrios in fact asked PRRM to review its programs before proceeding with community development....

In places where PRRM is just beginning, the usual high hopes are present but as the pattern suggests, these hopes are bound to vanish and turn into indifference. It is therefore quite clear that something should be done. As it appears, PRRM is losing credibility with the communities. In the first place, why is it that there is still a considerable number of barrios where people expect capital aids from the organization despite the fact that resident workers have been staying in the barrios for 5 to 6 months already? ...

Consciously or unconsciously, people are led to expect the wrong kind of aid. This fact partly explains why most people rely on PRRM for capital, for water service, for electricity supply or for free livestock if the mission of PRRM is made clear, that is, self-help. ...

Along similar lines, the needs people feel most do not seem to be the standard starting point in the operations. The expectations people expressed in a chain of community dialogues in 1971 and the projects PRRM has completed in part or is currently espousing appear not to coincide. It is known for a fact that for a program of development to succeed, it must directly or indirectly satisfy the needs the client community feels.

Another point of interest is the fact that the PRRM projects are left uncompleted. People in several barrios expressly attest to this fact. PRRM needs the people's confidence in order to successfully assist in the development of communities. This calls for a well documented and prepared plan that can minimize the frustrating effects of a project's failure on the people.

A considerable number of barrios feel insulted by the way PRRM has withdrawn its RRW; no notice, no reasons stated, no replacement yet.

PRRM did not dispute these findings, but it did see the necessity to include a prologue in the research report explaining the findings within their historical context. In this prologue, the management admitted that in spite of the training given to effect a conceptual integration of the community organization approach with PRRM's traditional fourfold program, the initial field work undertaken by the workers "leaned heavily towards 'selling' PRRM's fourfold program rather than developing a program of assistance tailored to a community's felt needs as is basic in the community organization approach." These initial contacts heightened the communities' expectations from PRRM-assisted projects, and the offer of the programs of assistance was interpreted as promises which the barrio community expected its RRW to fulfill. However, after the workers had been required to attend the additional one month of training in the CO approach in January and February 1972, "the more discerning RRWs continued their 'turnabout' from the admittedly deficient initial interpretation of the program of assistance."

But most of the workers, because of limited CO supervision, went to the other extreme. They "veered from aggressive project-orientedness to possibly the other extreme of not positively pursuing any programs, probably thinking that the 'process' on which they would be rated would happen by itself." In a further quotation from the prologue:

Discussion with the management staff of PRRM indicates their awareness of those problems which have attended the field implementation of the theoretical schema. The evolution of the approach in the minds of the field workers, the heightened and often-false expectations of the community as to what the proffered assistance entailed, the conscious refraining by the field workers from simply giving in to such expectations of the communities, the seeming lack of commitment of the organization to the barrios caused by the frequent changes of personnel assignments, and the absence of a specific program of material assistance pending analysis of the community surveys - all of these must have been reflected in the reactions of the barrio residents expressed to the ASI researchers.

PRRM has recognized the above limitations of the first year of implementation and is exerting efforts to stabilize the operations in order to successfully test the scheme of assistance.

The ASI survey findings emphasized what PBSP considered all along to be critically lacking in the Laguna Project, that is, the absence of full-time and competent CO supervisors who could have provided the day-to-day technical assistance needed by the RRWs. Many of the problems which were discussed in the ASI study could have been avoided if CO supervisors were available in the project area to provide the workers with necessary support. While CO consultants were at hand, the frequency of their visits to the barrios was not sufficient to be of significant use to the RRWs. Furthermore, the municipal coordinators, who were supposed to provide direct supervision, were merely performing administrative supervision, and were not adequately trained to provide the necessary technical supervision, even if they had wanted to.

This need for immediate identification and recruitment of CO supervisors was strongly emphasized by PBSP "to a point that there might not be any justification for continued operations for Year II in Laguna, unless a full-time CO supervisor is retained by PRRM" (letter of Castro to Canlas, dated February 2, 1973). PRRM acknowledged the need for full-time supervision of field workers, but could not locate CO supervisors who would be willing to work on a full-time basis in Laguna.

End of Year I Implementation

By February 1973, PBSP and PRRM staffs had started work on their presentation of the Laguna Year II program and budget for consideration by the PBSP executive committee. By this time, some of the barrio development plans had been completed and were incorporated into the Year II program planning. Ramos, as social laboratory manager of the project, made his decision about the RRWs who had been placed on probation in December 1972. He recommended that all of the workers be retained, because their capabilities could be further developed. He also proposed, however, that two of the municipal coordinators be terminated for reasons of incompetence. His action was intended to become effective February 28, 1973.

Implementation: Year II

On March 1, 1973, the PBSP executive committee received a staff recommendation for approval of a grant of ₱363,020 for Year II implementation of the Laguna Project by PRRM. The staff report indicated that PRRM had recognized the "gaps and limitations of the first year program and has taken steps to provide more systematic and efficient management of the project."

A high degree of improvement in PRRM operations was noted for the final three months of Year I (December 1972 through February 1973). Personnel staffing had improved with the dismissal of two municipal coordinators. There was also a marked effort to help the field workers understand better the concepts underlying the rural social development prototype aimed at in the project, and to translate these ideas into well-ordered plans of work. The target barrios were judged to be showing "signs of accepting the presence and purpose of the PRRM field workers by way of coordinating councils, and evolving barrio development plans to guide barrio activities in the solution of their perceived problems." Accepting the assessment and recommendations of the PBSP staff, the Executive Committee approved a second year of assistance to the PRRM-managed project at Laguna.

Laguna Field Worker Resignations

The termination of services of the two municipal coordinators, which the management had recommended in February, was publicly announced on March 12 at an area meeting attended by PRRM President Canlas, his senior staff, and all operations personnel from the Laguna Project. Canlas announced that personnel staffing had now stabilized. No other terminations would be made, with the exception of the two municipal coordinators. However, the periodic evaluation of PRRM rural reconstruction workers (RRWs) would continue. Canlas also announced that, according to a new PBSP policy, project funding by the foundation would be made on a year-to-year basis.

The March 12 meeting had an explosive aftermath. On March 21, 11 field workers from Laguna, including one group leader, submitted a letter of mass resignation to the PRRM board of trustees, effective April 1. The resignations, if accepted, would seriously affect operations at Laguna, for the resigning workers covered 40 percent of the assisted barrios in the development project.

The workers cited several reasons for their action in resigning. First, recent decisions by the PRRM management had fostered insecurity of employment. Second, members of the senior staff were prejudiced against old-time PRRM workers, and lacked rapport, diplomacy, and tact in personnel relations. The senior staff also was unable to provide supportive roles toward the workers. Finally, the announcement of termination of the two municipal coordinators was cited as threatening to other project employees.

No doubt existed that the March resignations at Laguna were an aftermath of the December manifesto by Nueva Ecija workers. The dismissal of the two coordinators was interpreted by old-time workers as a vindictive act by Canlas and the senior staff, for both had been parties to signing the manifesto. Word had circulated that if the coordinators could be terminated summarily, so could any of the RRWs. It is not surprising, therefore, to learn that all of the March resignees from Laguna had also been signatories to the December manifesto. Furthermore, the latest resignations had not been known beforehand by any of the senior staff because the letter of mass resignation went directly to the PRRM board of trustees.

If the December manifesto had created agony at Nueva Ecija, the March resignations did the same for Laguna. At the PRRM board level, chairman Andres Montecastro became personally involved in the matter. He wanted to know more of what was happening and sought better communication with the resignees. Toward these ends, he called upon Miguel Garcia, CO program specialist in the organization, to talk with the workers.

On March 29, a meeting attended by Montecastro, Canlas, PRRM senior staffers Paz and Ramos, and PBSP executive director Roberto Isidro, was held to discuss the situation and to hear a report by Garcia on his meeting with the disaffected workers.

The basic reason for the resignations, said Garcia, was the workers' employment insecurity. The periodic evaluation of their performance had assumed a negative connotation, and even when individual assessments were favorable, these were not being communicated to the workers concerned. The RRWs were normally hired on a three-year basis, but the year-to-year funding of PRRM Laguna operations by PBSP had diminished that security. Critical remarks made by the senior staff regarding discipline and lack of professionalism were threatening to the workers, who felt that the management was prejudiced against them in the first place. Workers also reacted against the tendency of some PBSP and PRRM staffers to judge them from a distance, unaware of the improvements that were taking place within them.

Garcia admitted that he himself had seen the struggle and anxiety the workers had undergone to integrate the new social development concepts, approaches, and techniques into their barrio activities. Although the RRWs generally showed a healthy attitude toward the concepts of supervision and evaluation, they reacted strongly against the manner in which these were carried out. They also missed the old PRRM camaraderie, missionary zeal, and way of life which Canlas and his senior staff, being overly associated with professionalism, could not understand or appreciate.

The management meeting produced a decision that the workers' motion to resign should be respected, and that Canlas should communicate this action to them at the earliest possible time.

The meeting between Canlas and the resigning workers was held on March 29. After reporting briefly on past events, Canlas announced the management decision accepting their resignations. He then attempted to clarify issues that had been raised. He explained the PBSP-PRRM contract in detail, and spoke about the significance of the last series of personnel evaluations. He expressed regret the official communication of March 12 had been thrown off balance by emphasizing the need to continue evaluations and to comply with performance criteria agreed upon by PBSP and PRRM. He denied that retaliatory measures had been taken against signatories of the December manifesto. In fact, Canlas told the group, he personally had endorsed the old-time workers during the evaluations in January and February.

The resignees, on the other hand, expressed their concern that events should have reached this critical point. They reassured Canlas that in leaving PRRM they did so without resentment or misgiving. Both parties reached agreement about changes that should be made within the organization, concerning such matters as the "army-style" management, the need for personnel support, the emphasis on professionalism, the method of worker supervision, and a desire to incorporate the old PRRM spirit of camaraderie once again into the Laguna operations.

Canlas met the next day, March 30, with the remaining workers, those who had not resigned. Some consensus was reached after various complaints triggered by the resignations had been thrashed out. First, the management needed to demonstrate its trust in the workers and in the work the latter performed; this was an essential requirement for successful project implementation. Second, better rapport and more two-way communication was required between individual workers and the PRRM management. Lastly, there was a general need for a more supportive role from management. While the latter must be firm and evaluative, it must at the same time be healing and productive to enable workers to attain personal and professional growth within the organization.

Any crisis in the PRRM operation at Laguna was also a crisis within PBSP, and even more so now when the series of resignations appeared to have no end in sight. On March 30, Castro, who still monitored the project for PBSP, met with the RRWs who continued to work at Laguna. He reported his findings to PRRM's social laboratory manager Ramos in a letter dated April 2. On the same day, Castro also wrote to Canlas, reviewing previous discussions between PBSP and PRRM:

Subsequent inquiries into the nature of the resignations indicated a positive defect in internal personnel management of the PRRM Laguna

[Project] , notably in the area of lack of rapport and very real communication and credibility gaps between the workers and the senior staff. The senior staff has recognized this defect and will take steps to bridge the gaps to prevent the recurrence of similar disruptions in operations in the future. . . . Likewise, the PRRM senior staff has positively promised that they will review their systems, procedures and attitudes in the Laguna operations to establish closer rapport between workers and senior staff . . . .

We shall anticipate your informing us formally of the steps you have taken to meet these unexpected developments in Laguna and to inform us should there by any changes in the programming report . . . .

Changes in Project Leadership

Regardless of whether or not the March 1973 resignations were a conspiracy against Canlas and the senior staff, the investigation did reveal inadequacies and limitations in the Laguna management. Many of the issues raised by workers who had resigned, as well as by those who remained, pointed to personnel management problems which at that time could be traced to Ramos as operations manager.

The PRRM senior staff felt that the pressure subsequently placed on Ramos was unfair. The insistence by PBSP on more tangible results meant that operations would have to be streamlined. Ramos had to be firmer with his staff, he had to push and to pressure them, and he had to monitor them. But, most importantly, his workers had to produce results. His management style, more demanding than that exercised by his predecessor Reyes, had been branded "army-style" by the workers. And it did not help his image any that he was, after all, a retired army major.

In spite of support for Ramos from some quarters, PRRM Board Chairman Montecastro wanted the Laguna social laboratory manager replaced. Canlas pleaded the latter's case, but heavy pressure was exerted within both PRRM and PBSP against Ramos's retention. Ramos's own uncertainty about his status was expressed in a letter to Canlas on April 21:

As for whether I should be replaced in Laguna or not, again I think you should try to negotiate. Perhaps the 15 June target date is a good breathing spell. If the pressure to get me out is really too strong for you to resist, don't resist it. . . . In the meantime, Laguna could go on as we planned, and could effect a smooth turnover to whoever you can find to take my place. . . .

I, of course, would be very happy if by June 15, you really, after superhuman efforts at looking for a replacement, cannot find one, and the [PRRM] board would agree to let me 'carry on' until at least the end of Year II. My only 'personal' stake in the project, is to see at least one or two barrios, reach 'Point A' on or before the end of Year II. But, then I suppose this may just be a pipe dream, as they say.

Canlas fou...   on April 24, the PRRM
Board of Tr...   only until June 30.
Ramos, ho...   Canlas wrote to
PBSP Exe...   rector Dionisio
Hizon w...   starting May 11,
1973.

Tran...

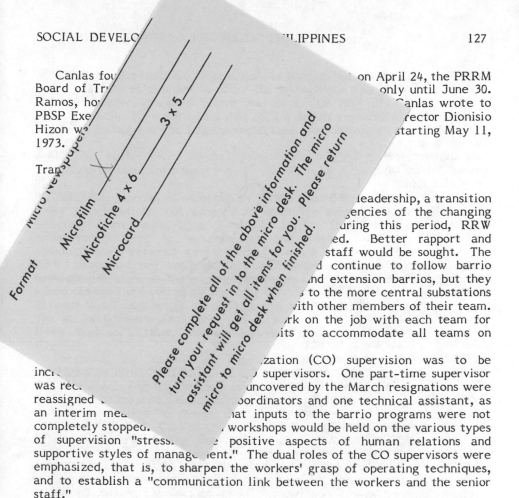

                                        leadership, a transition
                                    encies of the changing
                              uring this period, RRW
                         ed.   Better rapport and
                        staff would be sought.   The
                      d continue to follow barrio
                    nd extension barrios, but they
                  s to the more central substations
                vith other members of their team.
              rk on the job with each team for
            its to accommodate all teams on

                          zation (CO) supervision was to be
inc...   supervisors.   One part-time supervisor
was rec...   uncovered by the March resignations were
reassigned ...   oordinators and one technical assistant, as
an interim me...   at inputs to the barrio programs were not
completely stopped.   ... workshops would be held on the various types
of supervision "stress... positive aspects of human relations and
supportive styles of management."   The dual roles of the CO supervisors were
emphasized, that is, to sharpen the workers' grasp of operating techniques,
and to establish a "communication link between the workers and the senior
staff."

During this period, no significant development activities were achieved, as
it was only a transitional phase.   Economic activities were planned, but
problems anticipated were not effectively resolved.   As a result, no economic
projects were implemented.

After the March resignations, both PBSP and PRRM continued to face
implementation problems at Laguna.   These are well illustrated by the two
incidents described in the following sections.

Student Summer Task Force

In early April, the PRRM management asked PBSP for approval of a
budgetary item of ₱1,500 to be paid as honoraria to students who would be
assigned from April 23 to June 15 to the barrios vacated by the resigned
RRWs.   Castro withheld his recommendation on the request while he asked
PRRM program coordinator Paz to provide additional details for budgetary
justification.   Meanwhile, Castro was cautioned by PBSP associate director
Sison that the proposed operation should be carefully studied to determine

whether in fact it would truly promote attainment of Laguna Project aims. However, since Castro's instructions to Paz on April 17 had given the impression that the request would be granted once the requested details had been submitted, PRRM went ahead with implementation of the scheme.

On May 4, Paz submitted the additional information sought by Castro. Twelve students had been deployed in the barrio since April 23. Except for one, all were senior college students in social work. Before being assigned, all had passed psychological tests and a group interview, and were given one week of orientation to the project by the social laboratory manager and the municipal coordinators. The students were intended to maintain the presence of PRRM in the vacated barrios until new full-time workers could be recruited and trained. The planned activities initiated by the resigned RRWs would be continued by the students under supervision by the municipal coordinators.

Initially, PBSP reaction had been "to reject the idea as superficial efforts," but Castro asked for reconsideration of the scheme. He noted that the students were "even better than some of the remaining RRWs" and were representing PRRM in a manner "to avoid frustration from the barrio people." Sison, however, would not reconsider. On May 10, Castro had to inform Paz that the request would not be approved "since the original concept of the prototype operations in Laguna calls for fully trained, full-time workers to effective validate the concept."

PRRM disputed that decision. Canlas, on May 18, wrote a letter to both Sison and Castro, urging reconsideration and reviewing the sequence of events in relation to the requested funding. Canlas pointed out that the Summer Task Force was only part of the revised field strategy for the transition phase following the March resignations, and had been "discussed and apparently approved in several meetings with PBSP staff." He emphasized that Castro's letter of April 17 to Paz gave PRRM the "impression that PBSP had in fact no objection to funding the scheme." He further argued that the reason given for rejection of the request missed the whole point of the task force's role. As a temporary measure, it was intended to enable realization of the originally planned Year II operations. The students would provide continuity in barrio activities previously set in motion by the resigned workers.

Sison still would not reconsider, and she said so, definitely, in her response of May 24:

> ...even as a temporary measure, we find it difficult to justify a scheme in which students who did not train in community organization... can be entrusted with barrio development work, except as aides to regular RRWs, particularly when there is no CO supervisor to provide supervision. The MCs [municipal coordinators] are not yet in a position to provide technical supervision, and would therefore not be in a position to effectively guide the students in their working relationships with the barrio institutions and organizations.

Furthermore, Sison added, the agreement between PBSP and PRRM called for fielding the municipal coordinators in the vacated barrios where they would then be in "a position to continue to represent PRRM in the barrio officially, and be accountable to the organization for their work, behavior and performance." She also raised the question of project input relative to project costs:

Project inputs... for the last year and a half were not maximized in terms of anticipated and probable results due to mass resignations, unsatisfactory pre-employment procedures and the absence of full-time CO supervisors.... We wish to stress that project costs must be carefully monitored and controlled since an attempt at a cost-analysis will be a main factor in evaluating the duplicability of the prototype project. We hope you will identify in the above observations, some guidelines for future decisions in requesting for project funding.

Laguna Community Organization Supervision

The other incident illustrating internal implementation problems at Laguna concerned the need for fulltime CO supervisors. PRRM had earlier acknowledged the problem but had met extreme difficulties in recruitment. Castro and Sison, reflecting PBSP concerns, reiterated on May 4 the necessity to have at least two fulltime supervisors on the project. While the RRWs had been given CO theoretical training, this would have to be followed by guided field work. This training sequence, they pointed out, "has not been implemented since last year because of the continued failure of PRRM to locate and hire full-time CO supervisors." They also questioned the effectiveness, as a substitute, of the weekly strategy sessions conducted for the workers by the CO consultants, and made it clear that "we cannot appreciate the justification for continued operations in Laguna without full-time CO supervision."

As PBSP had requested "an effective solution to this critical operational requirement," PRRM on May 18 submitted a scheme for CO supervision. This would be implemented by the line supervisors - the social laboratory manager and the municipal coordinators - and would include individual supervision, team coordination, and group strategy sessions. The CO consultants would not attempt to provide direct supervision over the workers. They would, however, train the line supervisors, using the group strategy sessions directed by the social laboratory manager and the municipal coordinators. They would also offer assistance to individual RRWs upon referral by their respective coordinators, and to the RRW trainees undergoing field training.

The proposed scheme promised to serve as a total staff development program, not only for the RRWs but also for the social laboratory manager and the coordinators. It assumed that the line personnel themselves would develop faster if they exercised more direct supervision over their workers. PRRM considered this scheme as the most suitable to meet the existing situation. Canlas informed PBSP that Dionisio Hizon, newly appointed social laboratory manager, was ready to implement the scheme immediately.

PBSP, however, raised objections. Sison did not consider Hizon and the municipal coordinators fully qualified to exercise supervision in the CO approach. The coordinators had been trained briefly at Kaunlaran as direct-service CO workers only, and it would require a year of additional training in

CO supervisory techniques before they could be entrusted with CO supervision of the RRWs. Sison objected also that the scheme assumed there would be two fulltime CO consultants, when in reality reliance could be placed on only one. This was not sufficient to cope with the combined CO needs of the social laboratory manager, municipal coordinators, RRWs, and RRW trainees. Sison doubted very much that the weekly strategy sessions would be adequate to the task, and insisted that these be supplanted by regularly scheduled supervisory sessions for individual coordinators and workers. Because these issues continued to be unresolved, Sison asked for a fuller discussion of the scheme in a meeting called for May 28.

The meeting became a confrontation between the two organizations as PBSP management took issue with the CO supervision scheme proposed by PRRM. In an attempt to identify the cause for the apparent rift, Canlas suggested that both groups review how each was in fact interpreting and utilizing the concepts underlying the project scheme of assistance. PRRM's program coordinator Paz raised a question about CO methodology itself, and observed that PBSP wanted each PRRM worker to qualify for a "CO certificate" more demanding than PRRM personnel and recruits could manage. Strong reactions to these statements were expressed by both Sison and Castro.

Finally, it was agreed that the PBSP evaluations to be made after June 30 would provide a basis for determining whether the two organizations viewed the scheme of assistance in the same manner, and whether the Laguna staff was unable to meet PBSP objectives. Paz wrote later in an internal PRRM memo (undated) that achievement of these objectives was "strongly doubted by PBSP management team which assessed the field supervisors as poor and PRRM management style as ineffective."

From July to October 1973, additional CO activities were conducted in the barrios, but no economic projects were initiated. On September 1, however, PRRM made two basic decisions for improvement of field operations. First, it reduced the goal of project coverage from 50 to 26 barrios. The general strategy here was to concentrate operations in barrios with a relatively high development potential until those barrios had reached "the point of self-propulsion" (Point A; see Fig. 4.2), and then gradually extend project activities to the remaining barrios within the area complex. Second, PRRM would intensify CO supervision at all levels and provide its line personnel with CO competence equal to the requirement of the project and of project workers.

By October 1973, the 26 barrios were covered by 15 RRWs and 11 RRW trainees on guided field supervision.

Resignation of the PRRM President

By October 1973, PRRM president Eduardo Canlas finally decided that it was time for him to leave.

He had considered this move as early as January after the December, 1972 manifesto had exploded at Nueva Ecija, but to have resigned then would have meant vindication of the signatories, and all of his efforts to redirect PRRM activities would have proved futile. It would also have conceded too much, at such an early stage, to those within PRRM who opposed him and his ideas. So Canlas did not resign at that time. But funding still had to be secured to bolster up the Nueva Ecija operations, and that could only be realistically provided by Dr. Lee and the International Institute for Rural Reconstruction (IIRR). A compromise had to be achieved and, as mentioned, the PRRM board of trustees had named a special committee headed by Jose Gonzalez to look after Nueva Ecija as a first responsibility and to negotiate funding with Dr. Lee. Although Canlas continued as PRRM president, the existing operations in Nueva Ecija would continue in whatever manner the special committee, and IIRR as financial sponsor, might determine.

In April 1973, during the aftermath of the March resignations at Laguna, Canlas again considered whether or not he should leave the organization. He had decided then that if social laboratory manager Ramos was forced out, he would follow in sympathetic support. However, Ramos himself had urged Canlas to stay on as president. Therefore, Canlas did not resign, nor was he replaced by the PRRM board of trustees. But once more, as at Nueva Ecija, the board created an advisory overseer "to help in the management problems of Laguna." This was done by delegating that responsibility to PRRM trustee Bernard Du.

These moves, at both Nueva Ecija and Laguna, reflected the positive desire of PRRM trustees to become more involved in operational matters; but, if viewed negatively, they meant that President Canlas was no longer in control of PRRM operations.

The months of April to July were trying ones for the organization. Canlas knew that by this time PBSP felt that PRRM could no longer do anything right. "It was a tallying of errors," impositions, and threats of withdrawal of funds. In the face of all these, he felt that PRRM should do its utmost to maintain its own organizational integrity and self-determination. Policy differences with PBSP had become a personal problem so severe that official communication between the two groups had ceased at the management level. Canlas and his senior staff knew that PBSP had lost all confidence in their ability to manage. At no time was this more clearly evident than during these three or four months of 1973.

The Laguna Project, originally conceived as the phoenix which should arise from the old PRRM, was about to be aborted. The experiment, intended to prove that a deepening reactivation of PRRM's basic fourfold program was possible, had been branded a failure by the Nueva Ecija crowd. In less than one year, Canlas had suffered through the trials of the December manifesto and the March resignations, as well as the agony that accompanied the aftermath. Just so long as PBSP continued to support his position he believed he could still turn the tide and prove the experiment a success. However, the recent loss of confidence evidenced by PBSP marked the turning point; and in October 1973, Canlas moved to inform PRRM board chairman Montecastro that he would not stay on as the organization's president after December 31, 1973.

Transfer of Organizational Responsibility

On December 11, PBSP executive director Isidro formally wrote to PRRM board chairman Montecastro that, in view of Canlas's resignation and the findings of the PRRM annual review (March-June 1973), "we see an opportunity for PRRM to review at the present time, the management and organization of the Laguna project."
In the same letter, Isidro identified three important factors which

merit priority consideration, to enable us to continue to assist and support the project for the remaining three and a half years of this five-year project:

1. Competent management at different organizational levels of the project.

2. In view of the project being essentially a community organization for all personnel would be a working understanding of community organization principles and methods. This qualification would be most critical at the field operations level and we urge the appointment of two full-time community organization supervisors to provide adequate technical supervision and staff development for all field personnel.

3. Since the major expressed needs of the Laguna communities are increased income, increased agricultural productivity, employment, small scale industry, and skills training, the staff of the Laguna project should include a business expert who could provide technical support to the field workers and who could marshall technical resources available in Laguna and make these available to the project.

On December 27, Isidro again wrote to Montecastro, stating that "we would deeply appreciate hearing from you if possible before December 31, on the development towards the appointment of a new president and/or senior manager for the project. We wish to be informed in particular of the person who will be authorized to discuss aspects of the project operations with us, after December 31, as well as the extent of his authority." Isidro stated that PBSP's annual review of the Laguna Project would be shared with PRRM. He suggested that the review findings be utilized in preparing the 1974 program as well as in staff training and supervision of field staff. He reiterated that "this program plan as well as a competent organization will be necessary to secure approval of PBSP assistance for 1974."
Although frenzied preparations were being made by PRRM at the staff level to meet PBSP requirements for 1974 funding, board chairman Montecastro had serious doubts whether his organization should continue its Laguna operations.   With Canlas's impending resignation, Montecastro had become more directly involved with PBSP's top management in regard to the Laguna Project.   He felt obligated to see to it that the requests and recommendations of PBSP were properly attended to by his staff.   It was a

personal involvement that was beginning to take a heavy toll on his time.

Montecastro's doubts were further reinforced by PBSP's evaluation of the work at Laguna. The results of the annual review, covering the period from March 1971 until June 1973, were made available to the PRRM board chairman on January 1974 as promised. The results were not favorable to PRRM.

In early February, during a meeting attended by Montecastro, PBSP board chairman Nestor Pardo, and PRRM trustee Bernard Du, the PRRM board head suggested two alternative courses of action for dealing with the Laguna Project, in consideration of PRRM's organizational problems as well as its difficulties in identifying a senior manager for the project. One alternative was for PRRM to continue project implementation but with a schedule altered to allow time to elect a new president and to hire a new senior manager for the project. The other alternative was for PBSP to take over the management if it was ready to accept this responsibility.

Given these two options, both Pardo and Du took the position that PBSP should assume charge of the project "because we had given these [Laguna] people hopes and a promise, that it is important that to maintain this credibility, they be served without further delay." The two officials decided to refer the entire matter to the PBSP board of trustees.

On February 3, the PBSP executive committee accepted the recommendation by Pardo and Du that PBSP take over the Laguna Project management. It also approved a condition proposed by PBSP trustee Michael Cole "that in the event PRRM builds up the right organization and the capability for taking over, then we will gladly turn over the entire project again." To give PBSP management a free hand in the project, the executive committee agreed to ask PRRM to withdraw all field personnel as soon as the turnover date was agreed upon. This decision was officially communicated by PBSP board chairman Pardo to PRRM board chairman Montecastro the next day.

On February 6, the PRRM board of trustees accepted the PBSP decision and determined that turnover of the project should become effective on March 1. In a letter of February 8 to Pardo, Montecastro expressed the sentiments of his board:

> We reviewed and studied the implications of this change as far as Laguna is concerned and the effects on PRRM as an organization. As it is quite difficult to foresee and anticipate future developments in the Laguna project because of its nature, we are going along with PBSP's decision to terminate this relationship during the third year of a project that was conceived and planned for a five year period.

The operations personnel in Laguna, who still had no knowledge of the negotiations in progress between the two organizations, were officially informed of the final outcome in a memo addressed to them on February 11, 1974:

> This is to announce to you a joint decision taken up by the PRRM and PBSP Executive Committee(s) for PBSP to assume immediately the management of the Laguna project.

This decision was made to ensure a stable and continuing service to the people of Laguna involved in the project - to whom more hope for a better future has been given. With this in mind and in the light of the present circumstances that have given the impression that the needs of the people might not be served adequately considering the time constraints, this alternative has been chosen as the most prudent step in order to give the Laguna project a better chance for success.

We hope that you will understand and appreciate the reasons underlying this decision and support it sincerely.

Thus ends the narrative of PRRM's involvement in the planning and management of the rural social development project in Laguna.

PHASE 4: EVALUATION AND REFINEMENT

Project Identification and Formulation

From the initial stage of project identification, the Philippine Rural Reconstruction Movement (PRRM) and the Philippine Business for Social Progress (PBSP) were both interested in the basic idea of the Laguna Project and for similar reasons, mainly, experimentation with a rural social development prototype, the findings of which could be applied to like communities in other parts of the Philippines. Furthermore, both PRRM and PBSP would work in cooperation in developing the project.

PRRM desired to use the project as a test case for its own programmatic redirection. If the Laguna operation were successful, PRRM activities elsewhere could be implemented in a similar manner. In addition, PRRM had a more pragmatic reason for seeking PBSP assistance; the program, if approved, would alleviate its critical financial condition. Continued employment would then be available to many PRRM field workers whose barrio sponsors or donors had failed to renew their support.

The proposed operation faced no strong resistance or objections within PBSP, either from its trustees or its management. However, there was some hesitation or doubt expressed by PBSP executive director Isidro and associate director Sison as to whether PRRM, as an organization, could in fact see the project through to completion. Isidro, having previously sat on the PRRM board, knew the limitations of that organization. But he had confidence that Canlas, the new PRRM president, could achieve a successful conclusion of the operation. Moreover, the project was strongly supported by some PBSP trustees who were, at the same time, PRRM trustees. By securing PBSP funding, they would have contributed their share in raising the funds so sorely needed by PRRM.

However, strong resistance existed in some quarters within the International Institute for Rural Reconstruction (IIRR) which, as a sister organization of PRRM, viewed with some reservations PRRM president

Canlas's newly established relationship with PBSP. Another source of funding than IIRR had become available, and PBSP aid was suspect. Canlas was warned that PRRM would be dictated to by the funding agency in the course of the new project. Considering the long-standing historical and personal links between the staffs of PRRM and IIRR, it should not be surprising that some doubts lingered among PRRM employees who still valued the traditional ties with IIRR. A new approach to rural development was to be tried out, that is, utilization of community organization (CO) concepts and methods. Some questions arose among PRRM old-timers who could not see how the "CO approach" would enrich the implementation of the fourfold development orientation already espoused by PRRM and IIRR.

The next stage of project formulation proceeded with much participation and involvement from the more senior PRRM personnel. But if initial resistance on the part of PRRM old-timers dwindled to some extent, opposition from IIRR did not. In point of fact, the formulation phase of the Laguna Project remained primarily a PRRM task, which negated the earlier fears of some that PBSP would dictate the type of program to emerge.

When staffing of the Laguna Project was discussed, PBSP asked for a totally new roster of workers to be recruited and trained specifically to meet the unique demands of the project. PRRM, on the other hand, wanted to utilize its older workers, although, to be sure, the best from that lot would be selected. The principal consideration here was that PRRM had to find placement for many of its workers whose barrios were not being continued in the corporate sponsorships for funding. If PRRM fought hard for the inclusion of its older employees in the new approach, it was mainly for this reason.

PBSP had expressed opposition to employment of the older PRRM workers, even though they might be among the best. This was a carry-over from the initial reservations held by PBSP management during the project identification phase. PBSP executive director Isidro had hoped that a "new" PRRM would emerge from the experience gained in the Laguna Project. He had serious doubts whether this could be achieved by depending on the older PRRM workers, but to adopt the PBSP recommendation for a new field staff would be extremely difficult for Canlas. As the new president of PRRM, he had an obligation to take care of the organization's rank and file, and not to effect a mass termination as the PBSP suggestion would have him do. In the end, Canlas was able to convince the PBSP management that the older PRRM workers could be utilized effectively in the Laguna Project.

Although the project's nine-month planning phase was quite substantially financed by PBSP, the plans ultimately produced were not adequate for implementation of the subsequent operations. There were severe limitations in planning that would cause serious operational problems later on.

Recruitment of Personnel

If the transfer of older workers to the Laguna Project was financially convenient for PRRM, it turned out to be impractical for the workers concerned and therefore disadvantageous for the project itself. Most of the workers were recruited from existing PRRM projects in the provinces of Nueva Ecija and Pampanga, and most of their families continued to live there.   The workers themselves were being uprooted when they were transferred to Laguna.   Although salaries in their new assignments were higher, they could visit their families only on weekends, which was also the most convenient time for barrio residents to participate in their community activities.   Unfortunately for the project, this weekend activities situation as it applied in the Laguna barrios could not be utilized, because most of the PRRM workers spent their weekends at home with their families in Nueva Ecija or Pampanga.   The only attraction of the new Laguna jobs, therefore, was the higher salary scale.   When PRRM salaries in the other provinces were later standardized to the same level as those prevailing in the Laguna Project, many workers asked to transfer back to their former jobs in Nueva Ecija.

Training of Personnel

The training given to new and transferred field personnel during the preparatory stage turned out to be insufficient for the project's purpose. First, it was essential for the rural reconstruction workers to understand and to internalize the conceptual scheme of development assistance.   Second, they had to have the skills needed to operationalize the scheme in their barrio assignments.   Third, they required adequate technical support to guide them in their barrio activities.

At the time when the project was being formulated, both PRRM and PBSP accepted the notion that the CO approach was implied in the traditional PRRM orientation to rural development.   Consequently, it was thought that no formal CO training would be needed.   The judgment was that the better PRRM workers who were selected for Laguna could easily make the conceptual adaptation to CO methods.   For this reason, the initial training was conducted mainly as an orientation to the new project; but shortly thereafter, this was perceived by PBSP to be unsatisfactory, and representations were made for the formal inclusion of CO training after all.   This modification of training curriculum was only effected in January and February 1972, when operations were already scheduled to begin on March 1.

This inadequacy of worker preparation was even more evident after the RRWs initiated their motivational activities in the barrios, immediately following the November elections of 1971.   The results they achieved turned out to be disappointing, very much like those obtained from the traditional PRRM project packages.

Operational Planning

Although the individual barrio development plans were to have been finalized and submitted by February 28, 1972, no such plans were actually completed on time.   It is seriously doubted, considering the problems at this stage, whether barrio development plans could ever realistically have been made.   But this aspect of planning should have been rescheduled as soon as possible.   Because there were no operational plans, the scheme of assistance remained just a scheme.   It was left to each worker's interpretation of the scheme as to how it would be operationalized in the barrios.

Although the products of the planning phase were reviewed by the staffs of both PBSP and PRRM, the review was not exhaustive enough to be a thorough assessment. The plans submitted should have been appraised for their operational effectivity. If found to be inadequate, contingency measures could then have been drawn up. This was also the appropriate time to examine the organizational capability of PRRM and to determine whether in fact that organization could realistically be expected to meet the demands of the Laguna Project. Considering the earlier doubts of some PBSP staffers about the management capacities of PRRM, this was particularly important. When project operations finally started on March 1, after a delay of two months, specific barrio operational plans were still lacking, and the project's line supervisors were still in training at Kaunlaran.

PROJECT IMPLEMENTATION

Turnover of Personnel

Project implementation at Laguna was generally characterized by fast turnover of personnel, either by employee request or by management termination. The first group of resignations occurred just before July 1972, when 12 of the 24 RRWs departed, unable to accept or to adapt to the new development emphasis. Fifty percent of assisted barrios were thereby left uncovered. The next drop in personnel took place in September 1972, following the CO training at Kaunlaran. Finally, in March 1973, there were the mass resignations, an action directed at the PRRM senior staff.

There were various reasons for the turnover. One was the outright dismissal of workers unfavorably evaluated by PRRM. Another was related to the performance of RRWs who had been recommended for termination by PBSP. Most of these, however, were supported by PRRM in disagreement with PBSP on the qualifications desired for the workers. PBSP standards were admittedly higher, but PRRM held to the opinion that some of the negatively evaluated workers could still improve if they were given adequate assistance and supervision. Furthermore, internal PRRM problems would not be helped at all if too many terminations were executed. (5)

Resignations also resulted when workers would rather resign than be terminated. PRRM preferred to make transfers in those cases where the workers concerned could not internalize the new scheme at Laguna but were still effective as PRRM workers at Nueva Ecija.

Such personnel problems confirmed the earlier PBSP doubts and hesitation regarding the employment of older PRRM workers in the project. Retraining was admittedly necessary. PRRM was willing to have its workers retrained at Kaunlaran, but conflict later developed when PRRM disputed many of the Center's negative evaluations of workers. President Canlas resisted PBSP attempts to have the negatively assessed workers terminated. He could not understand why the training at Kaunlaran was made a standard requirement when the training itself was regarded as substandard or impractical by many of the worker trainees.

The series of resignations and transfers surprised PBSP as well as PRRM. The net result was the PBSP decision to monitor the Laguna operations extensively and to assign one of its own project officers to this task. However, this persistent monitoring eventually created tensions within the PRRM organization.

Changes in Organizational Structure

Partly because of the high turnover of personnel, PRRM had to revise its Laguna organizational structure several times. The first alteration occurred in March 1972, at the very start of the project, when the matrix relationship among the project's senior officers was introduced in place of the traditional PRRM line-staff organization. Later, however, area coordinator Reyes found he could not operate within the matrix system and gave this as one of the reasons why he was resigning from PRRM. Another major change took place in November 1972, when the matrix approach was changed back to a simpler line-staff relationship. Subsequent modifications were made in reassigning areas of authority when terminations and resignations followed the workers' disagreements with the management staff. These changes meant that the organizational capacity of the project did not stabilize until May, 1973, when Dionisio Hizon was appointed social laboratory manager for Laguna.

The frequent changes in organizational structure indicated the difficulties encountered by PRRM in managing a project of this magnitude, that is, a 50-barrio prototype. This was PRRM's first attempt on this scale. Previously it had operated only in a single barrios.

Because of the size of the project, the matrix relationship among the senior staff involved in the Laguna Project was established at the outset with the area coordinator operationally responsible. Unfortunately, the first person to serve in that capacity, Robert Reyes, did not fully understand how the matrix principle operated, and he misinterpreted the inputs of other members of the matrix as undue interference with his own function. When Major Ramos finally succeeded Reyes, the matrix management relationship was replaced with the more familiar line-staff relationship.

Feedback from Target Barrios

The fast turnover in personnel also produced much of the negative reaction issuing from the target barrios. Barrio activities suffered from lack of continuity when RRW replacements were made too frequently. In many cases, formal notice was not even given to the concerned barrio that its worker (RRW) had in fact already left the job. Stability of barrio work was therefore minimal. As workers came and went, projects were initiated but showed little or no continuity or follow-through. Negative responses from the barrio communities appeared as early as May-June 1972 (as reported later in the Asian Social Institute study), only two or three weeks after operations had formally begun. The same kind of feedback was still forthcoming 20 months later, in February 1974, when PBSP staffers met with people in the barrios for their own evaluation. (6)

The Asian Social Institute's evaluation research, reported in January 1973, was a third-party confirmation of PBSP's own assessment of the barrio operations. This report, coming from an uncommitted research institution, was embarrassing for PRRM. Program coordinator Paz acknowledged the accuracy of the survey findings that were based on data collected in May-June 1972. Before the publication of these findings, however, changes in PRRM strategy were in fact made following the appointment of Major Ramos as area coordinator. Nevertheless, whatever gains had been achieved since then were quickly forgotten by the PBSP management and staff, who saw in the ASI report a confirmation of their resolve to tighten up the monitoring of the project.

Area Management Supervision

Compounding the staffing problem was the inability of the PRRM management to respond effectively to both operational and personnel requirements of the project. The series of transfers, terminations, and resignations reflected the lack of an adequate personnel recruitment and stabilization policy. Training had to be provided continuously for new recruits, and the type of training itself became a subject of serious disagreement between PBSP and PRRM.

At the level of operations management, Robert Reyes, the first area coordinator, was appointed to this top responsibility on the assumption that he had the capability to supervise the project. But this decision was questionable. It was surprising that Reyes, previously a cooperatives technical assistant with no direct operations management experience, had been recruited to head a 50 barrio prototype operation. Furthermore, Reyes was allowed considerable leeway in the field when in fact he himself needed technical support from the senior staff. His periodic reports were apparently good enough that monitoring visits by his superiors were not increased in number of frequency. Some unfavorable comment was reported by the PRRM field director to the senior staff, but the latter did not consider this criticism sufficiently serious to create doubts about the area coordinator's effectiveness.

When Reyes later resigned, PBSP had already obtained substantial information that the Laguna Project was not moving along as well as expected. Consequently, PBSP felt compelled to take a closer look at the operation by monitoring it directly. The foundation assigned to this task a project officer from its own staff, one who had formal training and experience in management. When more serious defects in management were uncovered in the PRRM operation, PBSP stepped up its monitoring visitations.

PRRM had no choice but to appoint as the new project manager one who could keep abreast of the recommendations made by the PBSP monitoring officer. This resulted in a shift in administrative style, which some PRRM workers came to refer to as "army-style." Major Ramos, the new manager, had the task of stopping the downward slide of the project, and the only way he saw to do it was to make the workers produce more tangible results. But while this pressure was put on the workers in their barrio activities, no supportive structure from the side of management was operating to cushion the pressure. Line supervisors, with the exception of the CO consultants, were unable to meet the need of workers in this regard. The situation continued unchanged until March 1973, when the mass resignation of workers at Laguna produced a crisis both within the project and within PRRM generally.

Organizational Problems within PRRM

As a consequence of the retrenchment policy adopted by the PRRM board in December 1972, and with no new funding sources in sight, President Canlas had no alternative but to terminate a sizeable number of workers in the Nueva Ecija operations. This series of dismissals was resisted by the workers who were terminated as well as by those who remained. First, all of them signed the December manifesto and second, they opposed and downgraded the Laguna scheme. The latter would not have been so serious if the Laguna Project, as managed by PRRM, could have withstood the criticism. But this was not the case. In the view of the anti-Luguna forces (and even of PBSP staff members), the Laguna scheme was not effectively producing results. The struggle for power at the management level had finally spilled over to involve the PRRM rank and file, and had seriously disrupted all field operations. More specifically, this aggravated the operational problems at Laguna by undermining the morale of the RRWs, even of those who believed that the Laguna Project was a viable one.

Differences between PRRM and PBSP

Differences that gradually emerged between the two groups in the course of project implementation can be traced essentially to divergent views in their management philosophies and in the operationalization of the scheme of assistance. While both organizations agreed on the workability of the scheme, each had a different perception of how it should be operationalized. These differences are well demonstrated in the following specific instances.

Perception of the CO Approach

PBSP viewed application of the CO approach to field activities from a highly professional vantage point. For a CO-oriented project to be carried out effectively, there were certain prerequisites, which PBSP termed "ideal inputs." These demanded that workers be carefully screened, properly trained, and provided with adequate CO supervision in barrio activities. The RRWs should have internalized the conceptual scheme underlying the CO methodology. Periodic evaluation of field workers was also regarded as essential. PRRM, however, did not fully agree with this view.

Even after the additional training given to Laguna workers in January-February 1972, it was PBSP's assessment that the CO orientation provided was still not sufficient. By July 1972, because of the many resignations and transfers, a new batch of recruits had to be trained for Laguna. This time, all

PRRM workers and trainees were required to undergo one month of theoretical training at the Kaunlaran Center as recommended by PBSP. After the PRRM people started training there, however, the standards customarily operative at Kaunlaran came to be unacceptable to PRRM because its old-time workers were being "failed" by the center's staff. The differences which arose between Kaunlaran and PRRM on these issues continued to prevail until May 1973. PRRM, at that time, had to organize its own CO training, when Kaunlaran refused to accept any more PRRM recruits or workers in its program.

It is apparent that perceptions held by PBSP and PRRM differed also on the issue of workers' qualifications for the job at hand. Again, PBSP wanted to set higher standards of performance than PRRM considered necessary. Whenever personnel problems developed in the project's implementation, PBSP would always refer to the lower standards set by PRRM as the basic reason. (7)

Community Organization Supervisors

Agreement between the two organizations did exist that CO supervisors were essential to the Laguna Project. Although the municipal coordinators were originally intended to serve as CO supervisors, they were not qualified according to PBSP standards to perform the task of supervision competently. Therefore, part-time CO consultants were hired to fill in. But even this contingency measure was judged unsatisfactory by PBSP, which continued to press for recruitment of fulltime CO supervisors. None could be immediately identified by PRRM, nor by PBSP even after PRRM explicitly requested technical assistance. The continued lack of professional CO supervision meant that workers in the field were neither properly supervised nor effectively assisted. The municipal coordinators, furthermore, had a tendency to impose or to carry out their supervisory function in a rather highhanded manner, contributing still more to the deterioration of supportive structures within the PRRM organization.

Many of the problems and disagreements between PBSP and PRRM were related to operationalizing the CO approach. This was unfortunate because, as Canlas later wrote in reviewing a draft of this case study, the project was primarily "not to demonstrate [the effectiveness of] the CO Approach... but rather to see how enlarging the scale of PRRM operations to a 50-barrio complex, rendered into one organic whole by marketing and economic relationships, would pan out." But the project never reached that stage because it was handicapped by personnel problems related to training and standards of worker performance.

Management Philosophies

The management staffs of PRRM and PBSP had their separate views about how the Laguna Project should be conducted. PRRM envisioned the project as a prototype to be validated in the field, hence frankly experimental and open-ended in nature. An open-ended approach was certainly not viewed favorably by PBSP, which operated under conditions that were much more structured and planning oriented. These different philosophies eventually gave PBSP reason to suspect that PRRM could no longer control implementation of the project. Then, too, the project, although conceived by PBSP as a prototype to be applied later in other communities, was costing a lot of money. The PBSP management felt strongly about its responsibility to its own board of trustees for a successful conclusion of the venture.

On the other hand, PRRM thought that PBSP was willing to permit the implementing organization to operate its own project like any other PBSP-financed project, that is, to be directed by its own manager. PRRM strongly resented any interference by PBSP at the management level, if only to protect its own organizational integrity and "self-determination."

But PRRM president Canlas had no bargaining position, because PBSP refused to finance any activities not directly supporting the attainment of project objectives, no matter how strongly PRRM felt to the contrary. As PBSP became firmer in its own position about how the project should be implemented, Canlas' own perception of the funding agency changed. Rather than being "assistive," he saw PBSP emerging as a "contractor" of services. PRRM's role was simply to execute a job according to the preset specifications of the contracting party. This change of relationship, as interpreted by Canlas, was not welcomed, and what happened in the end was the ultimate irony. Canlas, in commenting on the author's case study draft, put it this way.

> The unfortunate net result of this was that an organization [PRRM] which was trying precisely to turn itself around has perhaps been irreversibly kept in the old mold. Precisely the hand that should have been stretched out in sympathy to help it to its feet and turn its face in another direction turned out to be the hand that chided it for not having been expert and experienced and trained and capable enough in its new function.

Just as the RRWs had looked for appreciation, understanding, and sympathy from the PRRM senior staff, so did the PRRM management expect the same from PBSP. But the "sympathy" sought by Canlas from PBSP was not forthcoming. While he had received strong support among PBSP trustees when the project was in the process of being approved, it was different now that PRRM performance in project implementation was being questioned. It was now up to him and his senior staff to produce the results desired, and in this area his dealings with PBSP were primarily with the management and operations staff.

Canlas could expect no sympathy from PBSP executive director Isidro. While the latter understood the constraints and limitations in the area of social development, he came from a business environment where professional managers either "have the qualification or get fired." Isidro wanted professional management standards maintained in the Laguna Project. He wanted rationality in its operations. If Isidro maintained this position to the very end, it was because he did not want Laguna to end up like other PRRM projects with which he was all too familiar. Furthermore, he was now executive director of the funding agency. He was responsible for operations and, in this particular case, for the validation of a rural social development prototype being managed by PRRM. Isidro could not permit PBSP to "turn its face in another direction," as Canlas wanted.

Nor could Canlas expect sympathy from PBSP associate director Clara Sison, although she and Canlas were personal friends. They moved in the same professional circles, but the two were in continuous disagreement over the CO approach to rural social development. As a professional social worker, Sison had definite expectations of training and performance from the RRWs if they were to function effectively as community organizers. Just as Isidro insisted that professional standards be maintained at the level of management, so did Sison when it concerned the RRWs and their work in the barrios.

Part of the insistence of these two was due to the fact that they were dealing with Canlas and his senior staff as professional social development managers. Isidro himself was very emphatic on this point. As professional managers, the PRRM people were being paid to do a job and to do it well. They should not expect to be treated with kindness and sympathy like a beneficiary community.

But the professional standards set for the PRRM senior management, as well as the creditable performance demanded of RRWs, proved to be too much to expect from the implementing organization. PBSP requirements of the project's management created a strain within PRRM. The expectations set by PBSP were unrealistically high and definitely beyond the capability of PRRM to deliver. While Canlas and the senior staff were indeed professional managers, their own attempts at professionalizing PRRM as an agency met with considerable opposition internally.

However, the experience of the Laguna Project was not lost on everyone, and especially not on PBSP executive director Isidro, to judge from his comment after reading an earlier draft of this case study:

This case could very well serve to crystallize for students of a management course, what I believe to be the fundamental professional question faced by social development management. The dilemma is the constant pull, seemingly in opposite directions, to give proper consideration to the human and humane factors in the project on the one hand, and the need for efficiency and effectiveness of the project on the other hand... both considerations must and can be served. It is not a mutually exclusive, either/or proposition. Seeing both considerations, and serving them efficiently and effectively, after all, is what social development managers are for.

NOTES - Chapter 4

(1) Statistics quoted are from 1970 Census of Population and Housing: Final Report, Vol. 1 (Laguna) (Manila: National Census and Statistics Office, 1974). Percentages are rounded off.

(2) The value of the peso varied during the period of Laguna Project operations, but on December 31 of each year, US$1.00 equalled ₱6.379 (1971); ₱6.671 (1972); ₱6.759 (1973); and ₱6.791 (1974).

(3) Letter from Canlas to the PBSP board of trustees, dated June 17, 1971.

(4) The Asian Social Institute (ASI) is an academic and research institute. It was commissioned by PBSP to do the research studies needed in the documentation and evaluation of the Laguna prototype operation. A report on the first study to be conducted was submitted in February 1972, entitled "Attitudes Toward Modernization in Laguna: A Socio-Psychological Study of Development Attitudes in Fifty Barrios in the Province of Laguna." This study was funded from the planning phase grant given to PRRM. The second study was a baseline study of the project. A report, entitled "An Evaluation Research of the Philippine Rural Reconstruction Movement's Barrio Development Program in Laguna," was submitted in January 1973. The cast of this study was also funded by PBSP.

(5) This position became a source of conflict between the two groups, giving rise to PBSP's impression that Canlas could not make the "hard decisions" on personnel that were required of a manager.

(6) One factor possibly worth considering, although its extent is difficult to ascertain, is that subsequent efforts to assist those communities where negative reactions had been reported fell upon deaf ears.

(7) On the other hand, it must be reported that some workers who had been initially assessed as favorable by PBSP turned out to be rather poor RRWs in the Laguna operation.

5 Bangkok Metropolitan Immediate Water Improvement Program: Thailand*

Chakrit Noranitipadungkarn

PROJECT BACKGROUND

Water is a necessity of life. Humans rely on it for drinking, washing, cleaning, bathing, and other essential purposes. In the more populated areas, any natural source of available water is usually insufficient, and it becomes the responsibility of the governing authority, by one means or another, to meet additional water requirements through planned development. Perhaps the most satisfactory solution is by way of pipeline system which transfers sanitized water from a treatment plant to each customer located in the area.

The provision of water to any highly urbanized area needs careful planning and effective administration, because it involves construction and maintenance of extensive water works, integration of several technical systems, accomodation to different categories of users, and distribution over a vast expanse of territory. To ensure an acceptable, sufficient, and timely output, which consumers can hardly do without, requires considerable engineering and public health skills and complex organizational and procedural arrangements.

* This case study has been adapted by the author, with the publisher's permission, from his "Bangkok's Metropolitan Immediate Water Improvement Program." which appears as Chapter 8 in Gabriel U. Iglesias, ed., Implementation: The Problem of Achieving Results (Manila: Eastern Regional Organization for Public Administration [EROPA], 1976), pp. 201-230.

The author wishes to thank both the former and the present managing directors of the Bangkok Metropolitan Water Works Authority, Mr. Chamras Chayapong and Mr. Kachok Suppakit-Lekhakarn, respectively, for kindly allowing the author to search the Authority's records for factual documentation. Appreciation is also due to the heads of the Engineering Department's Research, Planning, and Water Meter Divisions, who provided relevant information and ideas.

Should the water delivery system fail, it will cause immediate hardship to countless metropolitan residents who then will usually blame the administration for being incapable and inefficient.

The case of Bangkok's water supply from 1960 to 1970 presents a dramatic example of the difficulties noted above. The city's inhabitants suffered from chronic shortages and service inadequacies, which were due to faulty administration and to delays in enlarging the water supply capacity sufficiently to cope with rapid urban growth and constantly rising demands. Eventually, in 1966, a continuing effort to establish some order began with the conception of several remedial measures.

This case study will explore how the interim water improvement program* of 1969-1970, which was but one aspect of the total effort, was planned and implemented to fill the immediately critical vacuum until a more satisfactory long-term scheme could be prepared and carried out.

Growth of Metropolitan Bangkok

The city of Bangkok is the capital of Thailand. Its growth, especially after the Second World War, has been tremendous both in the absolute rate of expansion and by comparison with the rest of the country. In 1945, the population of Bangkok was approximately 0.7 million. This increased to 1.4 million in 1960, to 1.9 million in 1965, and to 2.3 million in 1970. (1) The municipal area expanded from some 50 square kilometers in 1945 to about 240 square kilometers in 1970. (2) Still there could be found clusters of housing projects growing farther out on the city's fringes which in the near future would be linked with the already congested urban center. The average annual rate of population growth during 1960-1969 for the whole Thai Kingdom was 3.1 percent, compared with 5.2 percent for Bangkok itself and 6.2 percent for the entire Bangkok metropolitan area. (3)

Such growth in numbers had resulted in large part from expanding employment, educational opportunity, and an increasingly active tourist industry. The rise in population was due both to new births in Bangkok and to immigration from the countryside and from small towns. Foreigners also contributed notably to the urban spread though on a much smaller scale. For a time, in 1965-1972, certain parts of the city constituted a rest and recreation destination for countless American GIs.

Physical expansion was both vertical and horizontal. New high-rise commercial, office, and hotel buildings and shopping center complexes were more generally located in the city's inner circle. Public and private housing units, or packaged developments, and associated small shops were concentrated off the main roads and in outlying areas. On the other hand, some blighted areas could be found in both the inner city and the suburbs on land developed insufficiently or not at all by the owners.

---

* A program is here considered as comprising several interrelated projects. Each project may further consist of one or several activities.

Owing to ineffective and unsatisfactory city planning, it was not only that zoning guidelines were lacking, but road systems were also inadequate. Many roads and highways were substandard and poorly designed. Streets were often very narrow and without sidewalks. Surfaces of the main arterials were paved with reinforced concrete, but this made it difficult to install new service facilities. Utility poles and lines along main and secondary roads had already multiplied both above and below ground so that added facilities had to be compressed into the limited space normally reserved for walkways.

The Bangkok metropolitan area had major physical, economic, and social problems similar to those usually suffered by other large cities. These included traffic congestion, overcrowded and unsanitary slums, pollution, flooding, robbery and other misdeeds, as well as inadequate public utilities, among the most critical of which was water supply.

Bangkok was governed as a municipality, but several other government organizations and public enterprises shared responsibility for providing local services to the people. Electric, telephone, and water services were maintained by public enterprises. Law and order, fire protection, local bus transportation, health services, and higher education were administered by central government agencies. Each operated quite independently of the others. Coordination, whenever it did occur, could be expected to be difficult. There never was any master plan for Bangkok that might reasonably have been accepted by all these varied organizations.

Bangkok Water Supply Administration

The introduction of a public water supply administration in Bangkok took place in 1914. The government, upon advice from the foreign adviser, first entered this field by constructing a small water treatment plant in Bangkok and a transmission canal from a tributary of the main river Chao Phraya, some 26 kilometers north of the city. New treatment plants were added as the city grew. After the Second World War, the Bangkok Water Works Authority shifted its attention to construction of deep water wells in various parts of the city. A single deep well had only a limited output, but wells had the advantage of being located closer to the client-users. However, the lack of any long-term or comprehensive planning for a full decade made it difficult, even impossible, for the administration to keep up with consumer demands.

A major development was attempted in 1960 when, under the government of Thai military strongman Field Marshal Sarit Thanarat, the Bangkok Water Works Authority was granted support to improve the water canal and to construct additional treatment plants and major service lines to serve both old and newer populated areas. A French construction firm was awarded a turnkey project contract to construct all that was necessary as determined by the firm's survey. Although more water did become available, this still did not meet popular expectations. Accusations of corruption were made against high officials in the government because the contract had not been reviewed by the Ministry of Finance. The construction costs were too high, and it took the contracting firm too long to finish the job. Such considerations as these provoked mounting dissatisfaction among Bangkok's residents. They also raised doubts about the Water Works Authority's control over the contractors that would allow the latter to work in such a leisurely manner.

Historically, there have been several changes in the organizational placement of the Bangkok water supply administration. It was first set up as a Water Works Unit in the Sanitation Department of the Ministry of Metropolitan Administration. When the Ministry was abolished four decades ago, Bangkok Water Works became a division in the Public and Municipal Works Department (PMWD) of the Ministry if the Interior. Later, the Bangkok Municipality, when it was established in 1939, assumed supervision of that division. In 1952, the Ministry of the Interior, considering the administration of water supply at that time to be unsatisfactory, requested return of the division to PMWD. And there it remained for the next 15 years until it was transformed into a public enterprise. In 1967 the four water works systems then serving the four contiguous cities of the Greater Bangkok area - Bangkok, Thonburi, Nonthaburi, and Samutprakarn - were consolidated to reduce costs and to increase efficient operation. The reorganized agency was named the Bangkok Metropolitan Water Works Authority (MWWA) and continued to be attached to the Ministry of the Interior. (4)

PHASE 1: PLANNING, APPRAISAL, AND DESIGN

Identification and Definition of Program Goals

At the height of the water crisis in 1967, it was estimated that the Metropolitan Water Works Authority (MWWA) was producing about 897,000 cubic meters of water per day in Bangkok-Thonburi, scarcely enough for the 205,700 metered clients per day (1,600 cubic meters per client per year). Thus, it was natural that consumers felt compelled to scramble for whatever water was available. Because only a few drops of water ordinarily reached the end of service lines in the daytime due to heavier use, many residents would rouse themselves during the night to draw off enough water for the next day's use. At commercial places and some residences, it was not uncommon for owners to install water pumps illegally in their bid for a greater and more regular supply of water. Although MWWA continued to approve the installation of water pipes to new buildings, some new housing areas were left without service because development funds were not sufficient to complete the job.

Complaints from users and nonusers alike were voiced constantly in the city's daily and weekly newspapers, demanding either new services or a cleaner, more dependable, and sufficient water supply. Many of these protests were forwarded to politicians and to the Ministry of the Interior, as well as to MWWA itself. The public was not generally aware that MWWA was just then constructing more water wells intended to augment the supply. Such an increase, however, would still fail to meet the mounting demand. Clients expressed their frustration and disappointments in whatever ways they thought might compel more serious attention by the authorities. The language they used in these communications ranged from gently phrased petitions and suggestions to emotional outbursts couched in harsh language. They even resorted to prayers for help in the distressing situation.

There were three principal reasons for the delay in a decision for an effective course of remedial action. First, officials were not confident about obtaining funds to support any new projects of major scale. The Bangkok Water Works Authority had only recently been discredited by its association with a much criticized water development project in which corrupt practices and inefficiency had been charged. Second, MWWA authorities were worried that the public would promptly suspect anyone who proposed a new plan as being motivated by self-interest to try once more to make some personal gain from it. Third, decisive action on any proposal would depend on the Minister of the Interior, who, as a strongman of the country, would have to be convinced of the fitness of the project. Finally, and most important, there was an urgent need to devise a more suitable organization and better problems associated with supplying water in the Greater Bangkok area. Those who could no longer tolerate delay included other officials, businessmen, and the people of Bangkok generally. However, all of these factions were seemingly left with no recourse but to rely upon the government service charged with responsibility for handling the water crisis.

Ad Hoc Committee on Bangkok Water Works Improvement

Earlier in 1966, the cabinet under Marshal Thanom Kittikachorn had decided to take steps toward certain reforms in the capital city. The initiative to do something about the water supply came from the National Economic Development Board (NEDB), (5) a central planning agency of the government. Members of NEDB were convinced that no more time should be lost in expanding and improving the several water systems in the metropolitan area. An ad hoc Committee on Bangkok Water Works Improvement was proposed, and this action was endorsed by the cabinet, the highest decision-making group in the nation. The committee was composed of the deputy secretary-general of the NEDB, as chairman, and representatives from the Bangkok Water Works Authority, the Public and Municipal Works Department, the Ministry of the Interior, the Budget Bureau, and NEDB. Its terms of reference were to suggest improvement measures and to plan for the future.

The committee's first recommendation was to reorganize the agencies that were providing water to the metropolitan area. These were the four water-works systems that served the four neighboring cities of Greater Bangkok, that is, Bangkok, Thonburi, Nonthaburi, and Samutprakarn. The cabinet agreed to the committee's proposal and, as noted earlier, the Bangkok Metropolitan Water Works Authority (MWWA) came into being under the direction of the Ministry of the Interior.

Another assignment the committee had accepted was to determine the type of studies necessary to formulate specific recommendations for improving the water supply itself. The committee intended to approach the entire matter scientifically. Its members, lacking the requisite knowledge and expertise themselves, agreed to recruit an engineering firm judged to be most suitable for conducting a thorough survey and preparing a master plan for both management and technical improvements in the MWWA operation. It was the committee's firm conviction that only by this strategy could supplies of water to the metropolitan area in the future be made sufficient and uninterrupted.

With the cabinet's approval, the committee circulated worldwide an announcement of its search for a firm of consulting engineers. A lengthy series of screening sessions were undertaken by the Committee in 1967-1968 for the job. Camp, Dresser, and McKee, of the United States, was finally chosen on the grounds that its time and cost estimate were the most reasonable and that it offered the most favorable conditions of experience and past performance, availability of skilled company personnel and copartner specialist firms and a convincing tentative plan of operations. After the necessary negotiations, the committee signed a contract with the American company to carry out its mandate.   This process of evaluation and approval, however, took several months, and many more months would be needed to get the new action moving. Under the circumstances, local consumer demand continued to exceed available water supplies, and the critical gap became even greater. The problem was obviously being felt much more keenly than it had been in the past, judging by the intensification of telephoned complaints to the authorities concerned. This greatly aggravated situation almost automatically forced the committee members to the realization that some intermediate plan was needed to provide the maximum amount of water in the shortest time possible. Such an intermediate proposal must be consistent with the more fundamental long-range plan. In the committee's view, the two together could best be designed by one well-equipped and intensely involved consultant firm of engineers. Even though additional expense would have to be borne in developing the intermediate plan, the emergency situation fully justified it.

Consultant Survey and Preliminary Report and Recommendations

Camp, Dresser and McKee accepted the job and began work in June 1968. After seven months spent in an extensive study of various possibilities, the consulting firm presented the committee with a preliminary report (6) which included a package of recommendations as emergency measures to meet the minimum water requirements for the metropolitan area projected to the year 1975. This was a proposal for a so-called Immediate Water Improvement Program (which is the principal focus of this case study) for work activities to be completed within the two fiscal years of 1969 and 1970. The governing criteria used in formulating these recommendations were that a maximum increase in water supply must be developed in the shortest possible time, with the least investment cost, and with minimum disruption of existing operations.

The committee appraised the report and indicated its satisfaction with the recommendations. The report was forwarded with committee endorsement to the governing board of the Metropolitan Water Works Authority. It was expected that the board would accept the recommendations, not only because these were based on a detailed feasibility study by experts, but also because the cabinet-endorsed committee had indicated its full support in obtaining the necessary government subsidy to implement the program.

The board, which had full authority to initiate new programs, agreed to go ahead with the proposal. The Immediate Water Improvement Program, as recommended, consisted of four major projects, or activities, designed to meet the stated goal. For each project, specific targets were identified, costs were estimated, time schedules were set, and details of needed improvements were set forth. The MWWA administration would bear responsibility for working out further details and procedures as the projects were implemented. The four major projects are outlined as follows.

Project 1: Improvement of the surface water transmission canal and water treatment plants. Both banks of the main canal would be raised one meter. In each of the ten existing treatment plants in Bangkok, a new water tank, larger in size, would be constructed, and pipelines, valves, and other accessories would be replaced as needed.

Project 2: Increase of groundwater production by additional deep wells and shallow aquifers. The latter would cost less than the deep wells but the quality of water would not be as good, although it should meet standards for treatment at the Thonburi plant then operating at only half capacity. The shallow aquifer alternative would require further setting.

Project 3: Repair of leaking pipelines for water conservation. New work units would have to be organized to survey the full extent and nature of leakage. Necessary equipment would be purchased and personnel would be recruited and trained to carry out this work for the entire metropolitan area. This activity would be critical for remedying the existing situation, but it would also have to be continued on a permanent basis as part of the long-range master plan.

Project 4: Repair, or replacement, of the large number of nonfunctioning water meters discovered in the firm's preliminary survey. A problem-oriented task unit would need to be created to complete this work within the two-year duration of the improvement program. The existing Water Meter Division would bear responsibility only for the installation of new meters.

In 1968, two-thirds of the water produced in Bangkok-Thonburi (598,000 cubic meters per day) was surface water, mainly river water transmitted by canal from north of the city. This was treated at ten plants in Bangkok and one in Thonburi. The consulting firm suggested that more raw water could be treated in Bangkok if all ten plants, or at least nine of them, were modified. Any such increase, however, would still fail to meet the ever-rising demand. It would be necessary to continue to rely on supplemental groundwater sources. The latter were the only potentially available water that could be tapped in the short period of two years called for in the improvement program. Groundwater sources already accounted for one-third of the supply provided in Bangkok and Thonburi and for all the municipal water used in Nonthaburi and Sumatprakarn. The problems faced in the last two areas, which were geographically separate from Bangkok-Thonburi, would be approached by another program.

According to the consulting firm's survey, 65 percent of the water consumed in Bangkok and 80 percent in Thonburi could not be accounted for. As already noted, a large number of water meters were defective. Many of these had been intentionally rendered inoperative by building occupants. Consequently, customers were often tempted to use more water than needed when they did not have to pay for all of the water they consumed. The consulting firm during its survey could find no meters at many client's places, and illegal connections were detected in many other locations. Furthermore, the system for collecting water fees was recognized as obsolete and inefficient. The Metropolitan Water Works Authority admittedly lacked enough staff to check out illegal situations or to file court suits against consumers for nonpayment of bills. Chronic leakage from the poorly maintained distribution system reduced still further the volume of water available to metropolitan users.

The consulting firm calculated that implementation of its recommendations would produce an additional 362,000 cubic meters of water per day, an increase of about 40 percent. A further increase, though more difficult to calculate, would benefit clients through the planned reduction of waste in the main distribution system. According to the firm's estimate, the total program of immediate water improvement could be achieved at a minimum cost of 92,600,000 baht, and the work could be completed within two years. Details of the recommended targets and required fiscal allocations are presented in Tables 5.1 and 5.2 respectively.

Preparation and Design of Project Activities

The Metropolitan Water Works Authority (MWWA) was a single organization unit in charge of administering and providing water supply to well over two million inhabitants of the Greater Bangkok area. It operated as a semiautonomous and state-owned public enterprise whose board of directors bore the responsibility for all major decisions and development projects. It also came under the general supervision of the Ministry of the Interior.

As noted, MWWA was the product of a merger in 1967 of the four waterworks authorities which had served the four cities of Bangkok, Thonburi, Samutprakarn, and Nonthaburi, making up the metropolitan area. Each of these authorities had suffered continuous losses and were constantly blamed for mismanagement. The new single integrated unit, operating on an economy-of-scale concept, was seen as more economical in overhead expense, more uniform in the services offered, and more amenable to changes introduced to achieve greater efficiency. MWWA managed ten water treatment plants in Bangkok and one in Thonburi as well as a number of deep wells in all four cities.

The reorganization of MWWA had not yet been completed when the intermediate program for immediate water improvement was launched. Rather, new management procedures were being devised and installed by Booz, Allen and Hamilton, International, an expert management consultant firm brought in by the engineering consultant group of Camp, Dresser and McKee. These new measures included such activities as computerized billing system, work reassignments, redistribution and expansion of work units, and

TABLE 5.1 - Project Activities and Production Targets,
             Immediate Water Improvement Program, 1969-1970

Project No.	Project Activity	Targeted Production Increase	Existing Production Capacity
1	Increased production of raw surface water (transmission canal and treatment plants)	145,000 cmd[a]	598,000 cmd
2	Increased production of groundwater from		
	(a) deep wells	131,000 cmd	
	(b) shallow aquifers (water to be treated at Thonburi plant)	86,000 cmd	299,000 cmd
		(362,000 cmd)	(897,000 cmd)
3	Detection of leaks and repair of distribution pipelines	99.7 percent (of entire system)	0.3 percent[b] (pilot tested)
4	Repair or replacement of defective water meters	120,000 units	165,000 units (considered in good condition)

[a]Cmd = cubic meters of water per day. This figure was for improving nine water treatment plants, but MWWA later decided to improve all ten plants, and raised the new water target to 168,000 cmd.

[b]Pitometer Associates surveyed 0.3 percent of the entire system as a pilot test.

TABLE 5.2 - Estimated Investment Costs,
             Immediate Water Improvement Program, 1969-1970

Project No.	Total Estimated Cost (in baht)[a]	Fiscal[b] Year 1969	Fiscal Year 1970
1. (Surface water)	31,000,000	8,500,000	22,500,000
2. (Groundwater)	19,500,000	4,500,000	15,000,000
3. (Leakage repair)	8,900,000	8,900,000[c]	---
4. (Meter repair)	33,200,000	18,100,000	15,100,000
Total	92,600,000	40,000,000	52,600,000

[a]Twenty baht = approximately US$1.00.

[b]The fiscal year runs from October through September of the following year.

[c]Establishing detection and repair work units and acquiring essential equipment would be completed in fiscal year 1969. Thereafter,
maintenance would have to be provided for in the regular budget.

recruitment of additional personnel. The organzational structure existing at the time the new program was being considered is presented in Fig. 5.1. This system was further reorganized in 1969, as shown in Fig. 5.2, in order to implement more effectively the various projects and new tasks assigned to MWWA.

As the responsible organization, MWWA has the initial task of translating the proposed program for immediate water improvement into several specific projects. Some of the proposals, when subjected to review in February 1969, could be carried out by utilizing the existing machinery of MWWA but other parts called for management and technical procedures that were new and sophisticated, requiring further assistance from the consulting firms. For example, the improvement of treatment plants and the deep-well system were construction projects of a type in which MWWA possessed prior experience. Construction techniques and procedures as well as cost estimating had been fairly well standardized. However, the proposal to enlarge the capacity of existing plants necessitated technical and administrative studies and particulars beyond MWWA's in-house capabilities. In this context, the four major activities in the recommended improvement program were approached as separate tasks, each to be considered and planned independently. Work assignments were made on a project-by-project basis and handed out to different organizations and work divisions.

Increased Production of Groundwater

The managing director of MWWA forwarded the recommendations on groundwater deep wells to the Engineering Department. This department originally consisted of divisions of adminstration, surveying and supervision of construction, and design (see Fig. 5.1). Later, with reorganization and enlargement, it was strengthened with new divisions of planning, research, and water analysis (see Fig. 5.2). Department engineers were sent out to inspect and select locations for the new wells. Subsequently, another team of technicians was assigned to make tests of water suitability. The necessary project documents were then prepared, with blueprints and specifications for each of the designated wells. Contracts were awarded through competitive bidding to individual companies to carry out the required construction.

The shallow aquifers that were recommended to increase groundwater production presented a relatively new kind of problem to the Engineering Department. The aquifer sources had to be checked out at specific locations with specialized testing equipment. Engineers from the department, with cooperation from the consulting firm and from the Public and Municipal Works Department (in the Ministry of the Interior), selected the sites according to specifications and conducted the necessary tests. Unfortunately, the water content of the shallow aquifers proved to be too salty for processing at the treatment plants, and the whole idea had to be scrapped.

Increased Production of Surface Water

As a consequence of the need to abandon the shallow aquifer project, the Engineering Department, assisted by the consulting firm, undertook a

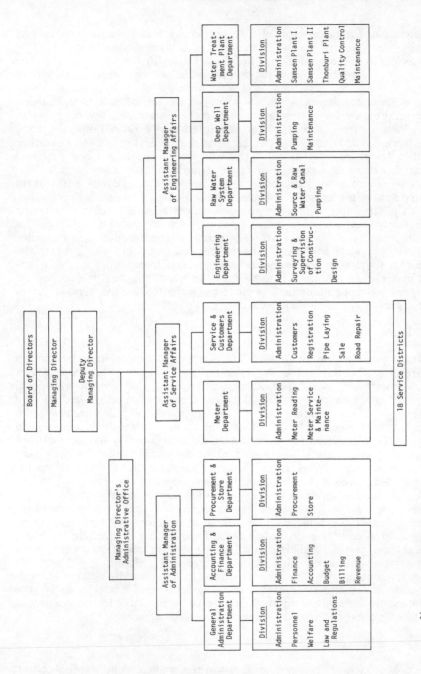

a/Metropolitan Water Works Authority, An Interim Report on the Organization and Administration of Metropolitan
Water Works Authority. (Bangkok: Camp, Dresser and McKee, and Booz, Allen and Hamilton, International, Inc.,
1969), Exhibit II (insert between pp. 5-6).

FIGURE 5.1 Organization of the Metropolitan Water Works Authority, 1967-1969 a/

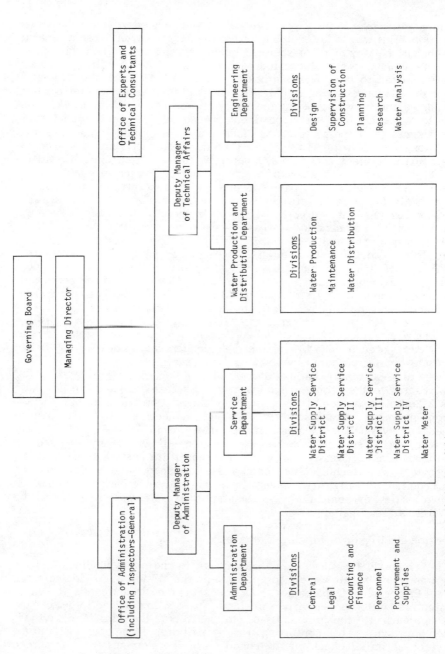

* Metropolitan Water Works Authority, ibid.

FIGURE 5.2 Reorganization of the Metropolitan Water Works Authority, 1969*

preliminary survey of an alternative solution suggested to increase water production. This was to lay a pipeline from the Bangkok transmission canal to the Thonburi treatment plant some 13 kilometers distant. When this option proved feasible, a proposal drafted with help from the consulting engineer was transmitted to the governing board of MWWA. Although the estimated cost of the new undertaking would be higher than the shallow aquifer project, it remained the only choice agreed to by the board, which approved it in principle. The Engineering Department proceeded with a detailed formulation and design of the project. Its Planning Division completed an intensive survey for use in drawing up the plan. Then the Design Division took over the preparation of project documents, blueprints, and specifications. Construction of this project was also to be contracted out to private companies, because MWWA itself did not have enough workforce to carry out the job.

It was MWWA policy to streamline its workforce. By awarding contracts for major development and construction work, there was no need to retain a large number of engineers and workers on the regular payroll. Nor was there a need to acquire and maintain a large inventory of specialized equipment and materials that would not be used after a particular job had been completed. MWWA always tried to maintain adequate staff and facilities to handle routine jobs and emergency calls. At this time, MWWA was in the process of expanding and improving its regular workforce by recruiting better qualified people and upgrading employee skills through training programs.

In the project described here, the acquisition of the necessary pipeline materials were achieved through outside purchasing. It is interesting to note that prices quoted in bids by commercial suppliers were considerably below the cost estimates prepared by MWWA. The reason was that oversupply of pipeline stock existed in Thailand at the time.

In regards to the proposed modification of treatment plants in Bangkok, MWWA accepted the consulting firm's recommendation but felt that formulation of the more detailed specifications and engineering designs had best be worked out by qualified experts rather than within MWWA. The board, therefore, appointed a team to represent it in meetings with the engineering consultants (Camp, Dresser and McKee) to negotiate costs and other terms for providing such technical service and also for supervising the construction work required. Finally, after several meetings and some bargaining between the two parties, agreement was reached and the results were referred to the MWWA Board for final approval.

Detection and Repair of Pipeline Damage

The proposals for surveillance of damage to the main pipelines and for their immediate repair were also approved by the MWWA board and referred to the Engineering Department. Officials of the department's Research Division met with representatives of Camp, Dresser and McKee to discuss the best approach to the problem and to work out the details of project implementation. The consulting firm's affiliate, Pitometer Associates, undertook an initial check on the condition of the pipelines. It was agreed that two new detection units would be set up within MWWA's Engineering Department with appropriate staff additions and budgetary support for a permanent detection operation. Pitometer Associates offered, at no extra cost to MWWA, to train new workers on the job. Repair work recommended by the damage survey would be carried out separately by regular staff in the 18 service districts (see Fig. 5.1). Subsequent reorganization of MWWA assigned these district offices to four separate Water Supply Service Divisions within the Service Department (see Fig. 5.2).

Repair or Replacement of Defective Meters

The recommendation to repair or replace the large number of defective meters uncovered in the consultants' preliminary survey was referred by the MWWA Board to the Meter Service and Maintenance Division (see Fig. 5.1), and subsequently was passed on to the Water Meter Division in the Service Department (see Fig. 5.2) for the drafting of an implementation proposal. With help from the consulting engineers, it was decided that the unusually large volume of work required to resolve the current crisis could not be handled adequately within MWWA either by the regular workforce or with conventional equipment and acessories on hand. As an indication of the size of the problem, in 1969 alone, the estimated loss of revenue resulting from defective meters was approximately US$3 million. About the same level of revenue loss had prevailed during the previous ten years. To cope immediately with the rapidly deteriorating situation, a temporary problem-oriented organization was suggested that could easily be dissolved once the targeted mission had been completed.

The envisioned temporary organization would not only carry out the repair and replacement of defective water meters, but would also survey the entire situation, locating existing meters whether defective or not and drafting a plan for future administration of the meter system. Following agreement on the essential goals to be achieved, an appropriate proposal was drafted in the Water Meter Division, detailing the organizational strucure and the requirements for staffing, funding, and purchase of repair equipment and meter replacements. Four years were judged to be necessary to complete the object. Consequently, as the proposal represented a multiyear investment, it had to comply with the submittal format directed by the National Economic Development Board (NEDB), that is: 1) objective, 2) rationale, 3) operational methods and targets for each activity, 4) financial requirements for purchasing and for new staff, and 5) expected benefits of the project. When the MWWA board finally approved the project proposal, the managing director transmitted it to NEDB to ensure that the operation would be consistent with established policy of middle-term national plan. With NEDB approval, the request for annual funding was forwarded to the Budget Bureau, and the new organization was finally set in operation.

However, the length of time taken to submit the meter project proposal for review by NEDB, to obtain funding approval, to draw up specifications for purchasing the new meters, and to await delivery from commercial suppliers, had the effect of putting the whole operation far behind schedule. Furthermore, it was discovered from the newly completed survey and workmen's experience in the field, that the volume of defective meters throughout the metropolitan area was far greater than had originally been estimated, amounting to 200,000 nonfunctioning units instead of 150,000.

This made it necessary to rewrite the project, taking this distortion into account and requesting a correspondingly larger support subsidy to accomplish the increased volume of work over a five-year period instead of four. After a while, when the new version had been approved by the MWWA Board, it was resubmitted as a long-term development project for review by NEDB and for final approval by the cabinet.

PHASE 2: SELECTION, APPROVAL, AND ACTIVATION

Project Review and Approval

As observed in the foregoing discussion, the National Economic Development Board's Sub-Committee on Bangkok Water Supply Improvement acted as an appraisal board, before transmitting recommendations of the consultant firm to the Metropolitan Water Works Authority (MWWA). However, the governing board of MWWA had the final word on all development projects conducted by the organization. The board reviewed, appraised, negotiated changes when necessary, and approved proposals and requests for funding to carry out work. The managing director carried responsiblity for supervising the Authority's activities, in accordance with major decisions handed down by the governing board.

It follows, then, that the time consumed in transmitting proposals up and down the lines of authority for review, modification, and approval was considerable. This happened because there was no scheduling to govern the limitations of the time that might be observed by each of the parties involved. As MWWA had been in existence only since 1967, no detailed study of this problem of work flow had yet been made.

Figure 5.3 outlines the relationships existing in 1969 between the major offices and agencies concerned in the process of project review and approval. In addition to the cabinet, at the very highest level, there were the National Economic Development Board (NEDB) and its Sub-Committee on Water Supply Improvement, and also the Budget Bureau. The last held authority to appraise and approve all requests for government funding.

MWWA was not a self-supporting enterprise. Its income from water consumption fees paid only one-third of its annual expenditures. The remainder was subsidized by annual grants from the government. It was expected that some time would pass before MWWA could rely entirely on its own resources.

To obtain the subsidies needed, MWWA had to submit its requests to the Budget Bureau, whose decisions to allocate government funds among various government agencies were guided by priorities set forth in the national policies within the limits of available resources. Actually, in the case of any major development project, the initial request for financing would be forwarded to the cabinet for approval in principle only. The cabinet's action then became a guideline for the Budget Bureau to follow. NEDB was, for its part, responsible for evaluating the economic and social contributions of any

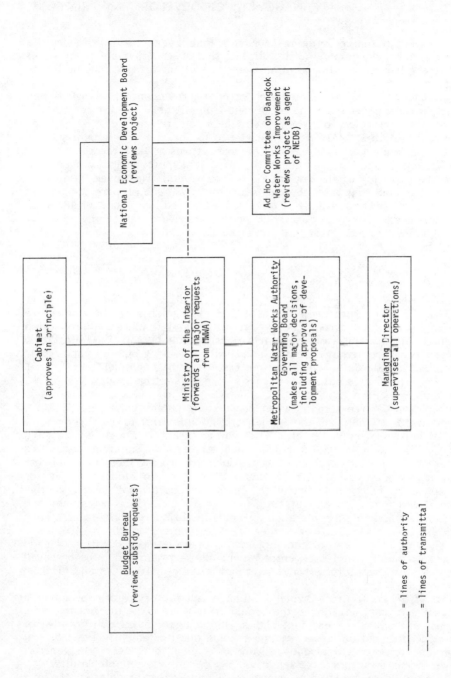

FIGURE 5.3 Lines of Authority and Transmittal for Project Review and Approval, 1969

project, especially one programmed for more than a year, toward meeting the goals of national development. It followed that an endorsement from NEDB would strengthen the likelihood of an agency receiving official funding for its activities.

The MWWA case for immediate water improvement in Bangkok had elicited strong support from the NEDB Sub-Committee. The latter kept the cabinet well informed of each step taken in the process of project development, in view of MWWA's urgent need to obtain a government subsidy for the emergency work required. Otherwise, it was argued, the government might well be blamed for not supporting a project most critically needed to relieve the suffering of the capital city's inhabitants. The government, well aware of the time that would be necessary for MWWA to prepare the project proposals in detail, had already in prior years allotted lump-sum subsidies for assistance even though the project documents were not completed for transmittal to the relevant offices for approval.

Project Activation and Organization

Of the four separate projects identified as segments of the Immediate Water Improvement Program, the two having to do with increased production of surface and groundwater were to be carried out by private contractors. The other two, directed at detection and repair of leaking pipelines and repair and replacement of defective water meters, would be implemented by either existing or especially created work units within the Metropolitan Water Works Authority.

In dividing the program between private and public workforces, MWWA relieved itself of much of the burden and complexities of management in favor of private companies that had won contracts through competitive bidding. The private firms, of course, would strive to manage those activities assigned to them, such as completing the job within prescribed time and cost limits, in such a way that they would be certain to clear a profit for themselves. They would have to calculate operational costs, recruit personnel and make job assignments, arrange for necessary equipment and instrumentation, and schedule their project operations economically. They would also have to be prepared to meet and overcome unanticipated problems arising during the course of the project. The agreed upon duration of each contract commonly carried an enforcement clause which had to be observed strictly by the contractors if they were to avoid penalty fines and lowered profits.

Most of the contractors involved did have satisfactory prior experience in deep well construction, though they could offer less in pipeline construction, and least in modifying treatment plants. In management capability, most of them still depended on rule-of-thumb to plan and implement their projects, though one or two had already advanced beyond that level. In general, however, the contractors' experience had produced fairly reliable results.

At stated intervals, MWWA supervisors would inspect completed segments of the work under contract. If all was satisfactory, payment of appropriate installments to the contractors would be endorsed. Supervision of construction work during modification of the treatment plants was assumed jointly by technicians from MWWA's Engineering Department and from Camp, Dresser and McKee, the consultant engineering firm.

When inviting bids for contract, MWWA stated only a few simple conditions, that the contractor should be in good standing (i.e., a good record of past performance) and be financially sound, well equipped to do the job, and capable of completing the work within the specified time. The lowest bidder was usually declared the winner, provided the tender he had submitted was in accordance with or close to the specifications set forth by MWWA.

Responsibility for inviting and reviewing bids and awarding contracts was divided among three groups: 1) receipt-of-tender committee, 2) opening-and-deliberation committee, and 3) contract-making committee. Officials from different but relevant divisions within MWWA were appointed to each group by the managing director. All final decisions were made by the governing board. The multicommittee approach had been adopted to avoid control by a single committee over the whole process of bidding and awarding.

Implementation of the two remaining projects was assigned directly to managers of various MWWA units. In each project, two different approaches were utilized. The first was to create special units for designated tasks demanded by the emergency situation. The second was to involve existing units within the MWWA organization for such work as could more easily be phased into regular service operations.

In the pipeline leakage project, the detection survey was to be conducted by two newly created units under the supervision of the Engineering Department's new Research Division (see Fig. 5.2). However, responsibility for pipeline repair was given to the existing Service District offices, of which there were 18 (see Fig. 5.1); later, this function was reassigned by the managing director to the four Water Supply Service Districts within the Service Department (see Fig. 5.2).

In the water meter project, authority for all repair work and replacement of defective units was handed to a problem-oriented unit, while new meter installation continued to be performed by the Meter Service and Maintenance Division (see Fig. 5.1) and, later, by the Water Meter Division (see Fig. 5.2). The new repair-and-replacement unit was conceived as an ad hoc organization the various functions of which are indicated in Fig. 5.4. As already mentioned, this special unit, like the pipeline detection units described earlier, would be phased out when the critical missions had been accomplished.

Consulting engineers played a role in advising MWWA on the organization of work units both old and new, as well as in aiding with preparation of special equipment and instruments and with other technical aspects of the extraordinary operations. For example, consultants suggested a doublecheck system whereby one MWWA unit would evaluate the performance of another. In the pipeline project, the leakage detection team worked independently of the repair team, but once a repair was made by the latter, the detection unit would check it out.

Similarly, in the meter project, the repair team and the meter-reading

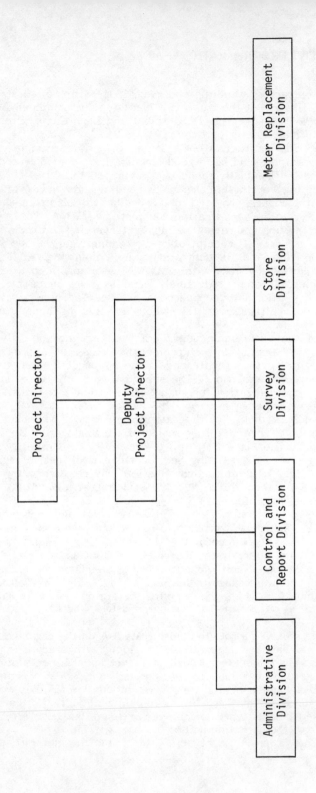

FIGURE 5.4   Ad Hoc Organization for Water Meter Repair or Replacement

groups operated separately, though the latter would report malfunctions in the course of routine reading. Also, each meter repair unit assigned to a given area would be rotated after a certain period of time. In the beginning, eight three-man repair teams were organized to do the job. Later, when the magnitude of the problem inflated unexpectedly and when additional workers could be trained, this number was increased to 24 teams of the same size. Each of these had its own construction equipment and was charged with excavating earth for installations as well as removing and replacing all defective meters.

Leakage detection and repair of the pipeline systems were facilitated by experiments directed by Pitometer Associates, a firm with expert knowledge and experience in this field. Pitometer also helped to train new personnel on the job in Bangkok, and arranged for other workers to train in Japan when a greater capability was called for in sophisticated aspects of the project. MWWA technicians were able to train their own employees in meter repair and replacement, because this work was less difficult and did not demand as much skill on the part of the workers.

PHASE 3: OPERATION, CONTROL, AND HANDOVER

We have described how certain work units within the Metropolitan Water Works Authority (MWWA) had to be modified, or created anew, to take over directly various functions in the several projects that were part of the Bangkok Immediate Water Improvement Program. Implementation of these structural innovations as soon as possible and their transition into a long-range master plan required MWWA to streamline its whole organizational structure and management procedures to accommodate the changes. In fact, when awarding the contract to Camp, Dresser and McKee, the National Economic Development Board, through its Sub-Committee on Bangkok Water Supply Improvement, specifically required the engineering consultant firm to devise an effective management system and appropriate procedures for the Water Works Authority.

Organizational Changes Within the MWWA

Modification in MWWA's organizational structure was the result of detailed world studies and analyses carried out continuously by the management expert firm of Booz, Allen and Hamilton, International, which had been called in by the prime contractor for this very purpose. The workload assumed by MWWA during the period of 1967 to 1970 grew rather rapidly because of the vigorous attempt to enlarge the Authority to serve more adequately the need represented by the metropolitan water shortage. The strategy of expansion was to take things step by step, so that one step became the springboard to the next.

Selection and recruitment of qualified people to manage the various assignments proved to be no easy task. Only when there was sufficient and qualified staff to deal with the increasing flow of work would the entire operation be processed to everyone's satisfaction. The planned alterations in work management were only partially realized in the period under review. Recommendations by the management consultants did include introduction of the concept of an integrated process of project management, but it would take some time before that concept could be fully implemented according to plan.

Reorganization of the MWWA structure was achieved in two major stages. In 1967, three assistant managers were given charge of three major functional areas, that is, administration, service affairs, and engineering affairs. What earlier had been designated as divisions were raised to departmental status, and more specialized divisional responsibilities were distiguished within each of these new departments. This was done mainly to cope more efficiently with the increasing volume of work in the many different activities. Thus, the functions of general administration, accounting and finance, and procurement and store were formalized as separate departments in the administrative group. Similarly, within the functional group of service affairs, the work of the Meter Department was differentiated from that of the Service and Customer Department. And the engineering affairs complex consisted of the Engineering, Raw Water System, Deep Well, and Water Treatment Plants Departments (see. Fig. 5.1).

In 1969, additional modifications were made to divide or realign work responsibilities further at divisional levels, regrouping all of these within four new departments, in place of the three functional groupings. The four departments were now Administration, Service, Water Production and Distribution, and Engineering (see Fig. 5.2). Two deputy managers, each supervising two of the four departments just named, were placed in overall charge of Administration and Technical Affairs respectively. The managing director was further assisted by two staff offices. One of these dealt with administration matters and included several inspectors-general; the other was concerned with experts and technical consultants. New, smaller units were created at the divisional level. Not included in Fig. 5.2 are the two pipeline leakage and repair units and the meter repair and replacement unit, which had been formed temporarily to resolve certain problems in the comprehensive water improvement program, as described in earlier sections.

The project manager of the water meter repair and replacement unit, after having secured appropriate budgetary support, managed to recruit the necessary complement of special workers. These employees were trained for the eight three-man teams set up during the project's first year of operation. As reported, these teams were increased to 24 in the following year. It was anticipated that this would be sufficient to complete the required work within the two years of the project's duration.

The newly renovated and computerized billing system, according to the plan, would go into operation after completion of the meter repair unit's assignment, so that when all of the repair work had been completed, the income from collection of water service fees could be increased accordingly.

The temporary work status of those involved in the water meter project was one disruptive factor in an otherwise smooth operation. Most of the laborers understandably preferred permanent employment. Therefore, they tended to remain with MWWA only until they could locate other, less temporary jobs. Several of the newly recruited workers, after but a short time on the payroll, misbehaved and upon being reported were immediately discharged. Replacements for these vacated positions had to be sought constantly.

One difficulty encountered in building up MWWA to be a more efficient operation was the general lack of incentive and sanction that had prevailed during the previous administration. Salaries were low, and the undifferentiated approach to reward for individual merit had demoralized employees, especially the better ones. When the volume of work increased far out of proportion to the number of new workers hired, some older employees were no longer willing to take their work as seriously. Under the circumstances, MWWA management found it necessary to revise pay scales more generously and equitably.

Monitoring of Work Performance

Direct responsibility for supervision and monitoring rested with two major organizational units of MWWA. These were the Engineering and Service Departments. In the first unit there were groups of engineers who could be assigned to oversee specific projects. Their criteria for monitoring were derived from terms of each contract and the specifications detailed therein. Periodically, they checked the work being done at the construction sites and notified the contractor in charge whenever a problem arose concerning engineering designs. They would endorse contractor's requests for payment of completed work segments only when the work had been performed to their satisfaction.

The detection of pipeline leakage was a responsibility of the Chief of the Research Division in the Engineering Department. For this undertaking, Bangkok was divided into several operational zones, and a schedule was set up to carry out the required job in each zone. This schedule was used by the Research Division head as the basis for monitoring the workers' performance, and he reported periodically to the Engineering Department head. It was anticipated that this project, for the whole of Bangkok, would be completed within one year. After that, the plan was to start over in the first zone, as part of a continuing cycle of checking on pipeline leakage as a regular maintenance chore.

The responsibility for repairing the pipelines, once leakage had been detected, belonged to the Service Department, more specifically to the several District Service offices whose supervisors would see to it that their field staff made the necessary repairs within a reasonable space of time. If there was any oversight on the part of these service teams, the detection crews from the Research Division, as noted earlier, would be expected to spot the malfunction during their next round of checks for leaky pipes.

As already pointed out, the repair or replacement of water meters was carried out by an ad hoc organization which became the special charge of the chief of the Water Meter Division in the Service Department. For purposes of this activity, 17 operational zones were differentiated for the Bangkok metropolitan area, and priority was given to any area or areas where the water supply problem was considered to be most critical. The special task force assigned to this project was expected, according to the plan, to have completed its work by 1976. Once the defective meters had been repaired or replaced, a foreman from headquarters would check out the work by resorting to a sampling method. If some repairs had been overlooked, the meter readers from the District Service offices were expected to discover such oversights on their regular check of home meters to record the monthly use of water.

Finally, periodic reports were submitted by chiefs of the various departments to their respective superiors, the deputy managers, and thence to the managing director according to the hierarchical line of authority. Upon completion of an entire project, a comprehensive report would be forwarded to the MWWA governing board for review and ratification.

Completion and Handover

Not one of the four separate projects in the Immediate Water Improvement Program was experimental or pilot in nature. All were identified at the outset as practical solutions to a crisis situation, and they were implemented as rapidly as possible. The Metropolitan Water Works Authority (MWWA) urgently needed to have the projects completed in order to overcome the water supply shortage in the Bangkok metropolitan area. Because the time spent on project preparation was relatively short, some discrepancies did develop between the estimated duration of the projects and the actual time required for their completion. Table 5.3 is a detailed statement of these differences.

The project on detection and repair of leaky pipelines was the only one completed on time. All of the others experienced unanticipated difficulties in adhering to the time schedules originally recommended by the consultant engineering firm.

The longest delay occurred in the case of the meter repair and replacement project. From the start, the situation deteriorated to the extent that several additional years had to be programmed. Unlike the other projects, this one required several preparatory stages before the work program itself could be tackled. This preparation included such matters as the organization of an ad hoc problem-oriented unit, a revised request for a long-term financial commitment from the national government, and the recruitment and training of special workmen. Furthermore, unexpected problems developed in the field when workers began the actual task of repair and reconstruction of meter facilities. The Meter Division itself estimated, while detailed planning was still underway, that about 900 to 1,000 additional water meters became defective every month.

Delays in the project to modify the water treatment plants were due largely to unforeseen construction problems and to the contractors' own

TABLE 5.3 – Estimated and Actually Completed Work Schedules, Immediate Water Improvement Program, 1969-1972

Date of Completion	Project 1 (surface water)	Project 2A (deep well)	Project 2B (shallow acquifer)	Project 3 (pipeline leakage)	Project 4 (meter repair)
Estimates in consultant recommendations	30 Sept. '70	30 Sept. '70	30 Sept. '70	30 Sept. '70	30 Sept. '70
Planners' revised estimates	29 Sept. '71	During '69	30 Sept. '71		30 Sept. '72
Same	23 Oct. '71	Dec. '71			
Same	17 Dec. '71				30 Sept. '76
Actually achieved	June '72	Dec. '71	25 Oct. '71	30 Sept. '70	about 85 percent by early '76

shortcomings on the job. Remnants of older facilities were frequently un-covered during excavation, which required more time and additional expense in clearing the land for the new construction. Service lines - for telephone, electricity, and drainage - sometimes needed realignment, and this neces-sitated time-consuming negotiation with relevant authorities. MWWA was sympathetic with the contractors' worries about these developments, but it meant that time estimates for the project's completion had to be revised continually (see Table 5.3, Project 1).

In general, however, most of the projects could not be completed on schedule because of the short period of time allowed to reorganize MWWA's management procedures and organizational structure. All projects, except the one on meter repair and replacement, were finally brought to an end before midyear in 1972. This accomplishment, although later than originally hoped for, did raise the total capacity of water production and distribution in the Bangkok metropolitan area to a new high of 1,200,000 cubic meters per day.

The governing board, basing its collective judgment on reports from the supervising engineers and other MWWA officials, including the managing director's own recommendations, finally took action to accept the construc-tion work completed by outside contractors, and properly credited the per-formance of MWWA work units involved in the emergency program. MWWA achievements were acknowledged in two principal ways - in the annual re-ports of the departments concerned, and in the final report on each project following its completion.

As already noted, the project on repair and replacement of defective meters was far from finished in 1972. Planners realized that it would not be possible to finish this project within the time limits of the Immediate Water Improvement Program. Considering the phenomenal increase in non-functioning meters reported monthly, it was likely that a new project to carry out this much needed rehabilitation would have to be formulated as a five-year plan and incorporated in the National Economic and Social Development Plan (1972-1976).

Transition to Normal Operations

There were two categories of activity that had to be transferred upon completion of projects in the Immediate Water Improvement Program. The first was concerned with the detection and repair of leakage in the main pipelines, where the specially trained personnel of the newly created de-tection and repair units had to adapt their labors to the continuing task of routine maintenance of the pipeline system. The second type of activity involved work assignments on the other three projects. For example, with the end of new construction, there was need to rehearse employees in the operation of the modified treatment plants, the new canal system for trans-mitting raw water to the Thonburi plant, and the new deep wells. These tasks, however, did not present undue difficulty or call for unusual effort on the part of MWWA. Personnel for the sections responsible for managing and maintaining the new facilities were available because they had been recruited and trained for the job during the process of MWWA reorganization.

In the case of meter repair and replacement, as explained previously, the ad hoc organization was to be phased out upon completion of the special project in favor of MWWA sections that regularly maintained the metering system. Executives of the ad hoc group already held posts of authority in permanent MWWA units, and the technical staff would simply be transferred to district offices of the Service Department where regular positions were being reserved for them.

MWWA did not face the problem of returning to the government those funds that had been invested in support of the Immediate Water Improvement Program. The government earlier had decided in principle that during the period of critical water shortage it should exercise responsibility for the special projects as a necessary public utility service for the people of the Bangkok metropolitan area. However, MWWA still had the responsibility for running an efficient water-works organization and for further improving its water supply capability in the years ahead.

MWWA continued to accept customers' applications for new water service installations so as to avoid new waves of citizen criticism and complaint. The need for water continued to be immediately and absolutely essential for the majority of Bangkok's inhabitants, although some residential projects and commercial plants relied on construction of their own deep wells and could wait a little longer before having to depend on the public Water Works Authority.

PHASE 4: EVALUATION AND REFINEMENT

It is readily conceded that projects undertaken as programmed action to achieve certain goals within a given time and cost expenditure will vary in objective, rationale, magnitude, complexity, and constraints. Nevertheless, the following observations drawn from the experience of the Bangkok Metropolitan Immediate Water Improvement Program should help to highlight certain critical factors in project planning and management that may occur elsewhere in the conduct of similar programs of planned change.

An Interim Program to Gain Time

The Immediate Water Improvement Program consisted of four projects, or activities, devised for implementation by the Bangkok Metropolitan Water Works Authority (MWWA) to alleviate as quickly as possible the very serious water shortage in the Greater Bangkok area. Under the circumstances, it was neither intended to, nor could it, solve the whole problem of water supply faced by the people and their government. Rather, quite frankly, it was designed to be an interim effort for the purpose of gaining time while the large-scale and long-term development program was being prepared.

A Program of Separate Projects

Instead of a situation in which a professional authority forecasts a crisis to occur some time in the future and recommends measures to cope with it, the concept of the Immediate Water Improvement Program emerged and was identified only in response to extraordinary public pressure issuing from the constant complaints of customers. As the organization responsible, MWWA was in fact not at all well prepared to take up the challenge. The severe limits of time available to prepare and activate a remedial program understandably contributed to a program implementation in which the four proposed projects were carried out independently instead of being coordinated within a single time schedule.

Actually, the lack of such coordination did not entail any disruption of one project by another, because they were not funtionally interrelated, and the completion of one project was not a prerequisite for beginning another. Any one or all four of the projects made a positive contribution in serving the common objective, that is, to increase the production and distribution of the public water supply. For any project to fall behind schedule, although certainly not desirable in itself, was not a critical factor in the program's overall success. Delays did occur and they did result in some increase in investment costs. And, of course, they also prolonged the inconveniences felt by the client-consumers of water in their daily living-condition.

A Test of Management Capacity

Originally the consulting firm attempted to devise its recommendations for solving the water supply problem in the form of a single program, that is, to integrate several activities or projects that would serve the single overriding objective and that could, or should, be carried out simultaneously. This strategy was based on the firm's feasibility study of the water service system, taking into account factors of demand and supply judged to be crucial for determining the scope of the remedial program and the engineering capacity to cope with the problem. At the same time, of course, potential sources of additional water supply were extensively explored. But the planning consultants sorely underestimated the time required to complete all of the projects.

Perhaps most important of all, they failed to gauge correctly the organizational capacity of the Metropolitan Water Works Authority to implement the whole program. In this connection, the consulting firm quite naturally had recommended specific courses of action on the assumption of accepted project management principles and practices. But MWWA administrators were not then totally familiar with, or experienced in, these concepts and their ramifications. Therefore, when the Water Improvement Program was finally launched, MWWA was still in the midst of reorganization aimed at modernizing its management structure and procedures. The result was that an unexpectedly long time was needed for total implementation of the program and its affiliate projects.

Recourse to Outside Assistance

While MWWA as an organization was not fully prepared to undertake a job of this magnitude entirely on its own, it was quite ready to call upon the services of outside consultants who assisted in laying out a basic approach to the emergency situation and in suggesting administrative and engineering solutions to various aspects of the problem. MWWA also proceeded promptly in putting out to bid much of the construction work, thereby relegating some of the task of implementation to outside contractors. If MWWA had attempted to do this work with its existing inadequate resources, there might well have been a great waste of labor and materials, and even more confusion and delay than eventually did come about.

Benefits of Strong Government Support

The Water Works Authority was unable to operate solely on the basis of its own financial resources. It was fortunate, therefore, in being beneficiary to strong moral and fiscal backing from the government. The support manifested within the National Economic Development Board, as well as the powerful personality of the board chairman, who was, at the same time, deputy prime minister, contributed significantly to receipt of the necessary funding from government sources. With such direct support in the present emergency, MWWA was not compelled to seek loan funds, either internal or external. To have had to resort to that option would have meant many months of negotiation and execution of loan agreements, forcing undue postponement of the desired accomplishments of the Water Improvement Program.

Emphasis on Physical, Not Social, Development

The kinds of work effort called for in the Bangkok program posed fewer problems than might be expected in other types of development projects. The principal reason for this was that the program involved almost entirely new construction or repair work, both of which were primarily physical in nature. No far-reaching changes in either attitudes or behavior of the city's population were contemplated, except for certain limited reorganization of personnel relationships and responsibilities in relevant MWWA work units. To have attempted any major alteration of Bangkok society or culture would have been very difficult to introduce or to maintain. Innovative elements in the water improvement projects, both physical and organizational, were, to a large extent, simply added on to what MWWA already had or was accustomed to, and this made the task somewhat easier. It may be noted, however, that in the meter repair and replacement project at least some client-users of water were delinquent in breaking meters and otherwise circumventing the system by illegal means, and would have to be educated to a more cooperative behavior in the future.

Organizational Changes to Aid Implementation

This case study has demonstrated how organizational arrangements may be modified or created anew to cope with problems arising in project implementation. Within MWWA there were some permanent structural units that were able to serve project demands with only minor adaptation. But, in other instances, ad hoc temporary units had to be established to accomplish a given mission. Another lesson learned was that organizational change proceeded more smoothly when it was carried out but one step at a time, moving ahead at a pace calculated to be not unduly disruptive, and building on what was familiar and well established. A third innovation, which promised positive gains for MWWA both then and in the future, was a doublecheck system whereby one work unit regularly reviewed the work of another toward the goal of achieving greater efficiency and integrity in services offered to the public.

Good Planning Means Flexibility

To program work segments in a project is a highly technical operation if the various elements are to be meshed accurately and consistently with each other. Even so, changes during the process of implementation must be expected, no matter how well the project is planned and estimated. Of course, the costs of a project depend upon close adherence to a time schedule. However, should the need arise to alter a planned course of action while the project is underway the process must be flexible enough to accommodate change even though this may add significantly to the cost. Planning is never achieved once and for all. To anticipate perfect management performance is only an illusion. However, the most desirable rule is still to hold any discrepancies between planning and action to a minimum, without endangering the ultimate success of the project.

NOTES - Chapter 5

(1) Official files, Division of Registration and Statistics, Bureau of the Under-Secretary of State for Bangkok Metropolis, Bangkok Metropolitan Administration.

(2) Official files, Division of Registration and Statistics.

(3) Jeff Romm, Urbanization in Thailand (New York: Ford Foundation, 1972), p. 10.

(4) Metropolitan Water Works Authority Act B. E. 2510, Royal Gazette, vol. 84, section 75, August 15, 1967.

(5) The name was later changed to National Economic and Social Development Board (NESDB).

(6) Camp, Dresser and McKee, "Preliminary Report on Water Supply and Distribution," February 1969.

6 The Malia Coast Comprehensive Health Center: United States

Nancy Crocco
Tetsuo Miyabara

GLOSSARY OF SIGNIFICANT ORGANIZATIONS

Community Action Program (CAP). A federal Government community development program under the administrative branch of the Department of Housing and Urban Development (HUD).

Comprehensive Health Planning (CHP) Advisory Council. The Hawaii organization that officially advises the CHP Agency on all health matters.

Comprehensive Health Planning (CHP) Agency. The agency responsible for overall health planning in the state of Hawaii.

Comprehensive Health Planning (CHP) Review Committee. The committee that conducts the investigations for the CHP Advisory Council's recommendations and decisions.

Department of Health, Education, and Welfare (HEW). The federal Government department responsible for the health, education, and welfare of all individuals in the United States.

Department of Housing and Urban Development (HUD). The federal Government department responsible for the welfare of metropolitan development in the United States.

Hawaii Medical Service Association. The only company in Hawaii that offers statewide prepaid health insurance.

Honolulu County Medical Society. A nonprofit professional society for doctors in Honolulu.

Malia District Comprehensive Health and Hospital Board, Incorporated (Board). The nonprofit corporation of Malia residents established to improve health care in Malia.

Malia District Neighborhood Planning Committee (MDNPC). The resident planning organization, required under Model Cities grants, to review Malia's proposals to Model Cities.

Model Cities. The special federal program that provides grants to poverty-designated neighborhoods for development projects. Model Cities is under the administrative branch of HEW.

Office of Economic Opportunity (OEO). The federal Government's anti-poverty program. It is under the administrative branch of HUD.

Office of Human Resources. The City and County of Honolulu office that administers Model Cities grants.

Planning, Implementation, and Evaluation Committee (PIE). The committee that conducts onsite investigations of the grants that RMP makes.

Regional Medical Program (RMP). The federal Government office that awards grants to upgrade the quality of medical care. RMP is under the administrative branch of HEW.

Regional Advisory Group (RAG). The decision-making body of each state RMP.

PROJECT BACKGROUND

In 1946 the United States Public Health Service and the National Commission on Hospital Care issued two publications reporting that the number of hospitals serving rural areas of the United States was sorely inadequate. (1) These reports provided the first empirical evidence that health care in rural areas of the United States had been neglected, and they spurred the federal Government into action. Soon after the reports were made public, Congress passed the Hill-Burton Act, which greatly expanded hospital services in rural areas. Because the authority to provide health care was constitutionally reserved to each state, however, the Hill-Burton Act could not permit the federal Government to directly implement or to centralize rural health services. Nevertheless, this legislation did grant money to the state governments to build and improve hospitals in those rural areas lacking health facilities.

By 1954, however, state health officials realized that it was impractical to build hospitals in small rural communities, and therefore the federal Government would have to provide grants-in-aid to the states to build smaller health facilities, which could be more feasibly located in these communities. Thus, in 1954, Congress amended the Hill-Burton Act to include financing for health centers, as well as hospitals. The federal Government further encouraged the development of these smaller facilities by passing legislation such as the Comprehensive Health Planning Act of 1966 and various amendments to the Public Health Service Act. (2) In addition, health centers were supported by special federal programs and federal agencies such as Model Cities, the Office of Economic Opportunity (OEO), and the Regional

Medical Program (RMP).

Despite this support and the millions of dollars spent on grants-in-aid, projects to build and operate health centers were plagued by numerous problems. Problems of coordination occurred because each health center required several grants, but each grant was provided by a different agency. Problems of overlapping jurisdiction occurred, since some funding agencies were loosely consolidated within the United States Department of Health, Education, and Welfare (HEW), but others were under the administrative branch of the Department of Housing and Urban Development (HUD). Finally, the projects to implement health centers were hindered by numerous "on-the-ground" problems - lack of community support, difficulty in hiring medical personnel, and lack of qualified administrators.

The following case study - a description of a project to build and operate a comprehensive health center in a rural area in the state of Hawaii - focuses on the management difficulties in dealing with these problems.

Malia, A Rural Community in Transition*

Located in the central Pacific basin, Hawaii is the western-most state of the United States and consists of several islands, the most populated of which is Oahu. Situated on Oahu's western shore is the Malia Coast. The Malia Coast is isolated from the rest of Oahu by the ocean to the west, the Malia mountain range to the east, and a nearly impassable jeep trail to the north. To the south lies the only road; it leads to urban Honolulu, which is about 30 miles away. Dry and rocky, the Malia Coast encompasses a land area of about 50 square miles, but the habitable land occupies a narrow corridor situated between the ocean and the mountain range. Along this seven-mile corridor are several closely grouped residential areas, whose residents identify themselves collectively as the community of Malia.

Malia has a multiethnic population of approximately 27,000 people. Hawaiians or part-Hawaiians make up 36 percent of the population, Caucasians 27 percent, Filipinos 14 percent, and Japanese 5 percent. (3) This differs considerably from the rest of Hawaii where Hawaiians and part-Hawaiians compose 15 percent of the population; Caucasians, 33 percent; Japanese, 28 percent; and Filipinos, 7 percent. Malia's population is also quite youthful, with about one-half the residents 17 years of age or younger. The major problem is poverty. Compared with the rest of Oahu, Malia residents suffer from high unemployment, lack of local employment opportunities, low family income, low educational levels, substandard housing, and poor health. (Table 6.1 contrasts the Malia Coast with the entire island of Oahu.)

---

* For reasons of personal and political sensitivity, the names of most specific places and individuals have been changed. When direct quotes are used, the pseudonyms replace the real ones. Citations that compromise true identities have been omitted. All other factual description is accurately represented.

TABLE 6.1 - 1970 Selected Indicators

Indicator	Malia	Oahu
Familes with Income under $3,000 per Year	17.0%	7.6%
Median Family Income	$8,950	$11,554
Unemployment	9.8%	2.6%
Median Years of School (persons over 25)	11.1	12.3
Substandard Housing Units	42.6%	28.9%
People over 65 Years of Age Receiving Old Age Assistance	12.5%	3.7%
Crude Birth Rate (per 1,000)	32.3	23.2
Infant Mortality Rate (per 1,000 live births)	25.0	20.1
Premature Birth Rate (per 1,000 live births)	114.5	91.9
Rate of Mothers without Prenatal Care (per 1,000 live births)	48.5	16.5

Sources: U.S. Census 1975, Model Cities Survey 1971, Department of
Health's Health Surveillance Study 1974, and the State of
Hawaii Data Book, 1974

Political jurisdiction for Malia is divided between and among the United States federal government, the State of Hawaii government, and the City and County of Honolulu government. The federal government has overall authority and mandates national policies with which Malia must comply. The state government mandates state policies with which Malia must comply. And, finally, the city government directly administers Malia, providing day-to-day services such as fire and police protection. In theory then, the federal government and the state government set the broad overall policy for Malia, while the city government implements this policy through an elected City Council, as well as an elected mayor and his administration. In reality, Malia retains considerable local autonomy, partly because Malia's geographic isolation from the city government in Honolulu has forced residents to solve their problems independently, and partly because grassroots community organizations have demanded to participate in making and implementing policies for Malia.

The residents not only support but also defend this de facto autonomy. In understanding Malia's special problems and unique lifestyle, they feel strongly that they are best qualified to manage Malia's affairs. Consequently, residents may be divided among themselves over many issues; but when outsiders come into the community telling them how to solve their problems, they unite against them. It is not that the residents do not want outside help. They welcome outside help. But they will not tolerate outsiders managing their affairs or telling them what to do.

In recent years, however, changes have forced Malia to become less insulated. The population has grown from 3,000 in 1940, to 16,000 in 1960, to over 24,000 in 1970. The city of Honolulu has sprawled out into the suburbs, leaving Malia closer than ever to densely populated areas. Most significantly, the economic underpinnings of the area have shifted. The area's major employer was a sugar plantation, which grew sugar cane in the valleys. The plantation, however, was unproductive and unsuited for commercial expansion: it had an inadequate water supply; it was too far from the processing plants; it had insufficient land; and its soil was too rocky. Thus, in 1946 the plantation closed down. Some residents converted the most fertile plantation land into truck farms; others started small pig farms; but, for the most part, Malia residents were forced to work as laborers outside of Malia. In the early 1960s, private developers planned to build the area into a resort location and the state government decided to use Malia for a low-cost housing program. To initiate these plans, Malia's southern road was widened and linked to the network of freeways into Honolulu.

By the late 1960s then, Malia was a rural community in transition; it was undergoing major economic shifts and its traditional autonomy and isolation were decreasing. Yet, beneath these changes, there was still strong sentiment to maintain autonomy and to preserve community control over community affairs.

The Problem

A major problem facing Malia was the lack of health services. One health facility, the Plantation Medical Center, served the area. But this had closed in 1946 when the plantation was shut down. Between 1946 and 1964 Malia's medical services were limited to two physicians who worked in the area. Then, in 1964, the Kaiser Foundation Health Plan began operating a Malia clinic. However, it did not meet the residents' needs. The clinic was open only during weekdays from 8:00 a.m. to 4:30 p.m., with no emergency service at other times. It was staffed only by one fulltime physician, a laboratory technician, and a nurse. Most significantly, the clinic limited its services to members of the Kaiser Prepaid Health Plan, which few residents could afford. In 1964 then, the medical needs of Malia's 20,000 residents were served essentially by two private physicians, a city and county ambulance station, and one dentist.

Clearly, the medical services available to Malia's 20,000 residents were inadequate. Moreover, a resident requiring emergency treatment or hospitalization would have to travel to Honolulu, a 45-minute drive away from Malia.

PHASE 1: PLANNING, APPRAISAL, AND DESIGN

Identification: A Grassroots Initiative

As early as 1946, Malia residents identified lack of health care as a major problem and initiated a grassroots campaign to obtain adequate health services. They held general community meetings, petitioned the governor, spoke to their city and state representatives, and met with state agencies. By organizing through mothers' groups, civic clubs, social clubs, welfare recipients groups, community action groups, and other community associations, they demanded that government help them obtain adequate medical services.

In response, federal, state, and city government did little. Although realizing Malia's health problem, they were strongly influenced by the American Medical Association, which opposed publicly subsidized medicine. Moreover, since Malia was a rural area and had a small population, it had little political leverage and could not make its problems salient political issues. Finally, Malia's community groups and associations dissipated their effectiveness by failing to unite in a single organization. Thus, Malia received no government support until 1966, when it was no longer politically feasible to ignore the health needs of 20,000 people.

In 1966 the Community Action Program (CAP), a federal government program that assisted poverty-designated communities to organize and solve their problems, assigned representatives to Malia. The representatives helped unify Malia's efforts by serving as a focal point through which the entire community could articulate their health care needs. They also coordinated the residents' activities through CAP committees. Representing a good working balance of residents, the CAP committees were assigned the vital task of formulating a unified health proposal for Malia.

The CAP committees began formulating the health proposal in late 1966, and were assisted by the Honolulu Council of Social Agencies and the Kaiser Foundation Research Institute, who provided outsiders' views and professional expertise. To complement the professional input, the CAP committees also held open community meetings at which residents argued their positions and articulated their health needs. Using the meetings and the professional aid for direction, the CAP committees worked arduously through 1966, and, in early 1967, completed the health proposal. Identifying as the primary project a centralized health center with a broad range of medical services, the proposal was submitted to the federal government's Office of Economic Opportunity (OEO), which granted funds for neighborhood health centers.

The OEO, however, rejected the proposal, pointing out that it lacked implementation plans, and that it had been criticized by the Honolulu County Medical Society because the health center's scope of services was too broad and its cost unjustified. The Society also objected to medical facilities and services financed with public funds. Kaiser Foundation Research Institute developed a second proposal and submitted it to OEO. It was also rejected for the same reasons.

Although the CAP initiative yielded no improvement in Malia's health services, advances had been made. Malia residents had achieved organizational cohesion. For the first time, a government agency had supported Malia's drive to improve health services; and, for the first time, a health care center had been formally identified as the primary project. On the strength of this concrete progress, Malia had made itself an extremely attractive candidate for federal government development project funds.

Surely enough, in 1968, Model Cities, a federal antipoverty program that provided "model neighborhoods" with funds to plan and operate development projects, designated Malia as a model neighborhood. At the same time, the Regional Medical Program (RMP), a federal program that gave development funds to health projects, was directed to coordinate funding with Model Cities. To receive Model Cities funds, residents would first have to organize a neighborhood planning committee, as required by Model Cities' funding provisions. The planning committee would have two purposes. First, by placing priorities on the neighborhood's development efforts, it would act as the community's policy-making body. Second, by requiring a majority of the committee to be local residents, it would guarantee resident participation in neighborhood planning.

Using the organizational structure of the old CAP committees, residents quickly organized a neighborhood committee and named it the Malia District Neighborhood Planning Committee (MDNPC). Like the grassroots organizations and the CAP committees, MDNPC was democratically organized and relied on active community participation to plan and make decisions. As a result, MDNPC meetings were well attended and characterized by animated, often heated, debates. This guaranteed that the committee's decisions - even controversial ones - were community decisions endorsed by a majority of Malia residents. MDNPC's first decision was noncontroversial. It made the improvement of health services the area's number one priority.

With the improvement of health care established as Malia's number one priority, residents organized a health task force. Composed of community leaders and residents interested in improving Malia's health services, the health task force's purpose was to formulate a comprehensive health plan for Malia and to identify specific projects to carry out the plan. Chosen as the chairman was John Hama, a resident of Malia.

As task force chairman, Hama first reviewed the studies that evaluated Malia's health needs. After examining the studies, he thought that several of them would be particularly useful in formulating a comprehensive health plan for Malia. He felt that one study - a community profile study, which had been conducted by the CAP staff in 1968 - would be important because it not only provided baseline data on the residents' poverty, but it also documented their strong traditional ties with community, neighbors, and kin. (4) He believed that another study - the Conway Report, which was a hospital feasibility study sponsored by the state Department of Accounting and General Services in 1968 - was useful because it provided an analysis in support of building a hospital on the Malia Coast. (5) Finally, he felt that a third study - the Gallimore and Howard study, a community structure analysis done in 1968 by anthropologists from the University of Hawaii - would be crucial because it specified the following medical behavior of residents: (6)

- They are almost totally crisis oriented.

- They defer medical attention.

- They have poor preventive health practices.

- They have poor personal hygiene practices.

- They conceal signs of illness.

- Men rely on relatives or friends for treatment.

- Women prefer home remedies and are likely to use traditional Hawaiian medications.

- Young couples are encouraged by parents to have families rapidly.

- An unempolyed head of household usually drops health insurance.

- They do not go for medical treatment - facilities are too far away, they lack transportation, and they are threatened with wage and job loss.

- They do not keep appointments.

Formulation: Some Outside Help

The Program Concept

After organizing this information, Hama and the health task force members tried to formulate the health plan. However, since the task force was composed wholly of community residents, none of whom were health professionals, Hama soon realized he needed outside professional help. He asked the state government for support. And in October 1968, John A. Burns, governor of the state of Hawaii, asked the University of Hawaii's School of Public Health to assist Hama, and it agreed. Specifically, the School of Public Health proposed to formulate a program concept of health services for Malia. The job was assigned to Dr. Roy Wilson.

In formulating the program concept, Wilson imposed three guidelines upon himself. First, because he was impressed by Malia's grassroots effort and because he advocated consumer-oriented medicine, he had to use Malia residents' participation and input in determining the major health needs of Malia. This was obtained by working closely with Hama and the health task force and by holding weekly community meetings, chaired jointly by himself and Hama.

Second, because Malia residents objected to being further scrutinized by outsiders, Wilson had to use only the existing data and studies. The task force provided Wilson with the information they had already collected and organized.

Third, since numerous health care providers, such as the state Department of Health, were interested in helping to formulate, and eventually to implement, Malia's future health services, he had to incorporate their suggestions and recommendations in the program concept. This was accomplished by holding combined working sessions, during which each group took primary responsibility for devising the section of the concept that matched their expertise. For example, the Malia CAP Committees contributed extensively in determining community health needs, the state Department of Health worked on extending and coordinating state services, the Honolulu County Medical Society helped to develop physician requirements, the Regional Medical Program (RMP) documented available federal funding, and the University of Hawaii School of Medicine specified desirable medical services.

In essence, then, Wilson and Hama coordinated work on the program concept, but actual formulation was the combined effort of numerous groups and agencies. Completed in March 1969, the program concept was called "Health Services for Malia: A Program Concept" (hereafter referred to as "Program Concept").

Wilson and Hama organized the Program Concept into four parts. Part one provided the health profile and health needs of Malia residents, along with general guidelines for all health projects. Part two described specific projects to cope with the health needs of residents. Part three recommended an activity sequence for implementing the projects. And part four identified the potential funding sources for the projects. The following paragraphs describe the Program Concept in more detail.

In part one, Hama and Wilson analyzed health needs within Malia's social, economic, and cultural environment, and concluded that, in order to succeed, the health program required community support. This meant that projects specified in the Program Concept would have to be staffed by residents and led by an organization clearly identified as a community entity. Additionally, because of resident discomfort with impersonal health environments, any health project would have to provide a traditional, personalized setting. This would both preserve the feeling of community and build the trust of residents. Finally, they reasoned that the community would need outside professional help; therefore it was vital to establish close working relationships with all health agencies and health professionals. Based on this analysis, Hama and Wilson recommended that:

- A community organization develop policies and provide guidelines for all health services.

- The community organization fully coordinate its efforts and cooperate with all professional health care providers.

- All ancillary health activities - social, welfare, and referral - be integrated into a single system.

- Services be provided rapidly and maintain the client's personal dignity.

- Community resources and manpower be trained, developed, and used whenever possible.

These recommendations, they stated, should be guiding principles for Malia's entire health program. They emphasized, in particular, the recommendation to develop a local community organization to set health policy, and the recommendation to use and train indigenous manpower.

In parts two and three, Wilson and Hama proposed an overall health program consisting of three component projects. Reflecting Malia's urgent need for a general health facility, the first component would be a comprehensive health center. In addition to providing 24-hour emergency service, the center would offer clinic services, special diagnosis, medical treatment, and education and training programs.

The second component would be home care, consisting of home health care and outreach workers. To be organized soon after the health center began operations, this component would emphasize preventive medicine, hygiene in the home, and patient rehabilitation at home. This would provide residents with health care in the safety of their own homes, and, at the same time, build the residents' trust in professional medical treatment. To implement home care, outreach aides - trained medical and social para-professionals - would be hired to work in the community, teaching residents proper health care, and informing them of the health center's services. The third component would be a hospital; this, however, was to be a future development. In parts two and three, then, Hama and Wilson identified a comprehensive health center as the immediate project.

In part four of the Program Concept, Hama and Wilson identified the several potential funding sources, including:

1. Model Cities. This federal government antipoverty program had already designated Malia a model neighborhood. To receive Model Cities funds, the health task force would have to submit a specific project proposal to the Malia District Neighborhood Planning Committee (MDNPC). MDNPC would then decide whether the project fit into the neighborhood's development priorities. If it did, MDNPC

would select it for funding and send the proposal to the City Council of Honolulu for approval (see Fig. 6.1).

2. Regional Medical Program (RMP). RMP, a federal agency whose objective was to upgrade medical services, coordinated health project funding with Model Cities. To receive RMP funds, a nonprofit corporation would have to submit a specific project proposal to the Hawaii Regional Advisory Group (RAG), which was RMP's decision-making body. RAG would decide whether or not to finance the project (see Fig. 6.2).

3. Department of Health, Education, and Welfare (HEW). Empowered by section 314(e) of the Public Health Service Act, HEW granted funds for developing and operating neighborhood health centers and family health centers (these funds hereafter referred to as HEW-HC). To receive HEW-HC funds, the task force would have to submit a detailed project proposal to HEW's regional office in San Francisco. The regional office would then ask the state Comprehensive Health Planning (CHP) Advisory Council to comment on the proposal. The CHP Advisory Council was responsible for the state's overall health planning and issued certificates-of-need to health facilities, if the facilities met community needs. After receiving CHP comment, the HEW regional office would internally review the proposal and give it a priority (see Fig. 6.2).

In essence, the Program Concept was an overall health master plan. It recommended general guidelines, identified health projects, established a schedule for implementing the projects, and suggested ways to fund the projects. It did not, however, detail specific project plans.

The Malia District Comprehensive Health and Hospital Board, Inc.

After reviewing the Program Concept, the health task force members decided to incorporate as a nonprofit health corporation. By incorporating, they could negotiate as a legal entity and qualify to receive federal health funds. Incorporation would also give them status as a serious, permanent group, and thus give them credibility as Malia's formally sanctioned health organization. This would add immensely to their political clout. In April 1969, they incorporated as the Malia District Comprehensive Health and Hospital Board, Inc. (hereafter referred to as the Board). The Board's purpose was "to improve the health of all citizens of the Malia District." (7)

Organized as a residents' participatory body, the Board was composed wholly of residents; many were community leaders, but none were health professionals or experienced in establishing health organizations. The Board was structured informally, had few procedural rules, and depended on resident input. For example, any resident who attended Board meetings was an official Board member and could vote on Board issues. Board members felt strongly that formal procedures could be worked out as the need arose, and that informality was the way to conduct business in Malia.

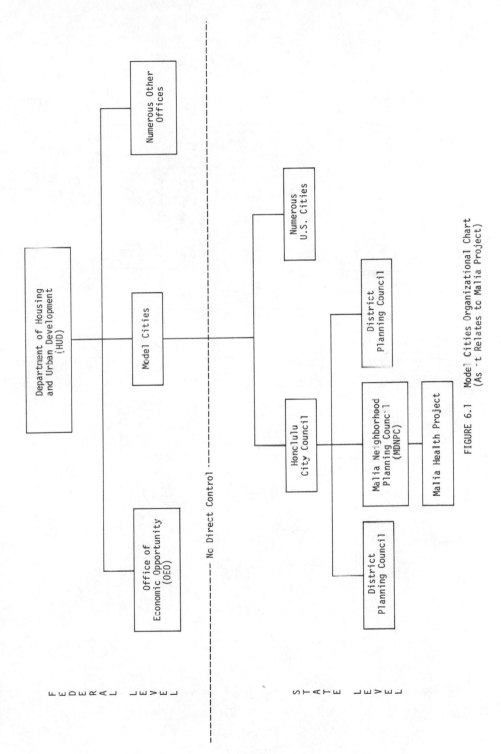

FIGURE 6.1   Model Cities Organizational Chart
(As it Relates to Malia Project)

187

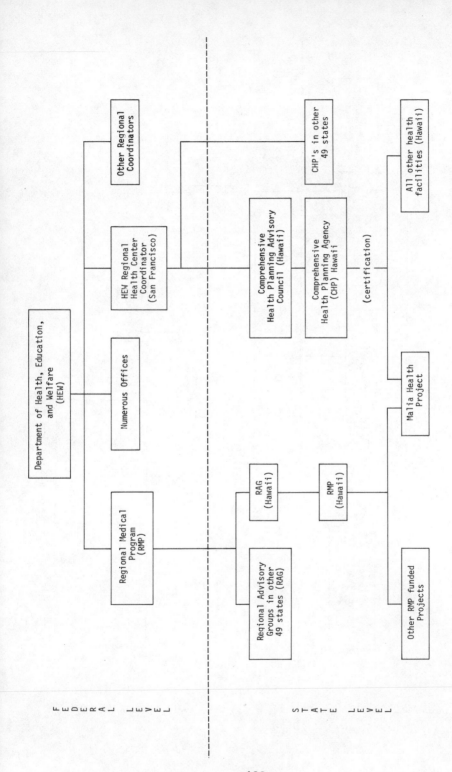

FIGURE 6.2 Regional Medical Program and Health Education and Welfare Organizational Chart
(As It Relates to Malia Project)

188

Informal Feasibility Discussions

Hama was chosen Board president, and he decided to discuss the Program Concept's overall feasibility with various health agencies. During April and May 1969, Hama and the Board held discussions with RMP, Honolulu County Medical Society, state Department of Health, and the Office of Economic Opportunity (OEO).

Briefly summarized, the discussions were as follows:

1. RMP told Hama and the Board that they totally supported the Program Concept, thought it was feasible, and would provide the technical assistance needed to complete detailed project proposals. RMP also told Hama that they could not grant money for health center construction, but could fund center operations.

2. The Honolulu County Medical Society reacted negatively to the Program Concept. They told Hama that there were too many federal agencies involved, none that could totally fund the concept; moreover, the comprehensive health center's proposed services were too complex and discouraged doctors from practicing in the area.

3. The State Department of Health pointed out to Hama and the Board that the Program Concept was not a project implementation plan. To implement the concept, Hama would first have to draw up detailed project plans.

4. The OEO similarly told Hama that detailed project plans were needed.

5. Several private health providers, Kaiser Foundation Health Plan, St. Francis Hospital, and Straub Clinic, also discussed the Program Concept with Hama. Basically, they thought the Program Concept was feasible, but only if it was implemented incrementally, and in coordination with private interests.

Initial Funding

Based on these discussions, which served as preliminary and informal feasibility studies, Hama and the Board decided the Program Concept was sound, but to implement it they would have to design detailed project plans. To do this, they needed money to hire outside experts. Hama again asked state government for help and Dr. Wayne Ott of the University of Hawaii volunteered.

Meeting with Hama and the Board, Ott explained that the best way to get project design funds was to write a federal grant proposal based on the Program Concept, and to submit it to both HEW and Model Cities. The Board agreed on this course of action and, over the next two months, Hama and Ott completed the proposal. In it they requested money to hire a planning staff, including the project director. Because Hama insisted on community input, they also stipulated that the planning staff and project director would work closely with the Board to develop detailed plans for the construction and operation of a comprehensive health center. Finally, anticipating questions about the proposal's financial management, Hama and Ott named the respected and well-known Research Corporation of the University of Hawaii to administer the grant.

The Board discussed the proposal, approved it, and submitted it to HEW for funding review. For four months, Hama and the Board waited in great anticipation but received no answer. Unable to restrain themselves, they wrote to their federal congressional representatives in Washington, D.C., requesting them to inquire about the proposal's status. Their representatives wrote back, saying that they would find out whether or not the Department of Health, Education, and Welfare (HEW) intended to fund the proposal. Questioning HEW, the representatives discovered that the regional office in San Francisco had ranked the proposal number one for funding; however, HEW could not grant money for planning new health centers because it had already overcommitted the current year's budget. Moreover, the entire HEW health center program was being reorganized and new guidelines were being prepared for health center proposals. Thus the representatives were told, until current commitments were honored and until the reorganization was completed, HEW would not fund the proposal.

Fortunately, during the four-month wait for HEW's decision, Hama and the Board had also submitted the grant proposal to the Malia District Neighborhood Planning Committee (MDNPC), as the first step to receiving Model Cities funds. In January 1970, the MDNPC noted that health care was Malia's top priority; and they therefore recommended that the Honolulu City Council approve the proposal. In February 1970, about a month after HEW's rejection, the City Council approved the proposal. Hama and the Board were jubilant. This was the first time government had granted Malia money for a health project.

The City Council had approved $84,000 to pay for a project director, his staff, consultants' fees, travel, office equipment and supplies, and an office. They had also approved a one-year planning period, June 1970 to June 1971, during which the Board and planning staff would:

1. Develop precise project plans for implementing a Malia Coast Comprehensive Health Center (hereafter referred to as Center),

2. Try to fund the plans through all possible sources - federal, state, city, and private, and

3. Complete a proposal for a Department of Health, Education and Welfare-Health Center (HEW-HC) grant.

Selecting a Project Director

To accomplish these objectives and the fundamental objective of completing the Malia Coast Comprehensive Health Center, Hama and the Board knew they would have to hire a versatile and exceptional project director. They reasoned that the project director would have considerable responsibilities. First, he would be responsible for planning both the construction and the operation of the Center; this meant he would have to coordinate the overall design. Second, if the design were funded, the project director would be responsible for managing the project; this meant he would have to provide day-to-day project administration - negotiating, supervising, scheduling, and monitoring. Third, assuming all objectives were accomplished, the project director would be responsible for implementing the initial delivery of health services. This meant that, at least until the transition to normal administration, he would have to mediate between medical and administrative employees, file health claims, organize medical services, implement the health records and financial operations, and set policy. Hama and the Board reasoned that because of these many potential roles, the project director would have to be someone experienced in both project management and health administration.

Hama and the Board began to screen applicants. Since Model Cities grants gave preference to local residents, they first tried to recruit a Malia resident, but could find no one qualified. Then they began screening outside applicants. It took four months before they hired David Wayne. Considered the most versatile and competent candidate, Wayne was an architect with a master's degree in Public Health. Although he had little experience as a project manager, he had both health and construction design expertise; moreover, he would be helped by the assistant director, who was a former aerospace project manager. The only drawback was that Wayne was not a resident and would not fully understand Malia's problems. The Board was not greatly concerned, however, since it set policy and would have considerable power over all project activities.

Having selected Wayne, Hama and the Board turned to two pressing business items - increasing the Board's credibility within the community and enhancing its image of professionalism. Since the Board's image would be enhanced by a more formal structure, Board membership was fixed at 12. Since its credibility would be increased by overt community participation, it was decided to hold a general community election for the 12 seats. The election would also give Board members community sanction. The Board publicized the forthcoming election by holding meetings, distributing leaflets, passing on information about the Center, and asking residents to vote. In September 1970 the community elected 12 Board members - many of them the original members. Like the original Board, the new Board was composed of community leaders, none of whom were health professionals.

The newly elected Board chose as president, Edward Kahele, a construction worker actively involved in civic affairs. Kahele would work closely with Wayne to design and implement the Center.

Design: A Complex Process

Some Ancillary Support Activities

As project director, Wayne's first action was to meet with Kahele and the Board to discuss preliminary planning criteria. From these initial meetings Wayne learned that, because the Malia Comprehensive Health Center's purpose was to serve residents and complement their needs, he would have to work closely with residents and community organizations. He also decided that it was absolutely essential to cooperate fully with the Board and to incorporate it totally in the planning process. This was partly because the grant had stipulated that he would work closely with the Board and partly because Wayne wanted to minimize the tension that was inherent between himself as the manager and the Board as the policy maker.

Following these initial meetings, Wayne organized his work schedule and set the planning staff's activities. Then, in October 1970, he met with the Board to discuss the planning strategy. At this meeting he explained that an immediate problem was the June 1971 deadline. The project was already four months behind schedule because the Board had taken so long to select him; and he anticipated further delays in the planning process. Wayne therefore recommended that the Board request a six-month funding extension. The Board concurred and asked Model Cities to extend the planning period to December 31, 1971. Model Cities agreed, allocating the project an additional $40,000.

With the extension approved, Wayne immediately initiated project activation tasks. Although not part of the design, these tasks would proceed simultaneously with it. This overlapping schedule would save time and would enable the project to begin immediately upon approval.

First, because the Board would have to be knowledgeable about formal health administration, Wayne initiated an informal training program to familiarize Board members with the types of health care delivery, the variety of health resources, and the federal guidelines for funding. As an integral part of the program, the Board took one educational and fact-finding trip to learn how other federally funded health centers throughout the United States organized services, set policy, and dealt with center administrators. They discovered that, theoretically, all health centers were intended to be financially self-supporting, but no center had yet achieved this goal. They were thus convinced that the Malia Center would need continuing outside support and they would have to plan for this.

Wayne then initiated a second activity. In October 1970, having concluded that the project would eventually receive federal construction funds, he decided to select and acquire a site for the Center. In selecting the site, he worked closely with Kahele and a special site-selection committee. Together, they chose five sites and evaluated them with regard to: 1) zoning laws, 2) central location in Malia, 3) room for expansion, 4) ease of installing electricity and water, 5) cost, and 6) ease of acquisition. After deliberating, the committee agreed unanimously on a parcel of state-owned land at Pahuna Point. The Pahuna Point site had 14.3 acres of land, was centrally located in Malia, already had water and electricity, and was near the site of a temporary health clinic built in 1969. In addition, the acquisition cost would be negligible since state law stipulated that public facilities - such as the proposed health center - had principal use rights on state-owned land.

In January 1971, before they knew whether Center construction would be approved, Wayne and Kahele began acquiring the Pahuna site. The land belonged to the Hawaiian Homes Commission (HHC) - a special state agency that provided homesteads for native Hawaiians. The Board could acquire Pahuna for one dollar if HHC agreed to exchange it for another parcel of state-owned land. To facilitate such an exchange, Wayne and Kahele met with the Executive Committee of the Hawaiian Homestead Association, which represented homesteaders. The Executive Committee was reluctant to exchange Pahuna for another site because it was an ideal housing location. The committee said, however, that it merely represented homesteaders; HHC actually controlled the land.

Over the next few months, while they were designing the Malia Comprehensive Health Center, Wayne and Kahele met with HHC. They also met with the State Department of Land and Natural Resources (DLNR), which would be responsible for finding comparably valued exchange land. Finally, in May 1971 HHC agreed to negotiate the exchange. Beginning the negotiations, DLNR appraised Pahuna. But HHC rejected the appraisal, feeling the land value would soon rise dramatically and DLNR had not included this in their appraisal. Negotiations dragged on. Then in September 1971, Wayne and Kahele decided they could wait no longer and they requested a right of entry so that they could analyze the land for construction. HHC granted entry rights and agreed to continue negotiating; but, until an exchange was agreed to, it would lease - not give up rights to - Pahuna Point.

Wayne began a third activity. Because he wanted health services to start before the Center formally opened, he began developing an outreach program as envisioned in the Program Concept. To begin the program, Wayne and the Board recruited residents, who would become outreach workers, employed by the Center to perform health and social services within Malia. Arrangements were made with Honolulu Community College to train the recruited residents.

A final support activity that Wayne initiated was a program to train residents to be aides and assistant workers at the Center. This was to be part of the ongoing training and educational program to develop local community manpower. The Board sponsored the training of two laboratory assistants; other residents would be trained later.

Organizing the Design

In January 1971 while these support activities were proceeding, Wayne and Kahele organized a voluntary consulting group, the Technical Advisory Committee. Composed of representatives from public and private health care providers, such as the state Department of Health, Regional Medical Program (RMP), Hawaii Medical Service Association, and Kaiser Foundation Health Plan, the Technical Advisory Committee was created to give the Board technical advice on the design. Theoretically, the committee was also to have considerable input in all policy decisions. Kahele and the Board, however, did not get along well with the committee; they felt it was too concerned with technical professional aspects of the Center and did not adequately consider community needs. Therefore, the Board largely ignored its policy recommendations. The Board did, however, use the committee for its technical expertise. In February 1971, the Board requested the committee to revise the Program Concept, and it consented.

While the Program Concept was being revised, Wayne and Kahele contracted an architectural firm to prepare preliminary Center blueprints and construction specifications. They felt that these documents would coordinate the overall design by matching proposed medical services with a physical model of the Center. Wayne and Kehele hired the Honolulu firm of Noda and Sons.

In April 1971, the Technical Advisory Committee completed their revisions of the Program Concept. They modified very little, but, in part one, specified that the Board was the resident organization in charge of Center policy. Then, in May 1971, Noda and Sons completed the architectural documents. In them, they sketched a physical model of the Center, specified space requirements, designed the preliminary floor plan, and provided a phased construction budget.

Wayne and the Board reviewed the documents and realized that construction would take longer than anticipated. Wayne and Kahele therefore decided to begin delivering health services as soon as possible, in a temporary location. After the Center was built, they would transfer operations to the permanent site. To expedite this plan, Wayne made the following two decisions:

1. He divided the design into two phases: construction design and Center operations design. This would allow both design phases to proceed simultaneously, and would also prevent delays in either phase from hindering the other.

2. He decided to contract out the final construction design so that he could concentrate on designing Center operations.

An Informal Feasibility Study

Before proceeding with this strategy, Wayne and Kahele decided to check informally the feasibility of the architectural documents and the revised Program Concept. They asked the Honolulu County Medical Society to conduct a review, confident that the review would validate the Center and provide it with a professional endorsement. However, after evaluating the architectural documents, the Society commented that the Center was economically unfeasible; its physical layout was unrealistically large and complex. The Center, they felt, should initially be built to provide basic services, adding facilities for specialities and sophisticated services only when justified by client demand.

Turning to the Program Concept, the Society identified a potentially critical problem. They pointed out that part one of the Program Concept never made explicit the relationship between the Board and the health center. Furthermore, it was impossible to determine any functional relationship between the Board and the Center, since the Board conducted all business informally, without due process. In such an environment, the Society emphasized, there was too much uncertainty; the Board could make medical decisions and become directly entangled in the Center's day-to-day management. This would be intolerable.

Kahele and the Board met with Wayne to discuss the Society's review. In discussing the criticism of the architectural layout, the Board and Kahele argued that since Malia had no hospital, the Center would be a surrogate hospital, and should therefore be built to house a complete range of health services. Moreover, Malia deserved a first-class public facility with room for specialists and sophisticated services. They also pointed out that the Society, like many other professionals they dealt with, was insensitive to community needs. They were adamant that Wayne use the architect's report. Wayne pointed out - as the Society had - that the envisioned Center would be extremely costly, and providing specialist services would be financially unviable. Wayne, however, could not press this issue since the Board felt so strongly. Instead, he agreed to use the architect's report - on a funding-available basis.

In discussing the Society's review of the Program Concept, Kahele and the Board agreed to work out policies and procedures that specified the Board would make no medical decisions. They stressed, however, that the decision to develop procedures would not be dictated to them by outside professionals and that they would work on these matters as they felt the need.

Problems and Solutions

In June 1971, Wayne, although apprehensive about the Board's decision, continued with the design. He faced two immediate problems - time and money. On the one hand, Wayne knew that the December 1971 planning deadline was unrealistic; designing the Center's operations would take until March 1972. On the other hand, he knew that he needed more money, both to complete the construction design and to guarantee that health operations could be started. To cope with the time and money problems, he wrote three grant proposals. He submitted one to the Regional Medical Program (RMP). If funded, this proposal would help pay the cost for both designing Center operations and implementing them. He submitted a second proposal to Model Cities. This proposal requested a six-month planning extension, money to prepare the Pahuna site for construction, and money to hire an architect. Wayne submitted a third proposal, this one to HEW requesting Department of Health, Education and Welfare-Health Center (HEW-HC) funds. He considered this proposal the most important because, if funded, it would pay for most of the first year operating costs.

In August 1971, the HEW regional office in San Francisco returned the HEW proposal, telling Wayne that they needed detailed plans of the Center's operations. They further advised Wayne to wait before submitting these plans because they were preparing new HEW-HC guidelines. If he waited, they would help him write a new proposal.

Wayne waited for a reply on the other two proposals. While waiting, he worked with Kahele and other Board members to seek private funds. The Board contacted trusts and foundations requesting financial aid, but were unsuccessful. Nonetheless, proceeding on the assumption that the proposals would eventually be funded, they continued all design activities. They continued designing Center operations, and they selected Noda and Sons to draft the final construction design, including specifications and blueprints. Noda and Sons were notified that they could start as soon as the Board received funds.

By late summer 1971, however, no agency had communicated with the Board. Thus, in August, Wayne and Kahele decided to visit the agencies in person. They first traveled to HEW's regional office in San Francisco and met with program advisor Irene Reed. They told Reed they were designing the Center but would need firm financial commitments to finish. In turn, Reed informed them that HEW's new guidelines for health centers were almost complete. Upon their completion she would personally visit Malia and help prepare an appropriate HEW-HC proposal. Wayne and Kahele thanked her and set February 1972 as the tentative date for her visit. Next, Wayne and Kahele met with Model Cities officials. They received good news - Model Cities had decided to fund their proposal. The Board would be given $52,000 for a six-month planning extension and $144,000 for architectural fees and site preparation. Although delighted with Model Cities funds, they knew that they needed RMP funds both to finish designing the health center operations, and to begin delivering health services.

In the meantime, the RMP proposal had passed preliminary screening and had been sent to the local decision-making body, the Regional Advisory Group (RAG). RAG was rigorously appraising the project, and was bothered - as the Honolulu Medical Society had been - about 1) the expense of the Center's specialist services, 2) the lay board that set Center policy, and 3) the lack of Board policies and procedures. They reached an impasse. Although recognizing the pressing need for the Malia Coast Comprehensive Health Center, RAG thought it was financially and administratively unviable.

In September 1971, RAG announced a final meeting to decide on the proposal. A national RMP representative was sent to Hawaii to evaluate the situation and offer an opinion. Before the final meeting, the national representative visited Malia and met with the Board. He was impressed by Board efforts, particularly their attempt to actively involve the community. Thus, during the final review meeting, he vigorously endorsed the project, telling RAG that the proposed Center complemented the new policy emphasizing support for medically underserved areas. Because of this strong endorsement, RAG approved the proposal. In October, RMP awarded the Board a first year allotment of $150,000. (There were, of course, conditions that the Board had to agree to before receiving the money; they will be discussed in the section on negotiation.) (8)

Completing the Design

Wayne notified Noda and Sons to start working on construction specifications and blueprints. Since they were thoroughly familiar with the Center's working requirements, they worked rapidly and finished in December 1971. The specifications and blueprints, which served as the final construction design, specified three construction phases.

1. Phase 1-the emergency facility,

2. Phase 2-the primary care facility, and

3. Phase 3-the dental and vision care facility.

Noda and Sons had carefully designed the Center. When the three phases were finished, the Center would consist of a cluster of buildings in a campus arrangement. This design would permit the emergency facility to begin operating while the others were being built.

Final design of Center operations took considerably longer, and, in fact, was not completed until after the Center began operating. Three factors contributed to the delay. First, Center operations were extremely complex; the Board had to hire outside consultants, review their work, and reconsult them if the work was unacceptable. Second, the Board and Center administrators had to fulfill a growing number of funding requirements from all agencies (these requirements will be discussed in the next section). Finally, and most significantly, the Board had previously decided to wait on developing Board policies and procedures. This meant that the rights, powers, and duties of the Board, in relationship to the Center, were undefined. Clearly, the Board could set policy. But it was uncertain whether the Board could also administer the Center. Until the Board developed policies and procedures that defined their relationship to the Center's administration, the management system for health operations could not be designed.

Wayne recognized the latter problem as one that RAG and the Honolulu Medical Society had previously pointed out, and he urged the Board to develop policies, establish procedures, and clearly delineate their relationship to the Center. But the Board reiterated that their informality was appropriate and they would develop policies and procedures as needed. They emphasized, moreover, that this was completely a Board matter.

Over the next few months, Wayne, Kahele, and the Board completed what they could of the design. By February 1972, the design of Center operations was organized as follows: (9)

A. Goals and Objectives. The principal objective of the project was to make adequate health care available to all residents in a setting that enhanced their dignity. The most important goals of the project included:

    1. Implementing a prepaid health insurance plan.

    2. Enrolling 4,000 residents in the plan by the first year.

    3. Providing 24-hour emergency care for the Malia district.

    4. Guaranteeing direct and indirect consumer participation in Center decisions and policy.

    5. Providing job opportunities and training for Malia residents.

    6. Developing a team concept for a family-oriented outreach program.

    7. Coordinating services with other health care providers and health agencies in Malia.

B. Operating Policies. The Center's formal operating policies were not drawn up for two more years. Wayne and the planning staff did, however, draft rough guidelines, which temporarily substituted for operating policy. These were divided into the following three sections:

    1. Personnel. This section included employee policy such as salaries, benefits, and working hours, but it lacked position descriptions, qualifications, authority, and appeal procedures.

    2. Finances. This section specified insurance needs, such as malpractice and liability; and it also identified the primary donors.

3. Operations. Although giving a general overview of Center operations, including emergency operations, diagnostic services, specialties services, transportation requirements, financial operations, and maintenance operations, this section did not comprehensively detail how the operations would actually be administered and who had authority to make final decisions (see Fig. 6.3 for proposed operational structure).

C. Activation Activities. Based on RMP funding requirements, the following activities had to be completed before operations could begin:

1. Obtain firm financial commitments, especially from HEW-HC, to build and operate the Center.

2. Advertise, screen, interview, and select core staff.

3. Contract a consulting firm to design a system for patient records, internal communication, and fiscal management.

4. Develop policies and a management system for the Center. Since the system had to be consistent with HEW guidelines, a consulting firm would have to be contracted to complete this system. Their work would also include an administrative procedures manual for Center operations.

5. Prepare and implement training programs for Center employees.

6. Contract a medical group for all medical services, including physicians to work at the Center, and a medical procedures manual to set medical policy.

7. Locate a temporary facility to serve as the Center.

8. Initiate all health operations by July 1972.

Although lacking detailed administrative and implementation plans, the design provided a fairly complete description of Center operations and provided Wayne, Kahele, and the Board with a rigorous schedule of activation tasks. The immediate tasks were to submit a proposal to the Malia District Neighborhood Planning Committee (MDNPC) for Model Cities' construction funds and to submit a proposal to HEW for first year operating funds.

In January 1972, Wayne and Kahele submitted a proposal to the MDNPC, requesting that the final construction design's estimated budget be funded. To review the proposal, MDNPC held a public meeting. At this meeting, the Board was criticized by the Hawaiian Homestead Association for using homestead land and was criticized for "trying to make a name for itself." But the MDNPC finally approved the proposal and sent it to the City Council for a decision.

The HEW-HC proposal was completed in February 1972 when, as promised, Irene Reed visited Malia. In assisting Wayne, Kahele, and the Board to prepare the proposal, she explained the new guidelines and pointed out the information that was expected. She also recommended that the Board meet with the state Comprehensive Health Planning Agency (CHP) because HEW

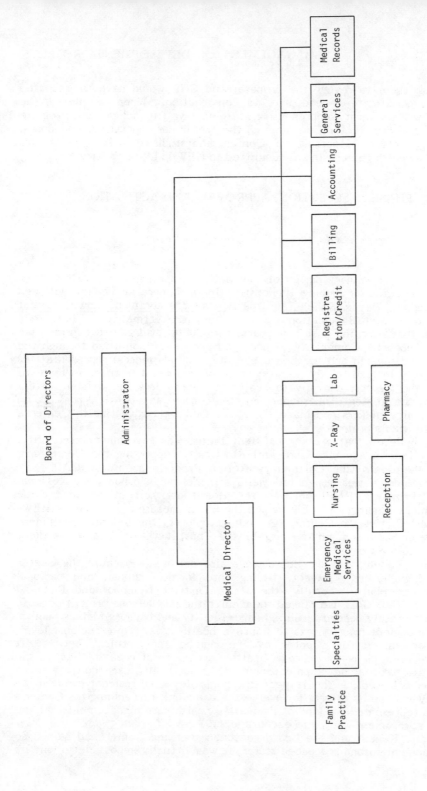

FIGURE 6.3   Malia Comprehensive Health Center Proposed Organizational Structure

would ask them to review the proposal and CHP would have to issue the Center a certificate-of-need prior to construction. When completed, the proposal was the most comprehensive statement yet; it included the Program Concept, the architectural documents, the preliminary operating procedures, the design, letters supporting the Center, and studies testifying to Malia's need for a health center. It was submitted to HEW in late February.

PHASE 2: SELECTION, APPROVAL, AND ACTIVATION

Selection: A Foregone Conclusion

Although preliminary design of the Malia Comprehensive Health Center had been selected for funding, its construction and operation had not yet been decided upon. Wayne, Kahele, and the Board were confident, however, that the Center's overall selection would be a mere formality. First, they reasoned that over the past few years, the Center had gained considerable political support. Community support had grown and solidified through the grassroots campaign and the Board election; Malia's federal representatives had actively lobbied for the Center; state officials had testified in favor of building the Center; and private health care providers had written letters endorsing the Center. This support exerted considerable political pressure on federal policy makers and made the Malia Comprehensive Health Center a politically viable project.

They believed that another political factor was government credibility. So many federal agencies were enthusiastically supporting the Center and helping the Board (the Community Action Program sponsored CAP committees; Model Cities designated Malia a model neighborhood; the Regional Medical Program (RMP) notified the Board of their intent to provide development funding; and HEW helped the Board prepare a proposal for HEW-HC funds) that if the Center were not completed, the federal government would be embarrassed and lose credibility. Thus, it was politically expedient to complete the Center.

Wayne, Kahele, and the Board were also optimistic because the Center was a high priority project, fitting into local, regional, and national development plans. Locally, the Malia District Neighborhood Planning Committee (MDNPC) had ranked the Center the number one project because Malia desperately needed a public health facility and because Malia's number one development priority was to improve health care. On a regional level, HEW had ranked the Center as the number one project because it complemented plans to improve health care in rural areas. Finally, the Center fit national development plans to make health care delivery more consumer-oriented. In this respect, the nonprofessional resident composition of the Board and its efforts to involve the community in deciding the Center's services represented the kind of innovative health care management that the federal government wanted to encourage. (10)

Finally, Kahele and the Board reasoned that the Center had gained so much momentum and proceeded so far, it was virtually impossible to halt its implementation. Already, proposals totaling $439,000 had been approved to plan the Center, design its operations, and prepare its site for construction. The completion of these activities had marked the passing of a halfway point and made it counterproductive to halt activities. Furthermore, once the initial design selections had been made, it was presumed that federal agencies would build and operate the Center. This implicitly committed funding agencies to complete the Center.

In sum, the Board was convinced that the Center had become so urgent - politically and developmentally, and had gained such momentum - it was virtually assured of selection, despite reservations about its feasibility.

In March 1972, after the state Comprehensive Health Planning Agency (CHP) endorsed the Center and issued it a certificate-of-need, HEW approved HEW-HC funds. These funds would be released in June 1972. In July 1972, Model Cities announced the Center's selection for $759,000 of construction funds, which would finance all construction for the first phase - the emergency unit. Added to the Regional Medical Program (RMP) selection in October 1971, these two selections meant that the Malia Comprehensive Health Center was close to becoming a reality.

Negotiation and Approval: Some Unanswered Questions

Despite its selection of the Center, Model Cities, RMP, and HEW were still concerned about its practicability. No formal feasibility study had been conducted; in its absence, the Board had solicited comments from professional health agencies. Generally, the health agencies had expressed doubts about the Center's financial and administrative viability. Specifically, they had questioned the competence of the Board and had voiced concern about the Board's lack of policies and procedures. Model Cities, RMP, and HEW now wanted assurance that the Board would deal with these problems.

To receive this assurance, Model Cities insisted on several conditions. (11) First, they stipulated that a staff member from the City Demonstration Agency (CDA) monitor project activities and act as the liaison between Model Cities and the Board. CDA was the city agency that administered and monitored Honolulu's Model Cities' grants. Second, Model Cities stipulated that the Research Corporation of the University of Hawaii (RCUH) monitor the project's management and finances. Since RCUH was already doing this, the Board readily agreed to the condition. Third, Model Cities required the Board to undergo an annual external review. This review would help the Board improve the project and inform them of any deficiencies. Finally, since Model Cities stressed neighborhood planning and participation, the Board had to report regularly to the MDNPC and attend open public meetings to discuss Center activities and progress. The Board also had to give preference in hiring to qualified residents - a condition to which the Board enthusiastically adhered. The Board did not negotiate any of these conditions; they simply accepted them as requirements for receiving Model Cities' funds.

RMP had selected the Center for funding in October 1971, after the Regional Advisory Group (RAG) had approved it with reservations. Reflect-

ing RAG's concern, RMP issued the following burdensome funding requirements: (12)

1. Review. RMP made it clear that the health center could be funded
   for a maximum of three years, but each year the Center would be
   strictly reviewed before new funds were approved. The Planning,
   Implementation and Evaluation Committee (PIE), which was RMP's
   onsite evaluator, would conduct the reviews.

2. Liaison. A professional RMP staff member would be the Board's
   liaison with RMP; the Board would have to cooperate fully with him.

3. Reporting. The Board had to provide monthly forecasts of expenditures and also submit monthly progress reports. The forecasts and
   progress reports would be evaluated by the RMP staff and then sent to
   RAG. The RMP liaison would also discuss the evaluation with the
   Board.

4. Expenditures. The Board had to consult with and receive RMP's
   approval before hiring consultants, traveling out of state, purchasing
   equipment over $100, and hiring employees with a salary over $10,000.

5. Monitoring. The Board had to cooperate fully with RMP's monitoring
   body, the Planning, Implementation, and Evaluation Committee (PIE).
   PIE would conduct site evaluations and send the results to RAG.

Because these conditions were required for RMP funding, the Board agreed to
comply. In determining their first year allotment, however, they negotiated
for a sum of $119,625, which was considerably less than the $158,000 they
initially requested.

In June 1972, HEW similarly insisted on certain conditions before
approving funds for the Center. They stipulated three routine conditions.
First, the Board had to cooperate fully with HEW liaison personnel, who would
occasionally monitor the project and make recommendations. Second, the
Board would have to undergo an annual Comprehensive Health Planning
Agency (CHP) review. In this process, the CHP Review Committee would
evaluate project progress and then report to the CHP Advisory Council. The
Council would then endorse or reject the Center and send their decision to
HEW. Third, and most important, the Board had to develop a prepaid health
plan, enrolling as many residents in it as possible. Because the development
of a prepaid health plan demonstrated fiscal responsibility, the Board had to
fulfill this stipulation promptly.

Since HEW was greatly concerned about the Board's administrative
competence, it also stipulated special conditions. In the funding agreement,
HEW stated that the Board had to:

Submit by February 1, 1973, a Board of Directors Procedure and Policy
Manual which delineates role and duties of Board members, officers
and functions of standing committees, including methods of operation
of each committee if such functions effect health center activities and
services. (13)

HEW further required the Board to agree to fulfill eight special conditions of administration.   These eight conditions were best summed up by the following two statements:

Submit by February 1, 1973, an Administrative/Personnel Policy and Procedure Manual governing operations of the health center, including detailed job description of duties, functions, lines of authority and responsibility, qualifications and salary ranges of each salaried position within the center.

Submit by February 1, 1973: Evidence of mechanisms for evaluation of personnel during probationary and permanent status; and reassessment of personnel allocations for most effective, efficient program operation; and evidence that salary level is commensurate with duties, qualifications and positions elsewhere on Oahu. (14)

Again, the Board did not negotiate these conditions, but simply agreed to them.   They did, however, negotiate for the first year allotment and compromised with HEW on a figure of $307,207.

Activation and Organization: Potential Problems

Activating Center Construction

Because they had been convinced that the Malia Comprehensive Health Center would be completely funded, Wayne and Kahele had decided to activate construction before receiving overall approval.   By immediately beginning visible activity, they hoped to give the Center credibility within the community.   Thus, in December 1971, prior to their completing the operations design, they invited contractors to bid on preparing the Pahuna site for construction.   Seventeen contractors submitted bids, but all were too high. So Wayne and Kahele revised their specifications and asked the contractors to submit new quotations.   After this second round, the lowest bid was accepted. The selected contractor prepared an environmental impact statement and began to grade the site.

Crucial Decisions

Then, in January 1972, with the site preparation proceeding smoothly, Wayne made a crucial decision.   He decided to resign, effective when the Center opened in its temporary location.   All along, Wayne had felt that he would only be interested in designing and activating the project. He did not want to get involved in implementing Center operations because he was unenthusiastic about administration. He, therefore, submitted his resignation to Kahele and the Board on very friendly terms.
The Board accepted Wayne's resignation, then decided to hire one person to assume his duties as project director, and to become the Center's permanent administrator when all health operations were implemented after

the first year of operation. To complement the project director's dual appointment, they also decided to hire a project team which would implement Center operations at the temporary location, then become the core staff at the permanent facility.

In February, Kahele and the Board recruited applicants through advertisements. In March, they hired the administrative project team consisting of: 1) an assistant administrator (who was the current assistant administrator), 2) an information specialist, and 3) a community health specialist. The project's medical staff, including resident outreach workers and trainees, would be hired after administrative preparations had been completed. They also hired the new project director, Ray Johnson. Johnson, a retired army officer, had considerable experience as an army hospital administrator, but he was not a Malia resident. This was to create some friction, as the Board had wanted the permanent administrator to be a resident.

An Ominous Review

After the administrative project staff was hired, Model Cities decided to conduct a review of the project. Kahele and the Board determined that this review would be particularly significant. It would be the first formal evaluation of the project and would therefore be closely scrutinized by all funding agencies. Moreover, as the first comprehensive analysis of the project, it would systematically evaluate all past and proposed activities, pointing out deficiencies, and indicating potential long-term problems. While the review would be desirable from the standpoint of remedying weaknesses, it would be undesirable if it encouraged other funding agencies to stipulate additional monitoring conditions. Since a negative evaluation would have serious implications for the Center's future, Kahele and the Board were quite anxious.

As could be predicted from the previous informal evaluations, the review focused on the administration of the project, the the Board's overall competence. In evaluating the administration, the review pointed out that certain key tasks had not yet been accomplished, particularly a formal feasibility study. As stated in the review:

> Project staff are proposing to begin construction of a center within a few months, prior to completion of all the detailed planning called for in the first-year work program. While not all such tasks need be completed before construction begins, it is recommended that, at the very least, the project complete a detailed analysis of the feasibility of at least those estimates which affect building specifications. These include the specific services proposed, staffing and equipment required for each service and space required for the staff and equipment. To confirm these estimates will require a careful determination of the need, potential use and ability to pay for the various levels of services proposed for the Center. (15)

Although basic oversights by the administration were serious problems in themselves, they were part of a larger question: Was the Board competent to administer the Center and to set its policy? The review never stated the question quite so bluntly, but it clearly implied the question by emphasizing that the Board should solicit professional advice and acquire professional members. For example, one section of the review stated:

> The development of a viable, ongoing resident health organization capable of planning and possibly administering health services on the Malia Coast should be viewed as an objective in itself. To accomplish this...agency and professional involvement should be strengthened. The Technical Advisory Council should be more closely involved in future development with more use made of the expertise of its members.... Project staff should facilitate more direct resident-professional interaction.... Members of the resident board should be exposed directly to more agency and professional views, and vice-versa. (16)

From the Board's perspective, it was not so much a question of avoiding professional input as it was a question of retaining community control of the Center.

Retaining community control had, of course, been a long-standing objective. It had been stressed from the Center's inception by residents who felt that they understood Malia's unique environment and therefore were most competent to set Center policy. It had been emphasized as the first guiding principle in the Program Concept; and it had been underscored when the Board had been criticized by the Honolulu County Medical Society for planning too many specialized medical services, but remained firm in retaining them all. Thus, given the intense feeling about retaining community control, the Board viewed direct professional involvement as an encroachment on their autonomy.

The report recognized the Board's concern, but also noted that direct professional input was necessary, both to provide the Board with technical information about the health services, and to provide it with information on how to administer them. In analyzing this situation, the review ominously forecast, "at some time soon, the key conflicts concerning... lay or professional control must be resolved." (17)

The Board discussed the review, dismissed it as an outsider's overstatement, and decided to continue with the activation tasks that were scheduled in the design.

Completing Activation Tasks

Several crucial tasks had to be completed before the Center could be opened; but Johnson, the new project director, was still becoming oriented to his job and could not oversee the operations. Rather than wait for Johnson to "catch up," however, Kahele and the Board decided to supervise the activation tasks and let Johnson help them when he was prepared.

The first task was to work on an integrated system of billing, patient records, and internal communication. Kahele contracted a private information systems firm, Control Data Corporation, to develop alternative systems, test them, and complete a final report of the findings. From these findings, Kahele and the Board would select a system for the Center. Control

Data submitted the report in March 1972. Kahele directed the community health specialist to review the report with physicians and information specialists. From these reviews, Kahele learned that the report was deficient in integrating internal communication, so he returned the report to Control Data and made them correct the deficiency. In May 1972, Control Data provided Kahele and the Board with a supplementary report, from which a system for the Center was selected.

In June 1972, Kahele began working on management procedures for the Center. He hired a special consultant to write an administrative procedures manual for Center operations. However, the consultant could not complete the manual because the Board's role in managing the Center was uncertain. Nonetheless, he did complete a preliminary document, which Kahele approved.

By June 1972, Johnson had become sufficiently oriented to the project to provide leadership in completing the activation tasks; he particularly wanted to help select the rest of the project team. However, Kahele and the Board had no confidence in his leadership and they still viewed him as an outsider, so they asked him to complete the monitoring forms, the progress reports, and the supplemental RMP funding request. Somewhat alienated from the activities, Johnson proceeded with the paperwork and completed the second year RMP budget request. Kahele and the Board, in the meantime, directed the project's activation.

In late June, Kahele began obtaining the project medical staff. To obtain a physician, he negotiated with Family Medicine of Hawaii, a medical group, which contracted physicians to work in rural areas. Some problems were encountered in negotiations because there was so much skepticism about the Center's administration. Nonetheless, Family Medicine finally agreed to find a physician because of the urgent necessity to implement health services. For a one-year period, July 1972 to June 1973, Family Medicine agreed to provide one fulltime physician, referral for special services, and hospital referral. For the first six months, consulting services would also be provided. Family Medicine, however, could not guarantee to continue its services after the first year; and it could not develop the Center's medical procedures manual.

Following the negotiations, Family Medicine contracted David Alexander to be the fulltime physician at the Center; Kahele and the Board, with the help of other health agencies, signed agreements with two specialist physicians who would work at the Center on a fee-for-service basis. To fill out the rest of the medical project team, Kahele hired one registered nurse, two medical aides, and one outreach worker. Unlike Alexander, who had a contract with Family Medicine, these employees would become Center personnel, directly accountable to the project director. The project administrative and medical staffs were now complete; one task remained.

In July 1972, the Board decided to use a deserted laundromat for the temporary Center. Although not the most attractive building, it was centrally located in Malia, had considerable open space, and would be relatively inexpensive to renovate. Renovations were begun in August and completed in October 1972. Health services were ready to begin.

Organization: Potential and Practical Authority

Because the project was both an experiment in resident-consumer control of health services and a professional medical center, two organizational structures with different lines of authority evolved. The first was the practical structure. In this structure, which was the day-to-day reality, the Board autonomously set Center policy, exercised considerable discretionary power over the project, and even directly administered project activities. These powers were vested in Kahele, as Board president. Kahele used these powers to act as the unofficial project director, accompanying Johnson to all meetings, taking part in negotiations, and sometimes directing the project staff. In the practical structure, then, Kahele and the Board exercised total discretionary power over the project and their duties conflicted with the project director's.

Superimposed upon the practical structure was the potential structure. In this structure, the Department of Health, Education and Welfare (HEW), Model Cities, and the Regional Medical Program (RMP) had final authority over the Board, based on their power to withdraw funding if the Board did not comply with their conditions and pass their reviews. Although these federal agencies were constitutionally restricted from exercising direct control over the health project, their authority was deceptively real. The numerous funding conditions were a form of indirect control that made the Board accountable to the agencies. Furthermore, the required reviews were open-ended and could evaluate any Board action. If a Board action was evaluated unsatisfactory, the agencies could mandate new conditions. This potentially gave the agencies direct authority over the Board.

By the time the project was to be implemented, the Board and funding agencies had reached an uneasy accommodation. The Board agreed to fulfill the funding conditions, particularly developing policies that defined their power over the Center. To insure the funding agencies of satisfactory progress, the Board also agreed to report regularly to RMP and HEW liaison staff, who, in turn, would advise the Board whenever progress was unsatisfactory. Finally, the Board agreed to undergo annual review by the Comprehensive Health Planning (CHP) Review Committee and the Planning Implementation and Evaluation Committee (PIE), which was RMP's review staff. Within this monitoring system, the Board retained direct control over the project, with direct authority over the project director and all Center staff (see Fig. 6.4 for potential and practical structure). They would retain this authority as long as they made satisfactory progress.

It is significant to note that, at this point, the Board was still composed totally of lay persons, whose professional advisor - the Technical Advisory Committee - had not been consulted about Center operations. Thus, from an organizational standpoint, the Board had no direct professional input.

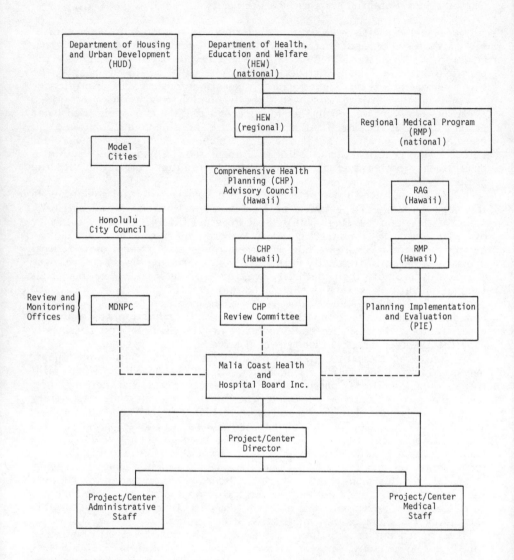

Potential Authority - - - - -

FIGURE 6.4   Potential and Practical Organizational
Structure of the Malia Project

PHASE 3: OPERATION, CONTROL, AND HANDOVER

Implementation: Critical Problems

Loose Ends but Immediate Progress

In October 1972, construction on the first phase of the Malia Comprehensive Health Center, the emergency unit, was proceeding smoothly; Johnson, Kahele, and the Board could do little to oversee the construction besides monitor progress. Thus, with the construction of the new emergency facility scheduled for completion in October 1973, they turned their full attention to the temporary facility and decided to begin health operations immediately. They acknowledged that opening the Center so soon was a calculated risk. Administration would be difficult because they had completed neither a medical procedures manual nor an administrative procedures manual. Moreover, Johnson, confused by Kahele's authority in the project, suspected that conflicts of authority would increase until the Board completed its own policies and procedures. Most significantly, they all acknowledged that the pressures of opening the Center might make it impossible to finish these tasks. But, if they were not completed, the Center would eventually fail. The lack of clearly defined procedures would create insurmountable administrative problems, and the lack of formal policies would jeopardize continued funding. By implementing the project immediately, then, the Board risked failure.

Nonetheless, the Board determined the risk was acceptable. The Center was already months behind schedule, and the community was growing increasingly skeptical. If the Board delayed the opening any longer, the Center's credibility might be damaged irreparably. Moreover, since the contract with Family Medicine had begun in July, the Board had to make available a facility for Dr. Alexander to practice in, or he would go elsewhere. Underlying these two factors was the Board's attitude that since the Center was merely a work place for doctors to treat patients, it was vital to hire doctors, but unimportant to complete formal Center policies and procedures. Family Medicine recognized the Board's underlying attitude and later commented that it had "stressed the importance of developing workable programs and systems prior to the opening.... The Board of Directors and staff, however, appeared to be interested only in securing additional physicians to work at the clinic." (18)

Despite initial apprehension, the Center was opened successfully. The delivery of health services began smoothly, in part because the medical operations functioned autonomously, much like a small private practice. Dr. Alexander, who had been hired by Family Medicine in August, served as the Center's only full-time salaried physician. He treated patients, and directly supervised the medical team - one nurse, two medical aides, and an outreach worker. Additionally, he coordinated the schedules of the two specialists who worked at the Center on a fee-for-service basis. Since the medical roles were well defined, little direction was necessary.

With medical operations requiring little administrative direction, Johnson succeeded in completing several key tasks. He organized his staff, the assistant administrator, secretary, information specialist, and community health specialist and assigned them specific tasks under his direct guidance. With the help of the information specialist, he successfully set up the system of billing and patient records. Since the system was necessary to the effective functioning of medical operations, the project team was extremely gratified to see it working efficiently after the first two weeks. Johnson and his assistant next performed a trend analysis. Indicating a steady rate of about 40 patients per day, the trend analysis allowed Johnson to set Center hours and plan for expanded operations. During the month, no administrative problems arose, and it seemed that the initial fears were groundless.

Johnson, Kahele, and the Board met in November and decided to set aside detailed planning for the second and third phases of construction. They reasoned that consolidating Center operations would demonstrate the viability of the present management and thus strengthen their construction grant proposals. Moreover, based on the smooth beginning, they believed it would take only a few months to accomplish the implementation goals specified in the design. After these were completed, they could begin construction planning in earnest. Kahele and Johnson thus specified the following new priority of objectives:

1. By December 1972, complete the provisions for the prepaid health insurance plan and, by January 1973, begin marketing it.

2. By February 1973, execute formal agreements with other agencies and health care professionals in order to (a) guarantee continuing service for the Center, and (b) provide 24-hour emergency service.

3. By February 1973, complete and submit the annual continuation proposal to HEW. This, of course, would be the first step to obtaining HEW-HC funds for 1974.

Each objective was crucial. Successful completion of the prepaid health plan was the primary criterion for HEW funding; formal agreements with doctors and other health care providers would guarantee that the Center could offer more health services; and, the HEW request would ensure enough money to continue operations.

Significantly, however, this new schedule of objectives overshadowed the completion of administrative policies and procedures.

A Tumultuous Period

By late November 1972, the Board had become so intent on completing the new schedule of objectives that it seldom conferred with the liaison personnel. The liaison personnel had never really been in a position to advise the Board, but now they could only report on Center progress and maintain indirect communication between the Board and the funding agencies. In essence, Kahele and the Board controlled the Center independently. The intensity of working on the objectives also prevented the completion of policies and procedures. Ironically, the lack of policies and procedures began to hamper work on the objectives.

In December 1972, with the Center settling into a routine operating pattern, Johnson decided that his immediate tasks were to guarantee continuing medical services and to provide 24-hour emergency service. He thus began negotiating with Family Medicine for 1) an extention of Dr. Alexander's contract, which expired in June 1973, and 2) for two full-time physicians, who would agree to be on call 24 hours a day.

Negotiations were a failure. No policies or procedures clearly delineated the project director's or the Board's authority, so Kahele assumed executive prerogative as Board president and oversaw all negotiations. He made Johnson report regularly to him and, whenever he objected to an offer that Johnson made to Family Medicine, he would make Johnson retract the offer and propose a new one. Johnson felt his work was undercut and his ability to negotiate was compromised. He could make no offer in good faith. Family Medicine viewed the situation as further proof that the Center's administration was unfeasible. In a terse letter to the Board, they terminated negotiations, saying :

> Family Medicine has continued its contract with Malia Coast Comprehensive Health Center (MCCHC) to provide physician services until July of 1973. At that time, no physician services will be provided to MCCHC by Family Medicine.

> Family Medicine is intensely interested in the provision of high quality medical care in a rural setting. The current disorganized, uncontrolled state at the clinic makes the chances of this outcome occurring very remote and the provision of any type of care quite slim.

> Federal and State governments have spent considerable sums of tax money on the creation of a small portion of the MCCHC which will not meet the needs of the community. Family Medicine recognizes that there is precedent for similar expenditures on the mainland but we certainly have hoped and worked to prevent this type of waste in an area of great need in rural Hawaii. (19)

Johnson encountered similar problems while working on the prepaid health insurance plan. He first had to guarantee the plan's health services by formally contracting other health care providers. For example, because many Malia residents received Medicaid and other federal government assistance, Johnson had to negotiate with the State Department of Social Services, which administered Medicaid assistance on the state level. Johnson also had to negotiate with the Hawaii Medical Service Association, the only Hawaii corporation capable of financing, administering, marketing, and monitoring a prepaid health plan. Finally, Johnson had to negotiate with specialists, such as psychiatrists and pediatricians, to get them to offer their services at the Center.

In negotiating with all the health providers, Johnson was closely supervised by Kahele, who emphasized that the Board would have to approve any plan and oversee its implementation. Inordinate delays occurred; Johnson would reach an informal agreement with the provider, have it rejected by Kahele, and then have to renegotiate the settlement. Since so many negotiations were involved, it was impossible to complete the prepaid insurance plan.

Johnson accomplished one objective; in February 1973 he finished the HEW continuation budget request. Preparing the request was relatively simple. Johnson assembled the new schedule of objectives, a prospectus of future activities, the budget for 1973-1974, and the Center progress report. In March, he sent the request to the HEW regional office in San Francisco and to the Comprehensive Health Planning Agency (CHP) in Honolulu. CHP responded promptly, informing the Board that it supported the new budget. HEW replied in late March, telling the Board that it was still reviewing the progress report.

Despite successfully obtaining CHP's endorsement for continuing funds, Johnson still viewed his situation as intolerable. He was totally frustrated in his relations with Kahele and uncertain of his role or authority in the project. Moreover, he realized that although the uncertainty was created by the lack of policies and procedures, there was an underlying factor of resident control. Kahele and the Board, as representatives of the community, were determined to retain total control of the Center. Since Johnson was still considered an outsider, he would continue to be closely supervised by Kahele. Beyond him personally, however, Johnson realized that Kahele and the Board were uncompromising; they were unwilling to give up any aspect of control to outside health agencies or to outside health care providers. Johnson knew, for instance, that Kahele did not really want to contract physicians through Family Medicine; he wanted to contract physicians directly, so that the physicians would be accountable only to the project director. Given this situation, Johnson felt he could no longer negotiate for vitally needed health services.

Seeing no alternative, Johnson resigned, charging that he was ineffective as project director, given the constant interference of Kahele and the Board. Furthermore, there was personal animosity between himself and Kahele.

Realizing the need for decisive action, the Board promptly accepted Johnson's resignation and appointed Kahele as acting project director. Board members then deliberated about offering Kahele the dual appointment of the project director and the Center's permanent administrator. They considered several factors. On the negative side was the possible charge of conflict of interest, as Kahele was also Board president. Moreover, there would be questions of Kahele's competence since he had no formal training or experience in health administration. But on the positive side, Board members knew from personal experience that Kahele was a strong leader. He was also a resident and thus understood Malia's needs. His understanding and leadership would be essential since the project had failed to meet major deadlines. At a meeting with Kahele absent, the Board decided to offer him the dual appointment. However, before officially appointing him project director/Center administrator, they had to get Regional Medical Program (RMP) approval, as required in the funding conditions.

Impending Crisis

In early April, while the Board waited for RMP to approve Kahele as permanent director, HEW returned the continuation budget request saying that it was unsatisfactory and that the Board would have to submit a supplemental report. HEW wanted more information about Kahele and about progress on the objectives. In separate discussions, HEW also asked the CHP Advisory Council to review the supplemental report, and to scrutinize the Board's progress on the prepaid health plan, The Board's and Center's policies and procedures, and the qualifications of the new project director.

Kahele and the Board submitted the supplemental report to HEW and CHP on April 17. On April 19, the CHP Review Committee completed their review and, after several days of discussion, told the Board they were not satisfied. In a letter dated April 25, the CHP Advisory Council noted that the Board had neither contracted physicians past June, nor established working relationships with other health care providers. But their greatest concern was Kahele. In somewhat veiled terms, the letter said:

> Some doubt was expressed by the Review Committee regarding minimum qualifications of the administrative staff positions of the health center. The questions raised whether personnel with such qualifications were capable of carrying out the involved difficult duties of running a complex health facility. For example, the minimum qualifications for the administrator position are optional allowing for so many substitutions that an individual totally without experience in the health field could qualify. (20)

The letter concluded by explaining that unless the Board was able to deliver health services and to institute the prepaid health plan by September 30, 1973, the CHP Agency would automatically withdraw its endorsement of the Center. A withdrawal of endorsement was tantamount to cutting off Department of Health, Education and Welfare-Health Center (HEW-HC) funds.

A few days after the Board received CHP's letter, HEW's regional Family Health Center Coordinator came to Malia to discuss HEW's concerns and see if some amicable, but satisfactory, arrangements could be worked out. Meeting with the Board, the coordinator discussed the failure to complete the prepaid insurance plan and the failure to contract physicians. He emphasized that these failures were merely symptoms caused by the underlying problems of the lack of a qualified director and the lack of professional Board members. In a lengthy letter to the Board, dated April 30, the coordinator summarized his positions on the two underlying problems. Concerning the director he wrote:

> Much discussion revolved about the Board's action in offering the position of Project Director to Mr. Kahele. Mr. Kahele stated that he had not yet decided whether or not to accept the position. While we have the greatest respect for Mr. Kahele's current accomplishments, we do not believe that he has the training and experience that we believe would be required in the future administration of a complex health care program. (21)

Concerning the Board's professional expansion, he noted:

We believe an expanded Board, representative of additional community interests, would ultimately improve the center's ability to market the plan and improve confidence in the program by other affected members of the community.... Other agency representatives expressed concern over the limited opportunities for participation. (22)

After completing substantive discussions, the coordinator told the Board he was going to continue Department of Health, Education and Welfare-Health Center (HEW-HC) funding through September 1973, provided that the Board:

1. Recruit and hire a qualified project director, acceptable to HEW.

2. Recruit three physicians, with one as the Medical Director.

3. Complete the prepaid health plan and complete a marketing strategy.

4. Develop policies and procedures to expand Board participation to include other representatives of affected health interests.

The coordinator then told the Board that an HEW team would visit the Center in August to follow up on these new conditions. At that time, the team would evaluate progress; and, if sufficient, it would approve 1974 HEW-HC funding. Since HEW-HC funding for 1973 would cease in September, the coordinator strongly recommended that the Board mail him a progress report prior to August.

A few days after being notified that their HEW funding might be cut off in September, the Board received an ominous letter from the Regional Advisory Group (RAG). Now alerted to the problems at the Center, RAG informed the Board that it had serious reservations about continuing Regional Medical Program (RMP) funding after December 1973. RAG cited the same concerns that HEW had articulated: lack of policies and procedures, lack of Center physicians, lack of a prepaid health plan, and lack of a competent project director. RAG also informed the Board that their review committee, the Planning Implementation and Evaluation Committee (PIE) would conduct an onsite study to evaluate these concerns. Based on the results of the evaluation, RAG would decide whether or not to continue RMP funding for 1974.

The Crisis

In June 1973, with the cutoff of operating funds now imminent, Kahele and the Board met to devise a plan that would not only satisfy the funding agencies, but also allow Kahele to remain as permanent Center administrator. It was decided that Kahele would first meet with the Comprehensive Health Planning (CHP) chairman to see if CHP would extend the September 30 deadline for withdrawing its formal endorsement of the Center. Extending the CHP endorsement would be the first step in getting HEW to reconsider Kahele.

The meeting began cordially, with Kahele pointing out that the deadline made it difficult for him to recruit physicians, because it created uncertainty about financing. He also pointed out that there were so many conditions from so many different agencies that the deadline was unrealistic. In reply, the CHP chairman stated that Kahele was in a conflict of interest since he was both Board president and Center administrator; it would be appropriate for him to step down as administrator and hire an experienced person. The CHP chairman also expressed the opinion that the Board had to expand to include some outside health representatives. The discussion became very heated and slowly degenerated into a shouting match. Nothing was resolved, and ill-feeling was created.

Later in June, the national RMP office informed the Board that Kahele was unacceptable as Center administrator because due process had not been followed in selecting him. Still resolved to appoint Kahele, however, the Board organized an Administrator Screening Committee consisting of six Board members. The committee advertised the position, interviewed four applicants, and unanimously selected Kahele. RMP, upon being informed that due process had been followed, had to approve Kahele since its stated objection to Kahele's selection had only been lack of due process. Bolstered by RMP's reluctant approval, the Board defied CHP and HEW, and formally appointed Kahele as project director/permanent Center administrator; Kahele then stepped down as Board president to avoid further charges of a conflict of interest.

While Center operations were being implemented from January-July 1973, construction on the permanent facility had proceeded on schedule. Thus, during July and August, Kahele spent much time planning the move to the permanent site. He decided to move all Center operations into the new emergency unit when it was completed in October. Although the emergency unit was inadequate for primary care, it was an improvement over the temporary facility. The large emergency area could be partitioned into offices, physician consulting areas, and examining rooms; this would serve until the Board secured funds to build the rest of the Center.

During July and August Kahele also spent much time dealing with personnel matters; he hired paramedics, laboratory technicians, and medical aides for the Center, mediated between Center employees, assigned responsibilities, and tried to recruit physicians. Recruiting physicians was especially time consuming. Normally, CHP and other health agencies helped to find physicians willing to work in rural areas. But Kahele was reluctant to communicate with the health agencies, and thus it took several months simply to identify physicians who would negotiate with him. When he contacted such physicians, few were willing to work at a Center whose policies and procedures were so informal, whose funding was so uncertain, and whose relationships with all agencies were so poor. Recruiting thus constituted much of Kahele's job. Kahele spent the rest of his time meeting with the staff and the Board, publicizing the Malia Comprehensive Health Center within Malia, and maintaining good community relations. He assigned all technical administrative matters, including the writing of monitoring reports and progress statements, to the assistant administrator.

During this time, Kahele seldom communicated with the funding agencies. He made all decisions independently and operated the Center as a self-contained, autonomous unit, accountable only to the Board.

Consequently, three of the four stipulated HEW funding conditions - selection of a new Center administrator, development of the prepaid health plan, and completion of policies and procedures - were ignored. By late August, however, the conditions could no longer be ignored.

On August 29, an evaluation team from HEW's regional office visited Malia to assess the progress that the Board had made on the conditions stipulated by the Family Health Center coordinator in April. The HEW team found that it could not evaluate progress because the Board had not prepared a progress report prior to the team's arrival. The team demanded to know why Kahele and the Board had not completed the report. Infuriated, Kahele and the Board replied that, with the site team suddenly appearing in Malia and demanding a report, it seemed that the regional office wanted to take over the project. Moreover, the Family Health Center coordinator had "strongly recommended" - not mandated - that the Board submit a report. The site team replied that they were only interested in guaranteeing high quality health care for Malia, and, to do this, they had to have the progress report, so now they were mandating it. The team then stressed the need for direct communication with the regional office and gave the Board until mid-September to submit the report.

At the Center, the uncertainty of funding, compounded with the move to the permanent facility, made it impossible to adequately coordinate and supervise all activities. Although medical operations proceeded without interruption, Kahele had to spend most of his time working on the progress report, meeting with the Board and concerned employees, and planning the move. He did not have time to perform administrative duties such as working out budget expenditure plans, planning medical support programs, or ensuring the fiscal stability of the Center. He did, however, accomplish the key task of hiring two physicians; they would become salaried Center employees, accountable to him directly. He also assigned to the assistant administrator the top priority task of working on the HEW progress report. The assistant completed the report, and submitted it to HEW on September 18.

On receipt of the report, the regional office told the Board it would complete its evaluation on October 12 and decide whether to continue the Center's funding. The Board was concerned about the timing, because HEW funding automatically ended on September 30. However, Regional Medical Program (RMP) funds, which were approved through December 1973, were sufficient to continue Center operations. During October, the Center was moved successfully to the permanent facility, but many of the planned services and programs had to be postponed because HEW funding had ended.

Then on November 5, HEW formally notified the Board that progress on the April 1973 conditions was unacceptable. If the Board wanted continued funding, it would have to:

1. Immediately write a position description for the Center administrator and then, through a nationwide search, recruit and hire an administrator acceptable to HEW.

2. Submit Board bylaws in one month, which provided for regular elections of new Board members, and which ultimately provided for the seating of 40 percent professional and agency representatives.

3. Complete a Board Policies and Procedures Manual, which delineated the role and duties of Board members and officers and the functions and methods of operation of standing committees. (23)

If the Board accepted the conditions, HEW would approve Center funding retroactive to September 30. The Board had ten days to agree to the conditions.

Seeing the conditions as outside intrusion and a direct encroachment on their authority, the Board called their federal representatives in Washington and angrily detailed the actions of the regional office of HEW. The Board emphasized that the regional office wanted to take over the Center and, to this end, had instigated a conspiracy against the Board. After all, they argued, the Board's troubles had begun in April 1972 when HEW notified CHP, RAG, and RMP that it considered Center administration unsatisfactory. The Board then asked their representatives to help in retaining Kahele and preserving HEW funding.

The Board also responded to HEW. In a letter dated November 15, it analyzed each condition for unreasonableness, and a compromise was offered: the Board would fulfill all original grant conditions if HEW withdrew all subsequent ones. HEW rejected the compromise and gave the Board until December 7 to send them a written notice stating that the Board intended to comply with the latest conditions.

The Board decided to defy the ultimatum; it would retain Kahele unless funding was terminated from all sources. Kahele himself vowed to keep the Center open and, if necessary, to use force to keep the Center operating. In mid-November, their resolve was aided by notification that RMP funding for 1974 was approved, provided that the Regional Advisory Group (RAG) send written notice to the national office of RMP stating that "it clearly understands the problems encountered by the 'Malia' District Comprehensive Health and Hospital Board and can ensure that RMP funds and program staff activities will be used in a coordinated manner to strengthen the capability of the 'Malia' Area to effectively manage programs locally." (24)   The notification also requested a clarification of all funding arrangements from all sources. Although the RAG letter constituted a very serious obstacle to renewing RMP funds, the Center was solvent for the immediate future.

Then, on November 26, the Board's problems were confounded when Dr. Alexander, the Center's first physician, resigned, saying that the administration of the Center had become too chaotic and Kahele had become overbearing. Alexander had been with the Center since its opening in October 1972 and he was upset because the planned training programs and special medical services had been postponed indefinitely. He had assumed that the failure to implement the programs and services reflected normal and expected delays; but now, given the problems with the funding agencies, he viewed the entire situation as an administrative disaster, unlikely to improve. To call attention to the situation, he submitted his resignation, not to Kahele, but directly to the Board. On receipt of the resignation, the Board realized that Center administration (or lack thereof) was now directly hindering the delivery of medical services; the Board therefore decided to reconsider the HEW ultimatum.   Separate meetings with Alexander and Kahele were scheduled for December.

Five days before the meetings, the Board received a petition signed by a majority of the Center employees stating that the Board's decision to meet separately with Kahele and Alexander reflected a lack of confidence in Kahele, and unless the Board supported Kahele they would all resign. The Board also received a letter from the two recently hired physicians stating their confidence in Kahele's leadership. Unlike Alexander, most Center staff had been hired by Kahele, and therefore had a sense of personal loyalty to him. Moreover, most staff were residents or sympathetic to resident needs. They thus felt that Kahele, as the resident most closely involved in the Center from its inception, was the person best able to serve the needs of other residents. They reasoned that, although he was having difficulty in dealing with the funding agencies, when this was worked out he would be the ideal person to administer the Center.

Given the employee support for Kahele, the Board decided it would defy the HEW ultimatum by retaining him as Center administrator. But it would meet separately with Kahele and Alexander to avoid a public confrontation. The HEW deadline passed without response from the Board. Then, on December 10, with HEW funding terminated, the Regional Medical Program (RMP) informed the Board that it was going to terminate funds on December 31 unless RAG provided the national RMP office with written assurance that it understood the Center's problems. RMP reminded the Board that this was the stipulation attached to the continuation funding agreement in November. The Board held an emergency meeting later in the day and discussed their options. There was heated debate, resulting in the resignation of one Board member, and they concluded that the only alternative was to close the Center and terminate Kahele as administrator.

On December 11, the Board informed Kahele of their decision, and directed him to cease operations on December 21. On December 17, the Board held a strategy session and by secret ballot decided to accept all HEW conditions.

Reorganization and Completion

By the time the Board decided to accept HEW conditions on December 17, 1973, no funds were left to operate the Center. But an obscure emergency clause in the Model Cities grant stated that if, for any reason, medical services at the Center ceased, the building and equipment would revert to the control of the City and County of Honolulu. Thus, on December 19, upon being informed that the Center was closing at 4:00 p.m. on Friday, December 21, the mayor of Honolulu organized a temporary project team, consisting of physicians and technical personnel from the City and County Physician's Office, as well as administrators and finance personnel from the City Office of Human Resources. The team would use the weekend to organize and reopen the Center on December 24. At an informal meeting with the Board, the mayor announced that the city would temporarily assume all Center responsibilities, but he would return authority to the Board once federal funding was resumed and the Board was reorganized.

Over the weekend, the temporary project team met and selected Daniel Ohana, the Director of the Office of Human Resources, as the temporary Center administrator. Ohana decided that the personnel from the City Physician's Office would provide continuous medical coverage and the personnel from the Office of Human Resources would both administer the Center and help the Board to reorganize.

After reopening the Center on December 24, the temporary project team met with the Board. Ohana told the Board that the team's major purpose was to give the Board administrative, legal, financial, and policy assistance in the reorganization. He then assured the Board that financial and patient record systems were still operative and thus the Center's medical services could continue uninterrupted. Finally, he told the Board that the team would: 1) conduct an audit of past Center administration, 2) complete professional position descriptions for the Center administrator, finance director, medical director, and marketing supervisor, and 3) send a representative to meet with HEW's regional office. The Board told Ohana that it was ready to cooperate fully, and Ohana suggested that the Board form a committee to recommend what personnel to rehire. The Board agreed to form the committee and also organized a finance committee to investigate the possibilities of resuming federal funding.

On December 28, a general meeting was held to discuss the strategy for the next few weeks. The temporary project team told the Board that a quick review of the administration revealed glaring financial problems. The Center owed $15,000 in back taxes, which had been withheld from employee wages but never paid to the federal government; the former administration had written an overdraft check for $7,400; and the only source of income was from direct patient fees. Over $47,000 was owed to the Center by patients, but, since there were no auditable records, the money might be lost. Ohana then reported that HEW had been contacted and it had assured him that interim funding would be granted to the Center under the authority of the Office of Human Resources. Irene Reed would visit the Center in late January to evaluate the reorganization and to confirm the funding.

The Board's personnel committee then reported and suggested that 16 core medical employees be rehired to relieve the temporary personnel from the City and County Physician's Office. Hiring the top administrators would have to wait. Ohana approved this plan and told the Board that the City would pay the salaries. Finally, the Board's finance committee reported that it had requested RAG to write the letter of assurance to the RMP national office as stipulated in November.

On December 31, the Board met with the RMP liaison to request continuation funding. They noted that core staff changes were being made, and that Center administration was presently being performed by qualified professionals from the Office of Human Resources. They further noted that the position description for the permanent Center administrator had been written to conform to professional standards, that RAG had been requested to write the letter of assurance, and that professionals would be added to the Board: lawyers, doctors, health, and finance professionals.

On January 3, RAG held an interagency meeting to determine how the agencies could help the Board. At the meeting the agencies were informed of the swift progress that had been made and were assured that Center administration was in competent hands. The agencies then agreed to assist the Board; the Comprehensive Health Planning (CHP) chairman, whom Kahele had initially confronted in a sharp exchange, volunteered to help write Board bylaws; various health care providers agreed to cooperate in developing the prepaid health plan; and RMP assigned a special liaison consultant to work closely with the Board. Finally, the agencies determined that the Board's immediate need was money, so RAG agreed to write the letter of assurance and send it to the national office of RMP. The letter, completed on August 17, was summed up in the first paragraph:

On January 10, 1974, the Regional Advisory Group (RAG) reviewed Project #30, Malia Coast Comprehensive Health Center, and approved funding for the three month period of January 1 - March 31, 1974.... The approval, however, is contingent upon: 1) RMP funds be used only for administrative costs and not for health services costs that are subject to reimbursement through service charges, and 2) the RAG receive detailed monthly reports on the progress of the project.

On January 24, Irene Reed, the program director from HEW, visited Malia and was impressed by the rapid progress and the cooperative effort between the Board and all health agencies. She subsequently approved interim funding for the Center, from February 1 to July 31. The conditions imposed on the Board were the same imposed on them in the November 5, 1973 ultimatum: hiring a competent administrator, completing Board bylaws, and completing policies and procedures. The funding would be overseen by the Office of Human Resources, but the Board would be closely involved in all policy decisions. On the same day, the national office of RMP notified the Board they had received RAG's letter of assurance and therefore would release funds retroactive to January 1. These funds would continue until March 31, when the Board would be reviewed for another three months of funding.

During February, control of the Center slowly reverted back to the Board and, at the end of the month, the Board selected an interim Center administrator to replace Ohana. The interim administrator was expected to perform a "holding action" until the Board completed the HEW conditions and hired the permanent Center administrator. Thus, for the next five months, the following tasks were accomplished:

1. Selecting a permanent Center administrator. The Board submitted the position description written by the project team to HEW, and it was approved. Then, with the help of professionals from the Regional Medical Program (RMP), the Board and interim project director prepared screening criteria, interview guidelines, and rating sheets - all of which would standardize their selection process. They then advertised the position in Honolulu and New York newspapers, and received 64 applications. Twelve applicants met the minimum screening requirements and two, who were both nonresidents of Malia, were chosen as final candidates. The Board interviewed both, found one acceptable, and offered him the position. He declined, however, because the salary was unacceptable. The Board began the entire process again and, out of 50 applicants, selected Donald Dell, who was experienced in health planning and health administration. He was approved by HEW and became the permanent Center administrator in June 1974.

2. Completing Board bylaws. Board bylaws were completed in June 1974 by a committee composed of two lawyers, several Board members, and several health professionals. One of the lawyers also helped satisfy HEW's requirement of obtaining professional Board members by becoming a member himself. The committee structured the Board as a legal corporation conforming to HEW conditions. The bylaws were also revised to delineate the membership of the corporation and to provide for the regular election of 12 Board members from the general membership. Three Board directors would be appointed by cooperating health agencies.

3. Completing a Board Policies and Procedures Manual. Completing the manual was such a complex task that the Board needed the assistance of MEDICUS, a national firm that helped family health centers with administrative problems. MEDICUS consultants gave the Board a model of recommended policies in February 1973, and the Board appointed a committee to work on the manual. MEDICUS consultants then returned in April, reviewed the committee's draft and recommended that the Board hire a consultant to complete the final draft. The Board hired a consultant, who finished the final draft in May. When completed, the draft provided comprehensive organizational policies and procedures for the Board, and delineated standing committees and their relationship to Center administration. The manual also made it clear that the Board was the general policy-making body of the Center, but once policy was made, it would be implemented and administered by Center management. The Board would have to work out in practice their actual relationship with the Center administrator, but the parameters between policy-making and administration were clear.

While the Board was working on these tasks, medical operations at the clinic proceeded smoothly, and the medical staff felt that they received adequate administrative support. The actual medical practice proceeded relatively independently and was facilitated by the new clarity in administrative authority. The interim project director, though working closely with the Board, performed all administrative functions. He coordinated all activities and prepared the Center for support systems, such as outreach, pharmacy, X-ray, and lab analysis. Implementation, however, would have to wait until the permanent administration began to perform.

The only real problem was lack of space at the emergency unit. The emergency unit was supposed to have housed all health operations temporarily, but had become the major facility because the previous administrative problems had prevented funding agencies from approving construction of the primary care unit. It would still take two years to complete all arrangements for the new unit. Until then, the cramped quarters in the emergency unit would be barely tolerable. This, however, was an unavoidable situation.

In June 1974, the permanent Center administrator, Donald Dell officially began his functions. First he completed the 1975 HEW budget request and submitted it to the Comprehensive Health Planning Agency (CHP) and HEW. CHP approved the request after meeting with the Board. Staff members from the HEW regional office decided to visit the Center to see how it was functioning and asked CHP to organize a special meeting of Honolulu agency representatives, health care providers, and the Board. At the meeting, the agencies testified that their working relationships with the Board had improved and cooperation was mutually beneficial to themselves and the Center. The Board articulated the problems they had in completing the prepaid health plan, but also knowledgeably outlined a strategy to overcome these problems. Their working relationships with the agencies also made it easier for them to complete the plan. After hearing this testimony, HEW approved 1975 funds for the Center.

With this approval, the Board was again in charge of Center policy, but now functioned with explicit procedures, had a definite structure, and possessed no administrative authority over Center operations. Although many administrative issues still confronted the Center, these would have to be resolved by the new administrator. The Board was no longer responsible for the day-to-day issues as it had been in the past. The transition to normal administration was complete.

PHASE 4: EVALUATION AND REFINEMENT

Evaluation and Followup

Since all funding agencies intended that the Malia Coast Comprehensive Health Center be an ongoing organization, they continually monitored Center activities, but did not evaluate the Center as a project with a definable lifespan. This section represents the first step in evaluating the life cycle of the project.

The Time Frame of the Project

The project formally spanned five years - from March 1969, when the Program Concept was formulated, to June 1974, when the Center was transferred to permanent administration. From beginning to end the project failed to meet major deadlines (refer to Table 6.2). No project phase was finished on schedule, and cumulative time overruns so exceeded the deadlines that the Board decided to implement the Center before completing the prerequisite activation tasks. This decision eventually culminated in the temporary shutdown and reorganization of the Center. As a result, the Center was handed over to normal administration about a year late, without the specific goals and objectives having been executed.

To analyze the dramatic events of December 1973 and the inability to complete the goals and objectives, we must view the project in total perspective.

Formulation: The Birth of the Health Center's Problems

By virtue of being both a community facility intended to serve residents, and a professional clinic expected to conform to national medical standards, the health center inherently created tension between residents and health professionals. The residents demanded that the Center be managed in accordance with local needs; health professionals demanded that the Center

TABLE 6.2 - The Time Frame of the Project

Project Phase	Starting Date	Scheduled Completion Date	Actual Completion Date	Time Overrun
Formulation	-	-	March 1969 (Program Concept formulated)	
Design	June 1970	June 1971	June 1974	4 years
Activation	January 1972	July 1972	June 1974	2 years
Implementation	July 1972	July 1973	(Not completed until 3 years after handover to permanent administration)	3 years, 5 months
Total Lifespan as a Project	March 1969 (Program Concept formulated)	July 1973	June 1974 (Date of handover to permanent administration)	1 year

be managed in accordance with national guidelines. The basic philosophy of the health center then - a facility intended to serve the community and, at the same time, to stand above it - established the potential for a conflict over control.

Exacerbating this inherent tension was the intense feeling of community within Malia, which made residents antagonistic towards outsiders who tried to exercise authority over Malia's affairs. The sense of community was especially applicable to the health center because residents had actively participated in identifying and gaining support for it through their grassroots initiatives and through the CAP and Model Cities efforts. Residents looked upon the health center as their project. Thus, before the project began, residents were committed to resident control.

Another problem inherent in the establishment of the health center was the complexity of multiple funding. The Center had to obtain funding from numerous sources to become a viable organization. This meant that manifold conditions would be imposed upon the project, inevitably creating conflicting priorities.   For example, contention occurred because a Model Cities condition gave top priority to hiring Malia residents, but an HEW condition required highly qualified professional administrators to implement the Center. Although these two conditions were not necessarily contradictory, the lack of professional health administrators in Malia, combined with the residents' feelings towards outsiders, made the priority conflict inevitable.

During formulation, both problems were recognized, and, in fact, the Program Concept recommended that the Center be implemented through a cooperative effort among community organizations, professional health care providers, and all funding agencies. The Program Concept, however, did not foresee the intensity of resident feeling nor did it accurately assess the great difficulties of multiple funding. Thus, although both problems were discussed, their deep-rootedness and their critical long-term implications were never emphasized as the fundamental obstacles to project success.

Design: The Time to Develop Mechanisms to Resolve Problems

The major flaw of the design, stemming partly from the formulation's lack of emphasis on the inherent problems of the health center, was inadequacy. Three major areas of the design were inadequate. First, the Board and project director never anticipated the complexity of multiple funding, thus never devised detailed administrative provisions for complying with the numerous funding conditions, for clarifying the funding agencies' overlapping jurisdiction, for scheduling the time delays in receiving approval, or for handling the large amount of negotiation.

Second, the Board and project director did not anticipate the complexity of operating the health center. Thus, they prepared no detailed plans for conducting statistical research, for coordinating the integrated system of health delivery, or for establishing the requirements of special training programs. Most importantly, they developed no administrative procedures. Thus, personnel qualifications and duties were unspecified; formal methods for resolving impasses were nonexistent; and the functional relationship between the Board and Center administrator was unresolved.

Third, the Board and project team omitted the major objective of developing a community organization capable of guiding the policy of the Center. Subsequently omitted were goals, such as the establishment of a rigorous training program to give the Board basic competency in setting health policy, or the preparation of ongoing programs to raise the Board's awareness of complex health issues.

A major factor causing the design's inadequacies was the Board's desire to ensure resident control of the Center. Since the Board represented residents, it could ensure resident control by maximizing its own authority over the Center and by preventing outsiders from having any input in Center policy decisions. Consequently, the failure to complete detailed plans for multiple funding and the failure to plan for the technical problems of implementation reflected the Board's inability to do all the planning - and its refusal to let outside experts help. After all, allowing outsiders to help would give them an opportunity to gain control of the Center.

The design's lack of policies and procedures reflected the Board's insistence on conducting business as a resident organization, which meant conducting business informally, without established procedures. The reluctance to develop procedures also reflected the Board's attempt to maximize its control of the Center, insofar as formal procedures would delineate the Board's authority and thereby limit its discretionary power over the Center. Finally, the Board could not make the development of its competence an objective because this would raise doubts about the Board's ability to guide the Center. Since such doubts would jeopardize the Board's authority, the Board was unwilling to acknowledge that expertise in health planning and administration was necessary to set Center policy.

Another major factor in the design's inadequacies was Wayne's inability to provide strong project leadership. Although Wayne recognized the problems of the design, he did not actually confront the Board. He urged the Board to correct the design inadequacies - especially the lack of policies and procedures - but he was not forceful. He did not fully assert himself and thus could not use the full range of his expertise to arrive at some amicable compromises with the Board. Moreover, he was unable to convince the Board that cooperation with outside professionals was essential.

Again, it must be emphasized that the full impact of resident control had never been fully addressed during formulation; thus, in the absence of forceful leadership, the Board could not foresee the problems that absolute resident control would entail.

Selection and Approval: Another Chance to Scrutinize the Problems

The selection and approval stage of the project introduced the complexities of multiple funding and thus highlighted some of the omissions of the design. The numerous funding conditions from HEW, Model Cities, and RMP created considerable confusion and led to conflicting priorities, which the Board neither planned for nor possessed the expertise to resolve. In addition, the deadlines that the Board and project team had initially set had to be postponed as the funding negotiations took much longer than anticipated. These problems, however, should really have been worked out during the design stage.

A major deficiency during selection was the failure of the funding agencies to insist upon an overall feasibility study.   Although informal assessments cast serious doubts on the Board's competence and the Center's feasibility, no formal assessment was conducted.   Nonetheless, the project was selected, partly because of the urgency to build the Center and partly because the funding agencies assumed that numerous funding conditions would remedy any problems.

Activation and Organization: A Last Chance for Correction

Activation afforded the Board and Johnson a last chance to correct any deficiencies in the design and to complete all detailed planning.   After beginning implementation, basic deficiencies and oversights could be corrected only at high costs and with long delay.

During activation the Board and Johnson never corrected the design's inadequacies. In particular, Center administrative policies were never drawn up. Without the formal policies and procedures, the project could not be effectively organized since: 1) no dependable mechanisms for resolving impasses existed; 2) no operational continuity and clarity could be established; 3) no clear-cut assignment of responsibilities could be made; and 4) no clear authority for project decisions could be determined.

The project's organizational structure reflected this confusion. In lieu of explicit policies or procedures the project was organized with overlapping internal jurisdiction. The project director administered the Center. But the Board, retaining conflicting interests, both administered the Center and set Center policy.

Organizational structure external to project operations similarly lacked clear definition.   The Board was accountable to three different funding agencies, but made no attempt to clarify and coordinate the overall relationships between and among itself and the agencies. Because the federal structure was exceedingly complex with offices on national, state, and local levels, the interrelationships of all agencies and the Board had to be clearly determined in order to secure and coordinate the necessary support from all offices.

Unfortunately, however, rather than spend additional time to clear up the organizational confusion and to complete all planning, Kahele, Johnson, and the Board decided to implement the project. And this decision resulted in a project that was insufficiently prepared for implementation.

It is significant that the organizational confusion and the lack of policies and procedures stemmed from the basic underlying issues of resident control. Thus, while the decision to begin implementation was prematurely timed, it was also a way to avoid the fundamental conflict of resident vs. professional control.   In this respect, Johnson and the Board failed to realize that the conflict could not be avoided indefinitely, only postponed until implementation.

Implementation: The Consequences of Unresolved Problems

During implementation, the issues that had been created earlier became critical problems.   Work on project activities came to a virtual standstill because the lack of administrative procedures caused uncertainty in carrying out routine tasks. The Board and Kahele were in constant dispute with the project director because of the confusing organizational structure. Multiple funding not only bogged down the project in a morass of red tape, but made it difficult for the Board to determine which funding agency, if any, had primary authority. The Board and Kahele's desire to retain control of the Center prevented them from cooperating with health professionals, and made them intransigent in dealing with the funding agencies. Moreover, the desire of the Board to retain control made them extremely defensive and isolated them from anyone who questioned their decisions. Finally, Kahele's lack of expertise, which the Board had never considered vital, prevented him from carrying out the Center's goals and objectives.

From this perspective, the dramatic events of December 1973 - though directly related to Johnson's lack of forceful leadership and Kahele's lack of competence - reflected the consequences of problems that were never resolved throughout the project's life cycle. It is useful to relate all these problems to specific project activities. Thus, as the final step in evaluation, we analyze and followup on the degree of success in achieving the specific goals and objectives.

Evaluation, Analysis, and Followup of Goals and Objectives

1. Implementing a prepaid health plan. During the course of the project, a prepaid health plan was never designed, let alone implemented. Three crucial administrative failures prevented the completion of the plan. First, the Board had never completed an administrative procedures manual that delineated who possessed what project authority or responsibility. Therefore, Kahele, as Board president, assumed responsibility for all project activities; and he constantly interfered in Johnson's dealings with outside health care providers. This interference prevented Johnson from reaching cooperative working agreements in offering the plan's services.

Second, after Johnson resigned, the Board appointed a project director who lacked the expertise to draw up the plan. Although adequate data was available, Kahele was unable to define the precise services required for the plan or to estimate its cost.

Third, Kahele was unable to negotiate with health care providers for their services in offering the plan. Health care providers were willing to participate in the plan, but only if they could be assured of the administrative integrity of the Center. The providers felt that administrative integrity could be achieved if the Board hired a more professional project staff, and developed policies and procedures. The Board and Kahele, however, were unwilling to compromise on or even to discuss these issues. Given their inflexibility, there could be no negotiation.

In December 1976, long after the transition to normal administration, Donald Dell, the permanent Center administrator, implemented the prepaid health plan. In developing the plan, he discovered a major substantive obstacle. The prepaid health plan depended upon large businesses or commercial enterprises to provide a financially viable base clientele. Malia, however, had no large employers, and therefore no target population. Instead, Malia had a large population of Medicaid and other medical assistance recipients who would be the plan's primary users. Consequently, marketing and guaranteeing the financial viability of the plan would be extremely difficult.

Realizing the problem, the permanent Center administrator contacted HEW and made arrangements for HEW funding to be awarded under a category of health center funding which did not require the implementation of a prepaid health plan.   Having eliminated the funding deadline for developing a plan, the Center administrator was able to cooperate with the Hawaii Medical Service Association and formulate a workable plan.

Significantly, administrative problems had prevented Kahele and the Board from even discovering the substantive issues. Once the administrative problems were resolved, the Center administrator was able to work on the real obstacles and complete the plan.

2. Enrolling 4,000 residents in the plan by the first year. During the course of the project, administrative problems prevented the completon of the prepaid health plan; consequently it could not be marketed. When the plan was finally drawn up in December 1976, it was competently evaluated and a new marketing goal was set: by the end of the fiscal year (October 1977) enroll in the plan 200 residents.

The new goal of only 200 clients, though realistic, was a far cry from the ambitious goal of 4,000 clients. However, the reason for initially setting such a high marketing figure was to achieve the Center's financial self-sufficiency, and the Center did become increasingly self-supporting from patient revenue. As indicated in Table 6.3 the Center expected to generate 65% of its own financial needs by 1978.

TABLE 6.3 - Center Operating Costs

Date	Operating Cost	Percent Federal Support	Other	Percent Center-Generated Income
1973	Cannot be determined because books unauditable			
1974-1975	$ 408,064	85%	0%	15%
1975-1976	$1,017,507	44%	33%	23%
1976-1977	$1,179,301	50%	6%	44%
1977-1978 (Projected)	$1,384,717	35%	0%	65%

Source: Health Center Records

3. Providing 24-hour emergency care. Kahele and the Board were unable to implement round-the-clock emergency service because they could not recruit enough physicians to work at the Center. Normally, health facilities recruited physicians through an informal statewide network of health agencies, which provided the names of doctors who were interested in beginning a practice or in relocating. The Comprehensive Health Planning Agency was especially helpful in passing on information, since it was in contact with health facilities throughout the state. Kahele and the Board, however, were never interested in cooperating with the outside agencies. They refused to cooperate because this would "open the door" for outsiders to gain influence over the Center. Moreover, Kahele was untactful and even abrasive in his dealings with the CHP chairman; he therefore had a miserable rapport with CHP. As a result, Kahele seldom communicated with CHP, and did not receive enough information to recruit a complete staff of doctors.

Following the transition to normal administration, the permanent Center administrator coordinated efforts with outside agencies and was able to recruit physicians. Additionally, he hired an experienced medical director who helped develop the support requirements and the schedule necessary to offer 24-hour emergency service. Nonetheless, the service was not implemented until November 1975 - more than two years past the deadline.

4. Guaranteeing consumer participation in Center policy decisions. During the course of the project, the Board failed to involve consumers in Center policy decisions. Only one Board election was held, that in 1970; and residents were able to directly address the Board only during the rare public hearings, which were held to satisfy the Board's funding requirements. As the project progressed, the Board became increasingly insulated, and felt it could not relinquish control of the Center until operations were proceeding on a routine basis. The Board, moreover, began to grow inflexible and defensive about its decisions, particularly its decision to support Kahele. Thus, although the Board initially intended to involve residents in Center decisions, it slowly isolated itself as the Center's sole policy-making body.

As a routine matter, the project director should have held regular community meetings at which residents had access to Board members. This relatively simple task seemed a prerequisite both to ensure community support and to achieve the goal of resident participation. Unfortunately, the project director failed, from the outset of the project, to open regular channels of communication between the Board and residents. This made it difficult, if not impossible, for the Board to obtain consumer participation once implementation began.

After the transition to permanent administration, the Board realized that its isolation was a major deficiency, and it attempted to involve residents in Center policy decisions. To stimulate consumer participation in the Center, Board members developed an information brochure, which they distributed to the community. Board members also held informal talks with community organizations to discuss the changes at the Center, and they initiated a membership drive. Finally, in June 1975, an open membership meeting was held, at which new Board members were elected. At this point, the Board scheduled regular membership meetings and elections.

5. Providing jobs and training for residents. The Board and Kahele intended the Center to become a major employer of residents; they therefore spent considerable time and energy initiating training programs. In 1972 they sponsored training for outreach workers, laboratory assistants, and medical aides at Kapiolani Community College. Kahele, however, was unable to provide jobs at the Center because he could not obtain the necessary cooperation of outside health care providers in expanding Center services. Without this expansion, he could not justify hiring the new trainees. When he did begin to expand services in late 1973, his squabbles with the funding agencies made Center income too uncertain to employ them.

In addition to disappointing resident hopes for employment, Kahele and the Board also failed to institutionalize ongoing training programs to increase the basic technical skills of the staff. The same problems that hindered employing the trainees hindered initiating the followup programs. The constant threat of losing funds prevented the scheduling of any programs; the lack of cooperation with outside health care providers made it difficult to arrange regular training; and the numerous funding conditions made Kahele too busy to plan training activities.

After the transition to normal administration, the permanent administrator clarified all funding arrangements with HEW and made continuous funding certain. He was also completely open and willing to work with outside health professionals and was thus able to secure their support. As a result, he was able to establish ongoing training programs in cooperation with the University of Hawaii School of Medicine and School of Public Health, and Duke University School of Medicine. Finally, his obtaining the cooperation of health care providers and his ensuring the receipt of HEW funding, enabled him to expand medical services effectively. By 1977, the Center employed 51 persons; most were residents who had graduated from the training programs.

It is significant that the accomplishment of a few routine administrative tasks - securing the cooperation of the health agencies, opening effective channels of communication with the funding agencies, and clarifying all funding arrangements - would have made this goal achievable during the course of the project.

6. Expanding the outreach program.   Approximately 12 residents had been trained as outreach workers in 1972, but Kahele could employ only two until he consolidated the administration of the Center's onsite health operations. Since the administration of the main services was never solidified until the project's end, the outreach program was not expanded.

After consolidating the operations, the permanent Center administrator was able to spend time on the outreach program. He budgeted funds for outreach workers and hired them. Then he coordinated their efforts internally, and he coordinated their efforts externally with community groups and other health providers. This resulted in cooperative outreach efforts, such as the Early and Periodic Screening, Diagnosis, and Treatment, which was a program sponsored in conjunction with the state Department of Health to promote preventive   health care, and the Special Olympics Program, sponsored with the City and County of Honolulu to promote physical activities for handicapped youths.

7. <u>Coordinating services with outside health care providers</u>. The key goal for achieving Center success was to coordinate efforts with health groups and health care providers, such as the Comprehensive Health Planning Agency, the Regional Advisory Group, the state Department of Health, and the Hawaii Medical Services Association. Two ingredients were necessary to coordinate services with these groups: the willingness to cooperate with them and the willingness to be flexible. Cooperation was necessary simply to be able to work with them. And flexibility was necessary to reach agreements. In this context, the whole essence of reaching an agreement was to compromise so that a mutually beneficial exchange could be worked out. In the case of the Center, however, Kahele and the Board were unwilling to cooperate or compromise because the health agencies and health care providers posed a threat to the Board's dominance of Center policy. Moreover, as the project progressed, Kahele and the Board became increasingly rigid; and their inflexibility made it impossible to reach agreements on coordinating services

In contrast, the permanent Center administrator was flexible, less threatened, and anxious to cooperate with the health care providers. Thus, after the transition to normal administration, he was able to work out agreements to coordinate services with the key groups. Additionally, the working relationships that he established with these groups helped him to secure the help of specialists, such as a psychologist, an internist, a cardiologist, and an urologist.

<u>The overall objective of the project was to make adequate medical care available to all residents.</u> During the course of the project, administrative problems, such as the inability to recruit physicians and the unwillingness to cooperate with support groups, interfered with the availability of medical services and actually led to the temporary closing of the Center. Moreover the administrative problems detracted from the overall quality of medical services by disrupting support from allied health care providers and by preventing the expansion of services. Nonetheless, primary medical care was provided throughout most of the project's life; over 5,000 patient visits were made to the Center before the transition to normal administration.

In the immediate period after the transfer to permanent administration, no professional evaluations or patient opinion surveys of the adequacy of medical care were conducted. However, the number of patients using the Center provides an indirect indicator of adequacy. If medical care was adequate - from the clients' viewpoint - then the clients would return, and would pass on by word of mouth their satisfaction. Thus, if medical care at the Center were adequate, one would expect the numbers of return patients to increase steadily, and the numbers of new patients to increase progressively. In Table 6.4, this trend was apparent for the first three years.

One indicator of the availability of medical care, was the proportion of residents that used the Center. By the end of 1977, a total of 45,000 patient visits were made to the Center. This represented about 12,000 residents, or about 40% of the Malia population; thus from the standpoint of patient utilization the Center was extremely successful, and medical care was readily available.

TABLE 6.4 -   Growth of Patient Utilization (monthly average)

Year	New Patients	Return Patients	Total
1974-1975	143	706	849
1975-1976	201	1,050	1,251
1976-1977	300	1,380	1,680

But the availability of medical services for residents cannot be evaluated solely in terms of numbers. The accessibility of the Center's medical services must also be scrutinized. And, from an economic perspective, the Board has progressed in making medical services accessible to all residents. The prepaid health plan was made available to residents and a sliding fee-scale, which charged clients according to their income, was instituted. The Board also expanded the Center's outreach program, increasing the time that workers spent in the community, and working on a system of transportation for clients who had no means to get to the Center.

Nonetheless, there is still much that can be done to increase the quality and availability of the Center's medical services. And, from this perspective, the project's objective has become the continuing objective of the Center.

Some Policy Implications

Although the case history has raised many health-related issues, the problems in implementing the Center were created not by substantive health issues, but by basic managerial oversights which could have hindered any project. These oversights can be generalized as the following four policy issues for management:

First, project management must be comprehensive. The project manager must be familiar with the project in its entirety. Although he cannot know every nuance of the project, he must be the generalist. He must know enough of the technical detail of all project tasks to make knowledgeable decisions, such as when and how to use temporary experts. And he must know enough of the administrative aspects of the project to deal effectively with personnel problems, organizational complexity, and conflicting priorities. This necessitates the project manager becoming familiar with every project phase.

In addition, comprehensiveness means completeness. The project manager must completely prepare the project for implementation. Not everything can be foreseen, but those activities and circumstances which are foreseen must be completely planned in advance. In addition, some procedures must be worked out to resolve special contingencies.

Second, project management must be integrative. During the course of the project many different groups perform different tasks, and it appears that the groups and tasks are independent. But all groups and tasks are interrelated. It is the job of the project manager to bring together, to coordinate, and to fit together the work of all these groups in a manner that assures a coherent and a unified project. To accomplish this, the project manager must open channels of communication between himself and each group. This means he will have to cooperate willingly with the designers, the funding agencies, technical specialists, and all other support groups involved in the project. Though obtaining this cooperation may be a difficult task, it is vital to integrate the project.

Third, project management must be flexible. The project manager will face many situations in which he must make tradeoffs. Often, he must compromise and negotiate in order to ensure the completion of the project's most important goals. Unless he is flexible, he will be unable to arrive at any satisfactory resolution of the necessary compromises.

In addition, the project manager will face many unforeseen obstacles. To deal effectively with these obstacles he must be willing and open to adjust to changing situations. Although, as much as possible, he must adhere to the plans and schedule, sometimes it is counterproductive to do so. The project manager must be willing to adjust his plans. In this respect planning is continuous, and project managers must not become intransigent.

Fourth, project management demands leadership. The project manager must deal with a broad range of issues: the needs of the many support groups, the demands of the funding agencies, the sudden unforeseeable obstacle, and the changing situations. All of these issues, and many more, become critical during implementation. And the project manager must make crucial decisions. This requires strong and steadfast leadership. Thus, the project manager cannot provide bureaucratic skills alone - he must also provide the leadership that is necessary to ensure project success.

NOTES - Chapter 6

(1) Milton I. Roemer, "Historical Perspective of Health Services in Rural America," in Edward Hassinger and Larry Whiting, Eds., Rural Health Services: Organization, Delivery and Use, The Iowa State University Press, Ames, 1976.

(2) Barbara O. Henkel, Community Health, Allyn and Bacon, 1970; Harold Herman, Mary E. McKay, Community Health Services, International City Managers' Association, Washington, D.C., 1968.

(3) The State of Hawaii Data Book, 1974, A Statistical Abstract, State of Hawaii, Department of Planning and Economic Development, Honolulu, 1974.

(4) M. Myers, A Community Profile Study on Oahu CAP Target Areas, Community Action Program, Honolulu, 1968.

(5) Ralph H. Conway, Hospital Consultant and Associates, Work Program for a New Hospital for the Leeward Area, Oahu, State of Hawaii Department of Accounting and General Services, Honolulu, 1968.

(6) Ronald Gallimore and Ronald Howard, Studies in a Hawaiian Community: Na Ma Kamaka O Nanakuli, Pacific Anthropological Records, Number 1, Bishop Museum, Honolulu, 1968.

(7) From the Articles of Incorporation of the Board.

(8) All documents to the Regional Medical Program are on file, as required by federal statutes requiring public disclosure.　Because the specific references compromise identify, however, only the general information of date and organization will be included in the rest of the footnotes.

(9) From the federal applications from the Board to the Department of Health, Education and Welfare, requesting federal funds.

(10) Arthur D. Nelson, "Introduction of Health Care Systems to Rural Communities," in Edward Hassinger and Larry Whiting, eds., Rural Health Services:　Organization, Delivery and Use, The Iowa State University Press, Ames, 1976.

(11) From the Model Cities grant proposal agreements, July, 1972.

(12) From the Regional Medical Program grant agreements, October, 1971.

(13) From the Department of Health, Education, and Welfare award agreement, March, 1972.

(14) Ibid.

(15) From the Model Cities liaison agency, the City Demonstration Agency, March, 1972.

(16) Ibid.

(17) Ibid.

(18) Letter from Family Medicine of Hawaii to the Board, March, 1973.

(19) Ibid.

(20) Letter from the Comprehensive Health Planning Council to the Board, April, 1973.

(21) Letter from the Family Health Center Coordinator, San Francisco, to the Board, April, 1973

(22) Ibid.

(23) Letter from HEW regional office to the Board, November, 1973.

(24) Continuation award agreement from Regional Medical Program to the Board, November, 1973.

7 Conclusion: Major Factors and Issues in the IPPMC

Louis J. Goodman
Ralph Ngatata Love

Because of the complex nature of a development project's life cycle, all of the issues in the IPPMC cannot be discussed in this volume. This chapter, however, lists in question form some pertinent issues and factors that concern managers of development projects during the operation of the various phases of the integrated project cycle.

The checklist of questions serves a variety of purposes. First, it provides a supplementary set of guidelines by which to evaluate the case histories in this volume. Second, the questions can be useful in the analysis of other case histories and ongoing projects which the reader wishes to understand within a comprehensive framework. Third, it gives the reader an appreciation of the number and complexity of the issues and factors affecting project management.*

PHASE 1: PLANNING, APPRAISAL AND DESIGN

In the first phase of the IPPMC, projects ideally originate from the identification, definition, and analysis of problems and needs within the context of larger development plans, policies, and programs. In most nations, this process is carried out through centralized government planning, the private sector, and mixed systems of private investment and government-sponsored activities, including unstructured entrepreneurial investments. A project can also be pinpointed from outside a country as well as from inside

---

* Because a more thorough treatment of the theoretical issues underlying the management of development projects would be valuable, a companion volume to this book entitled "Management of Development Projects: Theory and Practice," is being prepared. Louis J. Goodman and Ralph Ngatata Love are the general editors of this new book and the chapters are being written by an international cooperative team of senior scholars and practitioners.

it, by an international funding agency such as the World Bank or a multinational corporation. To translate a project idea into reality, the identification and formulation tasks must take into account community needs and preconditions as well as the social and political environment in which the project will operate. Strong agricultural lobbies, for example, may place pressure on government to favor projects in the rural sector.

Once the broad outline of a project idea has been formulated, planners must conduct a feasibility analysis to determine if available resources are sufficient to handle the many dimensions of implementation. Besides this systematic analysis of parts and details, an overall appraisal of the project as an entity is also necessary. Both feasibility analysis and appraisal must be focused on the project's likelihood of success; at this stage, therefore, planners must define goals, and assess whether or not they can be achieved.

If proper planning is an important prerequisite for a successfully executed project, then design is certainly a critical task within this phase. The success or failure of a project often depends upon the comprehensiveness of its design, which must strive to take into account all pertinent factors bearing on the project. Project design establishes in detail the responsibilities, activities, and resources necessary to operate the project.

Important questions during Phase 1 of the project include:

Identification and Formulation

- Was the project identified in the course of the national development planning process? If so, what was the policy-making character of this process?

- Can the national planning process ensure that policies and programs for economic and social development at the national level are translated into or integrated with counterpart plans at regional and local levels?

- Did the original project idea relate to problems identified in the national or sectoral or regional plan?

- What were the major environmental factors - political, economic, social, cultural, technical, or others - that led to the project?

- What was the primary source of the project idea?

- Who were the individuals or groups that first proposed the project?

- Did other organizations become involved in defining the project?

- What was the role of external donors or international funding agencies in project identification?

- Who, other than the earliest proposers, supported the project idea? Who opposed it?

- Were other groups or individuals involved in the preparation, such as: clients, users, beneficiaries, political supporters or opponents, resource suppliers, and potential project implementators?

- How and by whom was the initial idea justified in order to be included in the country's investment program? Should it be in the program at this stage? If so, how?

- Were prefeasibility studies done?

- How clearly and explicitly were the purposes and goals of the project stated or defined? Were the major potential problems also identified at this time? Were the time constraints taken into consideration?

- Was there general commitment to the goals of the project by all of the constituencies in its design? From whom could political and administrative support be initially counted upon? What recourses did these supporters have? What conflicts arose and how were they settled?

Feasibility Analysis and Appraisal

- How extensive was the preliminary design? Who prepared it?

- Was a formal feasibility analysis conducted?

- Who conducted it? Was it a national organization, an international assistance agency, a consulting team, or a combination thereof?

- How comprehensive and detailed were:

    - the technical feasibility studies (project location and layout, technology needs, training of technical personnel)?

    - the financial feasibility analysis (investment analysis, projected capital needs at various stages)?

    - the economic feasibility analysis (national economic benefits, demand forecasting, comprehensive economic analysis)?

    - the market and commercial feasibility studies?

    - the location studies?

    - the political feasibility assessment?

    - the administrative, organizational, and managerial studies?

- Did the studies reveal any weaknesses in the project that might affect future operations? If so, what were these weaknesses?

- What appraisal criteria were used? Who had the authority for the appraisal?

- What procedures were used during the appraisal process? How many stages did it go through?

- Did the appraisers and reviewers make an onsite inspection?

- Were there any reservations about the overall ability of the project to succeed? If so, what were these reservations? Were there any problems that other appraisers foresaw that were not included in the final appraisal?

- How were uncertainties and gaps in the reliable estimates or projections affecting project appraisal dealt with?

Design

- What were the major sources of data or of information used in designing the principal components of the project?
- How well did the project design reflect the initial objectives and targets of the project idea?
- How clearly and explicitly were the purposes and goals of the project defined and stated? Were immediate goals distinguished from longer-range goals? Were project objectives related to broader development policies?
- Did the proposal include measurable targets for attaining objectives and specifications for the project's outputs?
- Did the source of the project's identification influence how it was prepared and designed?
- Was an attempt made to identify the potential project manager and to involve him in project design?
- Were the project's activities, functions, tasks, and components clearly identified and defined?
- How many and what kind of design alternatives were considered and analyzed? How were these alternatives evaluated and chosen?
- Were preconditions or prerequisites of success considered during the design task? Were potential problems or bottlenecks to successful implementation identified?
- Were potential social and cultural impacts of the project taken into consideration in its design? Were adverse affects identified? If so, how was the design modified?
- Did the project design indicate an adequate mechanism for internal and external communication requirements?
- Were linkages and relationships with complementary or competing projects examined?
- In how much detail were plans, specifications, job descriptions, and work schedules prepared?
- Were alternative organizational arrangements for project execution and operation considered? Were plans made for expanding administrative capacity of the potential project implementation unit?

- Did the project organization maintain a balance - appropriate to the project task - between technical and managerial persons and functions?

- Were the different elements of the project design integrated into a coherent whole?   Was there one person responsible for this integration?

PHASE 2: SELECTION, APPROVAL, AND ACTIVATION

Preliminary work on a project is well under way long before it is actually selected and approved for operation. For this reason, the analysis and preparation that has gone into designing the project should also provide sufficient information for policy makers to make a final decision about its funding. A project must compete for selection on the basis of extremely diverse factors: sophisticated forms of cost analysis, political and economic priorities, competition between pressure groups, and many other considerations. Even within government, departments are often competing for scarce resources for their own ministries, with top officials including ministers pressing their case for particular projects. Thus, educationalists may consider their claims for more funds for schools outweigh those of defense experts concerned with expanding defense capabilities. To provide convincing evidence of their project's priority, development project administrators must be able to perform such varied tasks as preparing loan documents, assessing public reactions, obtaining necessary ministry approvals, negotiating agreements with international assistance agencies on the content and scope of their project, and resolving proposed loan covenants.

In activating a project that has been selected and approved, the project manager faces a complex task of coordination. The commitment of professionals, technicians, resource suppliers, and policy makers to the project must be formalized. The project manager must decide on the type and location of the organization that will be responsible for executing the project, and he must determine what work structure best translates operating plans into project activities. He must coordinate a number of outside resource persons, delegate responsibilities within the project, and make a wide range of related administrative decisions.

Critical questions during Phase 2 include:

Selection and Approval

- What appraisal and selection criteria were used?

- How many stages of review were necessary before final selection and approval? Who participated in the review, selection, and approval processes? Did these stages involve:

-    obtaining legislative authorization?

-    obtaining executive approval?

-    confirming procedures for budget operation, personnel management, and interagency operation?

- Did any changes occur in the project environment from the time of the
  feasibility study that affected project approval?

- How long did the appraisal, selection, negotiation, and approval
  process take? What were major sources of delay, if any?

- What major factors - political, social, technical, economic, administrative, or others - influenced decisions at each stage of the review?

- How were uncertainties and gaps in the reliable estimates or
  projections affecting project appraisal and selection dealt with?

- Was the proposal in competition with others ones? If so, was the
  project appraised and evaluated comparatively with these others?

- Which of the following criteria were used in selection:

  -    linkage with national or local development thrusts?

  -    accelerating the pace of economic and social progress in the
    area?

  -    availability of natural resources and raw materials?

  -    considerations of priorities dictated by political pressures?

  -    cost and duration?

  -    other criteria?

- From what sources was the project to be financed and funded? Which
  organizations - national or international - provided other basic
  resources or inputs?

- Who was involved in negotiation of loans or grants or other forms of
  funding for the project? What were the major issues of negotiation?
  What were the positions of the negotiators? How were differences
  resolved?

- Were constraints and conditions placed on the project's design or
  operation by the selection, approval, or funding authorities? Was the
  plan modified to conform to those conditions?

Activation

- What criteria were used in choosing a project implementation unit or
  executing agency?

- What variables influenced the choice of organizational structure?

- What was the relationship between the project implementation unit and higher organizational authorities in terms of responsibilities and support?

- Who was included in the project team? Were they transferred out of their previous responsibilities temporarily or permanently? Were they on a part-time basis or on a full-time basis?

- What were the criteria used in personnel selection for the project team and for the project manager? What recruitment methods were used?

- Were the project leader and the project team given their job responsibilities clearly? Were they provided an orientation or a period of retraining?

- What working contracts and activation documents were used? Who prepared them?

- Was an adequate information and control system provided at the activation phase? If not, why not?

- How was the project organized internally with regard to:
    - work and task division?
    - authority, responsibility, and supervision?
    - communication channels among divisions and with supporting organizations?
    - relationships between technical and administrative divisions?
    - resource procurement and allocation?
    - monitoring and reporting?

- What types of systems or procedures were established for bidding and contracting?

- Were the major sources of projects inputs:
    - financial resources?
    - materials, supplies, equipment, and facilities?
    - manpower?
    - political support?
    - technology?
    - public participation?

- Were detailed and realistic project operation plans formulated for:
    - budgeting?
    - recruitment and training of personnel?
    - data collection?
    - work and activity scheduling?

PHASE 3: OPERATION, CONTROL, AND HANDOVER

The startup of the project will result in intense activity as the various tasks and functions become operational. The project manager must coordinate and control the many diverse operations and resources which may be working together for the first time. After basic administrative blueprints have been established, the project manager allocates tasks to groups within the project organization, making sure that the flow of necessary resources is properly scheduled. The initial implementation task requires close coordination and control. While equipment, resources, and manpower are being procured, timetables and communication, information and feedback systems must also be set up.

As implementation continues, good supervision, control and information procedures must provide the project manager with rapid feedback which isolates, as quickly as possible, problems and bottlenecks. A good control system not only pinpoints problems that arise during the project cycle, it also measures progress by evaluating not just the quality of performance but also the extent to which output adheres to preliminary plans and specifications. Control procedures provide the basis for guiding project operations and redirecting them, where necessary, to achieve the goals that have been set. Setting up an adequate supervision and control system means that the project manager must coordinate activities that occur both inside and outside the formal limits of the project organization.

Ending a project properly is just as important a part of its operation as beginning it. Project completion in this sense means that the project is prepared for its inevitable termination and handover to a different type of administration. Completion involves scaling down project activities, transforming experimental, pilot, and demonstration projects into institutionalized programs and production units, transferring output to beneficiaries, and diffusing project results. Within this task also falls the reallocation of unused or excess resources. Generally, the project manager must closely supervise the slowing down of the project and the transfer of personnel and equipment in such a way that assets are liquidated to maximum benefit.

Important questions during Phase 3 of the project include:

- How were work activities and project tasks scheduled?

- Did the project management team make use of such techniques as CPM and PERT analysis? What other techniques were used and why were they selected?

- Was there an adequate management information system? Did it define:

    - information requirements?

    - sources of information?

    - systematic procedures and organization for collecting data?

    - a coordinated design to integrate internal and external project activities?

- Were feedback channels and feedback elements identified? Was adequate use made of these channels? Was adequate use made of the information received from these channels?

- Were formal problem-solving or troubleshooting procedures established?

- What arrangements were made for coordination of project activities with supporters, suppliers, and clients?

- What was the nature of the leadership style of the project manager during the implementation phase? Could it be characterized as:

  - management by control?

  - management by objectives?

  - management by exception?

- Was the project redesigned or modified to meet unanticipated problems during implementation?

Supervision and Control

- Were formal systems or procedures created to:

  - procure, inspect, and inventory at optimum levels raw materials and other resource inputs?

  - ensure vigorous recruitment and optimum manpower utilization as regards their efficiency and output?

  - monitor budget performance, cash flows; forecast deviations in funding requirements?

  - test and adapt transferred technology?

- Were formal management techniques such as network analysis or operations research used to:

  - provide information on project progress to constituents and beneficiaries?

  - coordinate the work of contractors?

  - reallocate resources to behind-schedule activities?

- What methods were used to report progress and problems to higher authorities? What type of information was reported? How frequently were reports made? To whom were they addressed?

- How were remedial actions initiated and performed when monitoring and control procedures indicated problems?

- Did conflicts occur:

  - between technicians from different disciplines or specializations?

    - between administrators and technicians?

    - between project managers within the parent organization?

    - between the project implementation unit and other organizations?

Completion and Handover

- Were project completion reports prepared and reviewed?

- Was a plan prepared either for replication or for the transition of a successful experimental, pilot, or demonstration project to full-scale operation?

- What arrangements were made for diffusion of project outputs and results?

- Were replicable components of the project identified?

- Were arrangements made for followup investment or multiphase funding?

- Were extension or technical assistance services created to assist clients or users to adapt project output and results?

- Were the procedures and methods of handover and a continuation in an ongoing organization well established? Were they complied with? If not, why not?

- What kinds of arrangements were made to transfer unutilized or excess resources - human, financial, physical, and technical - from the project at completion to other projects or organizations?

- What arrangements were made for the transfer or disposition of the capital assets of the project?

- What arrangements were made for credit or loan repayment?

- Would levels of outside funding change considerably upon handover to an ongoing organization?

- Were project personnel reassigned to new duties at the project's completion? Were they prepared and trained for this?

- Did the handover mean that new persons took over the project activities, or were the same persons transferred to a different organizational setting?

- What restructuring or modification was required of the receiving agency or institution?

- What difficulties arose as a result of the transfer and handover:

    - to the project team?

- to the receiving institutions?
- to the beneficiaries?
- to the funding agencies?

PHASE 4: EVALUATION AND REFINEMENT

An often neglected task of project management, evaluation is in fact the means by which the entire success or failure of the project is measured, and the only means by which useful information about its impact can be transmitted. More than simply an after the event examination, evaluation should also be an ongoing process during each phase of the integrated project cycle. Project evaluation includes both financial auditing, to ensure that assistance funds were used for the purposes of the loan, and postassessment of project results. Postassessment consists of examining the following factors: the effectiveness of the project in attaining its goals; the impact of the project in attaining its goals; the impact of the project on sectoral, regional, and national development; and the degree to which the goods and services provided by the project have been made available on a continuing basis through normal administrative channels.

Followup is the action taken on the basis of evaluation, and can include both corrective action on unmet needs arising from the project or implementation of smaller related "piggyback" projects.

Refinement of procedures is the last necessary task in the life of a project, because this modification, based on lessons learned from the old project, will be the foundation of projects yet to begin. It is the function of refinement to pass on the project experience both to new projects and to improved national policy. This refinement of procedures, as much as the work actually accomplished, constitutes the project's real contribution to the well-being of a country.

Important questions during Phase 4 include:

Evaluation and Followup

- Was the need for the evaluation adequately perceived?
- Were the objectives of the evaluation sufficiently clear?
- What type of evaluation was decided upon? Was the focus to be on short-term, medium-term, or long-term effects/benefits of the project?
- Were formal evaluation procedures established? Was an evaluation timetable set up?
- What techniques were used in the evaluation (cost/benefit analysis, baseline measures, etc.)?

- Who did the evaluation? Was it an individual or a team? If a team, was it composed of individuals independent and outside of the parent institution, or of individuals from within, or both? Why?

- What level of seniority did the evaluator(s) have?

- Was adequate background information and data provided for evaluation purposes?

- Was the evaluation team provided with adequate administrative support?

- What were the results of the evaluation? Were the intended benefits realized? If not, why not?

- Was project efficiency measured from time schedule, budget, and performance output considerations? What were the major factors causing delay, cost overruns, lack of meeting project performance criteria?

- Was variance analysis used to measure the difference between projected and actual results?

- Did the evaluation consider the appropriateness of the following aspects of the project:

    - management information system?

    - level of technology?

    - operating design?

    - manpower capabilities?

    - organizational structures and flexibilities?

- Did the outcome of the project support the program and national policy goals for which the project was intended and of which the project was a part?

- What was the overall impact of the project on the local, sectoral, or national setting?

- What was the prevailing attitude and reaction of the end users at the start of the project? What was it at the end? Did they perceive the project objectives in the same way?

- Did the evaluation identify unmet needs? Did the evaluation identify piggyback or followup projects?

- Did the evaluation identify replicable components of the project? Did it identify followup investment or multiphase funding?

- Did it detect unforeseen side effects of the project, whether fortunate ones or unfortunate ones?

- Were formal evaluation reports written up and presented? To which individuals or agencies were they given? When? How were they used?

- Did the project team see the reports or participate in their formulation or preparation?

Refinement of Policy and Planning

- Were the results of the evaluation followed up? If so, by whom and how soon afterwards? If not, why not? If so, what were the results?

- Did evaluation results lead to the formulation of proposals for further projects? Did they lead to improvements or modifications of national policy?

- What lessons and insights were learned from the project? Was there an analysis of the reasons for deviations in implementation from the operating plan? Did the analysis reveal both long-term and short-term lessons?

- How can these lessons be applied to refine the project or future similar projects?

- How can these lessons be applied to future policy decisions on project management?

As the foregoing list of questions demonstrates, the issues and factors affecting development project management are numerous and complex. To bring order out of this maze of diverse factors, the IPPMC organizes management tasks and issues into an integrated concept which views development projects in their entirety - from identification to followup - and places them in a cohesive framework. This conceptual framework provides a comprehensive and balanced approach to project management.

Selected Bibliography

PHASE 1: PLANNING, APPRAISAL, AND DESIGN

Ahmad, Yusuf J. "Project Identification, Analysis, and Preparation in Developing Countries." Development and Change. Vol. 6, No. 3 (July 1975).

Avots, Ivars. "Projects in Developing Countries." Business Horizons. Vol. XV, No. 4 (August 1972).

Chadenet, Bernard, & King, John A., Jr. "What is a 'World Bank Project'?" Finance and Development (September 1973).

Cracknell, B.F. "Some Problems in the Application of Project Appraisal Techniques." Journal of Agricultural Economics. Vol. XXII, No. 3 (September 1971).

Diamond, J. "The Analysis of Structural Constraints in Developing Economies: A Case Study." Oxford Bulletin of Economics and Statistics. Vol. 36, No. 2 (May 1974).

Lal, Deepak. Methods of Project Analysis: A Review. Baltimore: Johns Hopkins Press, 1974.

McColl, G.D., & Throsby, C.D. "Multiple Objective Benefit-Cost Analysis and Regional Development." The Economic Record. Vol. 48, No. 122 (June 1972).

Merrett, A.J., & Sykes, Allen. The Finance and Analysis of Capital Projects. 2nd Ed. New York: Halsted Press, 1974.

Organization for Economic Cooperation and Development. Manual of Industrial Projects Analysis in Developing Countries. Paris: OECD, 1968.

Rondinelli, Dennis A. "Project Identification in Economic Development." Journal of World Trade Law. Vol. 10, No. 3 (1976).

Solomon, Morris J.   Analysis of Projects for Economic Growth: An Operational System for Their Formulation, Evaluation and Implementation. New York: Praeger, 1970.

United Nations, Department of Economic and Social Affairs. Administration of Development Programmes and Projects: Some Major Issues. New York: United Nations, 1971.

Waterston, Albert.   Development Planning: Lessons of Experience. Baltimore: Johns Hopkins Press, 1974.

PHASE 2: SELECTION, APPROVAL, AND ACTIVATION

Crowston, Wallace B. "Models for Project Management." Sloan Management Review. Vol. 12, No. 3 (Spring 1971).

Frankwicz, Michael J.   "A Study of Project Management Techniques." Journal of Systems Management. Vol. 24, No. 10 (October 1973).

Gemmill, Gary, & Wilemon, David L.   "The Power Spectrum in Project Management." Sloan Management Review. Vol. 12, No. 1 (Fall 1970).

Hodgetts, Richard M. "Leadership Techniques in the Project Organization." Academy of Management Journal. Vol. 11, No. 2 (June 1968).

Schaefer, M. "A Management Method for Planning and Implementing Health Projects." World Health Organization Chronicle. Vol. 29, No. 1 (January 1975).

Shah, Ramesh P.   "Project Management: Cross Your Bridges Before You Come to Them." Management Review. Vol. 60, No. 12 (December 1971).

Srinivasan, V.   "Project Reshaping."   Washington, D.C.:   World Bank, Economic Development Institute, 1976.

Thamain, Hans J., & Wilemon, David L. "Conflict Management in Project Life Cycles." Sloan Management Review. Vol. 16, No. 3 (Spring 1975).

United Nations Industrial Development Organization. Contract Planning and Organization. New York: United Nations, 1974.

United Nations Industrial Development Organization. "The Initiation and Implementation of Industrial Projects in Developing Countries: A Systematic Approach." New York: United Nations, 1975.

Westring, Gosta.   "Procurement Methods."   International Procurement - A Training Manual. New York: United Nations Institute for Training and Research, 1974.

PHASE 3: OPERATION, CONTROL, AND HANDOVER

Ahuja, H.N. Construction Performance Control by Networks. New York: Wiley, 1976.

Anthony, Robert Newton. Planning and Control Systems: A Framework for Analysis. Cambridge, Mass.: Harvard University Press, 1965.

Burman, P.J. Precedence Network for Project Planning and Control. New York: McGraw-Hill, 1972.

Cleland, David I., & King, William R. Systems Analysis and Project Management. New York: McGraw-Hill, 1975.

Holden, Ian R., & McIlroy, P.K. Network Planning in Management Control Systems. London: Hutchinson, 1970.

Johnson, R.A. Operations Management: A Systems Control. Boston: Houghton Mifflin, 1972.

Kaynor, Richard S., & Schultz, Konrad F. Industrial Development: A Practical Handbook for Planning and Implementing Development Programs. New York: Praeger, 1967.

Kramer, Robert. "A Control Program for Construction Projects." Management Accounting. (October 1970).

Lock, Dennis. Project Management. London: Gower Press, 1968.

Martino, R. Project Management and Control. New York: American Management Association, 1965.

Saitow, Arnold R. "CSPC: Reporting Project Progress to the Top." Harvard Business Review. Vol. 47, No. 1 (January-February 1969).

Staffurth, C. (ed.). Project Cost Control Using Networks. London: Operational Research Society and Institute of Cost and Work Accountants, 1969.

PHASE 4: EVALUATION AND REFINEMENT

Bateman, Worth. "Assessing Program Effectiveness: A Rating System for Identifying Relative Project Success." Welfare in Review. Vol. 6, No. 1 (January-February 1968).

Berger, Michael. "Divesting Project Resources." Vanderbilt University: Graduate School of Management, 1974.

Hansen, John. "Summary of the Principal Methods of Economic Industrial Project Evaluation." Washington, D.C.: World Bank, Economic Development Institute, July 1971.

Harberger, Arnold C. Project Evaluation: Collected Papers. London: Macmillan, 1972.

Haveman, Robert H. The Economic Performance of Public Investments: An Ex Post Evaluation of Water Resources Investment. Baltimore: Johns Hopkins Press, 1972.

Hayes, Samuel P. Evaluating Development Projects. Paris: UNESCO, 1966.

Hyman, Herbert H.; Wright, Charles; & Hopkins, Terence. Application of Methods of Evaluation. Berkeley: University of California Press, 1969.

McFadden, D. "The Evaluation of Development Programmes." The Review of Economic Studies. No. 97 (January 1967).

McKusick, Robert B., & Snyder, J. Herbert. "A Regional Approach to Project Evaluation." Water Resources Bulletin. Vol. 8, No. 3 (June 1972).

Rady, Hussein. "Instrument for Evaluating Public Projects." International Economics. No. 4 (1974).

Weckstein, R.S. "Shadow Prices and Project Evaluation in Less-Developed Countries." Economic Development and Cultural Change. Vol. 20, No. 3 (April 1972).

Index

Activation
    discussion of, 6-7
    mention of, 5
    of Bangkok project, 161
    of Laguna project, 114
    of Malia project, 203, 204, 206
    of Rabona project, 37-38
    questions about, 240-241
Activation tasks
    for Malia project, 198
Appraisal
    by Rabonans, 23-28
    definition of, 5
    discussion of, 6, 88-89
    of Bangkok project, 159-160
    of Laguna project, 109-113, 136, 137
    of Rabona project, 21, 22-23, 36-37
    of Way Abung project, 68
    questions about, 236-237
Approval
    discussion of, 7
    mention of, 7
    of Bangkok project, 160-162
    of Malia project, 201-203, 225-226
    of Rabona project, 30-31, 36-37
    questions about, 239-240

Authority
    for Bangkok project, 160-162, 173
    for Laguna project, 104-105, 130, 133-134
    for Malia project, 186-189, 207-209, 226-227
    for Rabona project, 38-39
    for Way Abung project, 69-77, 83-84

Budgeting
    discussion of, 92
    for Bangkok project, 154, 155-158
    for Laguna project, 114, 120, 123, 132-133, 142
    for Malia project, 190, 191-192, 196, 201, 227-228
    for Rabona project, 30-31, 36-37
    for Way Abung project, 67, 80
    of Laguna project, 104

Case history
    in training, 10-11
Completion
    discussion of, 9
    mention of, 8
    of Bangkok project, 168-170
    of Malia project, 220-222
    questions about, 244-245
    see also Hanover

Control
    discussion of, 8
    mention of, 8
    of Laguna project, 139, 141-142
    of Rabona project, 42-46
    of Way Abung project, 76-77
    see also Feedback; Monitoring;
    Supervision
Coordination
    discussion of, 92, 232-233
    of Bangkok project, 174
    of Malia project, 230-231
    of Rabona project, 39-41
    of Way Abung project, 80, 81
Cost-benefit analysis
    See Feasibility study

Design
    discussion of, 6
    mention of, 4
    for Rabona project, 31-36
    for Way Abung project, 63-64
    of Bangkok project, 151, 153
    of Laguna project, 105, 107
    of Malia project, 195-199,
    224-225
    of Way Abung project, 66-68
    questions about, 238-239
Development program
    definition of, 1-2
    mention of, 2, 11, 48

Evaluation
    discussion of, 10
    of Bangkok project, 171-174
    of Laguna project, 117-123, 130,
    132-133, 139
    of Malia project, 204-205,
    215-216, 219, 222
    of Rabona project, 47-49
    of Way Abung project, 87
    questions about, 245-247
Expatriate aid
    See Foreign assistance

Feasibility analysis
    discussion of, 5
    mention of, 4

Feasibility study
    and cost-benefit in Way Abung
    project, 87, 88-89, 124, 153, 159,
    212
    discussion of, 5, 6
    in Bangkok project, 150-151, 152,
    154-155
    of Malia project, 187, 194-195
    of Rabona project, 22-31
    questions about, 237-238
    see also Appraisal
Feedback
    in Laguna project, 112-113, 138
    in Way Abung project, 69
    see also Control; Monitoring;
    Supervision
Financing
    See Budgeting
Flexibility
    discussion of, 174, 233
Followup
    discussion of, 10
Followup action
    in Malia project, 227-233
    in Rabona project, 48
    in Way Abung project, 82
Foreign Aid
    See Foreign assistance
Foreign assistance
    for Rabona project, 18, 19, 47, 49
    in Bangkok project, 148-149, 173
    policies, 1-2, 49
    related to Laguna project, 97-98
Formulation
    discussion of, 92-93
    mention of, 4
    of Bangkok project, 148-150
    of Laguna project, 105, 106
    of Malia project, 182-185, 222-223
    of Rabona project, 17-18
    of Way Abung project, 63-64
    questions about, 236-237

Handover
    discussion of, 9, 92, 161
    mention of, 8
    of Bangkok project, 170-171
    of Rabona project, 46-47
    of Way Abung project, 84-86
    transfer of resources, 9

Identification
    discussion of, 4
    mention of, 4
    of Bangkok project, 146-147
    of Laguna project, 99, 100-104
    of Malia project, 181-183
    of Rabona project, 15-17
    of Way Abung project, 63, 64-65
    questions about, 236-237
Implementation
    discussion of, 8
    of Bangkok project, 155, 156,
    160-161, 165-166
    of Laguna project, 114-115,
    136-137
    of Malia project, 203, 208-211
    of Rabona project, 39-41
    of Way Abung project, 76
    questions about, 242-244
Integrated Project Planning and
    Management Cycle (IPPMC)
    definition of, 2
    diagram of, 3
    discussion of, 4
    phase 1, 2-3, 235-236
    phase 2, 7, 239
    phase 3, 8, 242
    phase 4, 10, 245
International assistance
    See Foreign assistance

Leadership
    discussion of, 93, 400
    in Bangkok project, 173
    in Malia project, 212-213,
    217-218, 227
    of Laguna project, 112, 115-117,
    126-127, 130-132, 139-140
    of Rabona project, 40-41, 46,
    47-50

Manpower
    See Personnel
Monitoring
    in Indonesia, 92, 93
    of Bangkok project, 161-162,
    167-168
    of Laguna project, 116-117,
    129,130, 138, 139

of Malia project, 213-215, 216-217
of Rabona project, 39-41
see also Control; Feedback;
Supervising

Operation
    discussion of, 8-9
    mention of, 8
    of Bangkok project, 163, 165, 168
    of Laguna project, 115-116, 119,
    123-126, 137-138
    of Malia project, 209-212, 215-216
    of Rabona project, 39-46
Organizational structure
    discussion of, 93
    of Bangkok project, 152-157,
    158-159, 163-165, 173-174
    of Laguna project, 108-110, 115-116,
    138, 141
    of Malia project, 187, 188, 199,
    207-209, 226
    of Rabona project, 20, 38-39
    of Way Abung project, 69-73

Personnel
    development of, 46, 47, 52, 53
    skilled, 40-41, 52
    specialist, 115-116
    trained manpower, 11
Phases 1 - 4
    See IPPMC
Planning
    discussion of, 88-92
    in Indonesia, 92-93
    of Laguna project, 104-105
    of Malia project, 191-193, 195-197
    of Rabona project, 28-36
    of Way Abung project, 63-66
    see also Design
Program
    related to Bangkok project, 172
Project
    definition of, 1
    life cycle, 5, 8, 222
    unity of process, 2
    see also Development project
Project director
    leadership style of, 78
    of Malia project, 190-191, 218-219
    of Way Abung project, 78-79

Project manager
    for Rabona project, 27-28
    of Malia project, 203-204,
    212-213, 215
Project objectives
    for Bangkok project, 148-149,
    151, 153
    for Laguna project, 105, 107, 108,
    109
    for Malia project, 197, 210,
    227-232
    for Rabona project, 30-31, 32-35,
    50, 52-57
    for Way Abung project, 63, 64-68,
Project organization
    discussion of, 7
    see also Organizational structure

Refinement
    discussion of, 11
    mention of, 10
    questions about, 247
Reorganization
    of Bangkok project, 165-168
    of Laguna project, 127
    of Malia project, 218-222
    of Way Abung project, 87-91

Sector
    and the IPPMC, 2, 4
    agricultural, as related to
    Rabona project, 14-17
    infrastructure and public works,
    as related to Bangkok project,
    145-146, 147-149
    social, as related to Laguna
    project, 97-99, 102-103
    social, as related to Malia
    project, 177-178, 181
    social, as related to Way Abung
    project, 52-55
Selection
    mention of, 7
    of Malia project, 200-201
    questions about, 239-240
Supervision
    mention of, 8

Transfer
    See Handover

About the Authors

LOUIS J. GOODMAN is Assistant Director of the Resource Systems Institute, the East-West Center, Honolulu, Hawaii. He holds degrees from M.I.T. and Harvard University.

RALPH NGATATA LOVE is Director of the Management, Education, and Development Center, Massey University, Palmerston North, New Zealand. He holds degrees in Business Administration and a Ph.D. in Policy Formation.

NANCY CROCCO is the Assistant Executive Director of the Professional Standards Review Organization in Hawaii, and was previously the Director of Community Health Services for the Regional Medical Program of Hawaii.

ERNESTO GARILAO is Regional Manager of the Philippine Business for Social Progress (PBSP), in charge of the overall supervision of PBSP-funded projects in the Visayas.

TETSUO MIYABARA is a research intern at the Resource Systems Institute of the East-West Center in Hawaii, and has been a lecturer in Public Administration at the University of Hawaii.

CHAKRIT NORANITIPADUNGKARN is Professor of Development Administration and former Director of the Research Centre, National Institute of Development Administration in Bangkok, Thailand.

BINTORO TJOKROAMIDJOJO is Deputy Chairman for Administration of BAPPENAS (National Development Planning Agency) of Indonesia.

Pergamon Policy Studies

No. 1   Laszlo—*The Objectives of the New International Economic Order*

No. 2   Link/Feld—*The New Nationalism*

No. 3   Ways—*The Future of Business*

No. 4   Davis—*Managing and Organizing Multinational Corporations*

No. 5   Volgyes—*The Peasantry of Eastern Europe, Volume One*

No. 6   Volgyes—*The Peasantry of Eastern Europe, Volume Two*

No. 7   Hahn/Pfaltzgraff—*The Atlantic Community in Crisis*

No. 8   Renninger—*Multinational Cooperation for Development in West Africa*

No. 9   Stepanek—*Bangledesh—Equitable Growth?*

No. 10   Foreign Affairs—*America and the World 1978*

No. 11   Goodman/Love—*Management of Development Projects*

No. 12   Weinstein—*Bureacratic Opposition*

No. 13   De Volpi—*Proliferation, Plutonium, and Policy*

No. 14   Francisco/Laird/Laird—*The Political Economy of Collectivized Agriculture*

No. 15   Godet—*The Crisis in Forecasting and the Emergence of the "Prospective" Approach*

No. 16   Golany—*Arid Zone Settlement Planning*

No. 17   Perry/Kraemer—*Technological Innovation in American Local Governments*

No. 18   Carman—*Obstacles to Mineral Development*

No. 19   Demir—*Arab Development Funds in the Middle East*

No. 20   Kahan/Ruble—*Industrial Labor in the U.S.S.R.*

No. 21   Meagher—*An International Redistribution of Wealth and Power*

No. 22   Thomas/Wionczek—*Integration of Science and Technology With Development*

No. 23   Mushkin/Dunlop—*Health: What Is It Worth?*

No. 24   Abouchar—*Economic Evaluation of Soviet Socialism*

No. 25   Amos—*Arab-Israeli Military/Political Relations*

No. 26   Geismar/Geismar—*Families in an Urban Mold*

No. 27   Leitenberg/Sheffer—*Great Power Intervention in the Middle East*

No. 28   O'Brien/Marcus—*Crime and Justice in America*

No. 29   Gartner—*Consumer Education in the Human Services*

No. 30   Diwan/Livingston—*Alternative Development Strategies and Appropriate Technology*

No. 31   Freedman—*World Politics and the Arab-Israeli Conflict*

No. 32   Williams/Deese—*Nuclear Nonproliferatrion*

No. 33   Close—*Europe Without Defense?*

No. 34   Brown—*Disaster Preparedness*

No. 35   Grieves—*Transnationalism in Politics and Business*